Many Threads

The Saga of an Electronics Engineer

MANY THREADS

THE SAGA OF AN ELECTRONICS ENGINEER

Arch C Luther

ISBN 978-0-557-02199-4
Copyright © 2008 Arch C Luther

Contents

Chapter 4   71

Management at RCA   71

Chapter 5   81

Electronic Recording   81

Preface

Welcome to my memoir. Before we begin, I would like to cover some important items.

My life spans from 1928 until the present — 2008, as I write. Included in this period were the Great Depression, World War II, Cold War era, the Korean War, and many other world events that I didn't participate directly in. More important to this book, however, are the technology events, particularly in electronics. These, I did directly participate in. During my career, there were at least five technology "sea changes" that occurred. You will find these in the book, with my observations about them.

Because technology and its progress is such an important part of my life, I need to tell you about it in the book. That means I have to sometimes get technical. I have tried to do this in a way that is understandable to anyone, whether of technical background or not. Occasionally, I may use explanations that seem trivial to a technical reader. This cannot be avoided in order to reach a wider audience.

However, a non-technical reader may have trouble with the concept of "engineer" and what such a person is like and what they do in life. For these readers, there is a discussion about engineers and engineering at the end of this preface that may help with understanding of these matters. Also, non-technical readers may be tempted to skip completely over the chapters that look to be technical; don't do that, you will miss a lot of the story and my comments. Instead, browse over those chapters and pick out the stories and comments to read, skipping only the sections that are actually too technical for you. That way, you won't miss anything.

My objectives for this book are:

To show some of the things that make a person want to become an engineer, and how you can recognize when they occur.

To tell what I think are the attributes of a good engineer.

To document the accomplishments of my life.

To tell from my perspective about the advances of technology that have occurred during my life.

To tell some interesting stories.

Things in my life that contribute to these objectives are in the book. Other things may not be in the book.

An important concept I have used in this book is that of *threads*. Threads are interests that have been with me throughout my life. As the book progresses (it is mostly chronological), I will highlight new threads as they appear. You will then see them reappear again and again in the later chapters of the book. If you are familiar with the thread concept in computers, you know that a computer has to continuously switch between the threads of the program that is running, or even between programs themselves. The process of switching between threads to keep "all the balls in the air" is called *multitasking*. People do that too, but maybe on a longer time scale. For example, when you are driving a car, you have to steer the car to stay on the road, watch for other cars, watch the instruments, and perhaps carry on a conversation with your passengers. Each of these activities is a thread; you switch your attention periodically between them. Everyone does the same thing with the threads of their life.

The thread concept is a metaphor. I have reservations about metaphors because they are dangerous in that the reader may extend them into concepts unintended by the author that are not relevant to the subject being described. However, I use them anyway because they are helpful in explaining things. But don't extend my metaphors beyond what I say about them because that may lead you into soft ground (a metaphor). For example, my threads here are weaving among themselves in only one dimension (time), not in two dimensions as with the threads of a fabric.

This book has been written from November, 2007 to May, 2008, at the age of 79 years. When I am writing about an event that happened earlier in my life, I may remember the chronology of the event, but I may or may not remember what I thought about that event at the time.

I may also at times make comments about the event from my perspective of today (2008). To help the reader distinguish between the chronology and comments made from the present perspective, present-day comments are shown in italics. These comments may also show how my perspective has changed over time from earlier days until today. I feel those comments are important, because they give my analysis of what happened.

My sources of information are: my recollection (not very complete); documents and papers I have saved (a lot, but also nowhere near complete); my letterbooks (1963 to 1984); RCA Broadcast News Magazine; RCA Engineer Magazine; tens of thousands of my photographs, talks with friends and colleagues; and others. There are many observations I want to make about my thoughts when reviewing things that happened or that I wrote 40 or 50 years ago. These are in the book.

The narrative is not always chronological; sometimes I have to follow one thread through time and then go back to other threads. For example, in the chapters related to my RCA career (1950 - 1987), I do not say much about my personal life outside of work. To make my personal life during those years easier to understand, I have put most of it in a separate chapter (chapter 8).

You also can learn more about me on my personal web site, **www.archluther.com**. My current threads are shown by the menu list on the home page of that site. A page at the end of the book explains more about using my web site.

What follows is the memoir of a person who is primarily an engineer, but there are many other aspects to a life.

Arch C Luther
October, 2008

x

About Engineering

This book is about someone who is an engineer and who did (and still does) engineering things. Although you will get a picture of an engineer from the book by the time you finish reading it, if you don't know about engineering already, this introduction to the concepts of engineering and engineers as people may speed up your understanding.

An engineer is a person who *makes or builds things*. "Things" refers to any man-made device or structure, ranging from the tiniest microchip to the largest structures such as skyscrapers, ocean ships, or airliners. An engineer is a different person from most of us, a person whose whole life is focused on the concept of making or building things.

Most engineers show the tendency and aptitude for engineering while they are still in grade school. They are interested in how things are built and how they work, and as soon as they learn some math in school, they begin figuring things out analytically. As they grow up, more and more of their time is spent in engineering activities. In many cases, this leaves less time for sports and social activities. This behavior may cause them to be seen as anti-social or as geeks.

After high school, potential engineers choose to continue their education at an engineering college, where they select curricula such as Electrical Engineering, Mechanical Engineering, Biomechanics, Computer Science, or many others. In the course of undergraduate college, they learn the fundamentals of science, such as physics, chemistry, materials, etc. These fundamental sciences underly all engineering. They learn that these fundamentals apply to anything, any problem, any design. This equips them to design and build almost anything and to solve problems in any discipline. They might choose a career in one discipline, such as computer science, but as they mature, they will apply the engineering mentality to everything in their life.

An engineer facing a problem will try to analyze it carefully, look for solutions, invent when necessary, and then carry out the solution. When designing and developing a product, they will use the same approach to achieve the best design within the constraints of time and cost. However, there is only so much that one engineer can do by himself or herself. A large project requires more than one engineer -- sometimes thousands, working to complete a single product. A large team of engineers needs to be organized to the task, with the total project broken down to one-person pieces. Each piece of the project must have design goals, time schedules, and cost goals both for design cost and the resulting product cost.

This is where the job of engineering management comes in. Many engineers strive in their careers to move to management positions, and apply their engineering skills not to design, but instead to the organizing and managing of design. This proves to be just as rewarding to the engineer--he or she is accomplishing designs through subordinates.

If an engineer marries a non-technical person, the spouse has to learn to live with this probing and analytical approach to everything, including areas such as family finances, purchasing items for the home or garden, or deciding where the family will go on vacation. This behavior can often be taken as uncaring, or overbearing by the non-technical spouse. Many marriages have failed because this discrepancy was never resolved.

Engineers are *different* people. They are compelled by their background and training to behave this way, no matter what their family and friends may want. But this is just the behavior that will make the engineer successful in his or her career, and it is difficult for engineers to turn it off when dealing with other parts of their lives.

All of these aspects of engineering will show up in the life story that follows. Look for the engineer attributes introduced here as you read on.

Acknowledgements

Although this book is about me and was begun solely by me, any book becomes richer when it includes input and review by others. The other people who assisted me one way or another in this task are listed below, in alphabetical order.

Dr. Oded Bendov, Tom Boag, Bill Dischert, Lee Hedlund, John Hersh, Louisa Lavelle, Lulu.com, Bill Luther, Kayle Luther, Niki Luther, Dr. Alex Magoun, Catherine Osterbye, Elena Scola, Dr. Raymond F. Skryja, Jim Sparkman, Dr. Ken Wilkes, Dr. Scott Workinger, Cora Wright, and Tom Wright.

Thank you all.

Chapter 1

Early Years

This book is about someone who, at 12 years of age, wrote and published his own newspaper at school, using only a manual typewriter and carbon paper to make six copies at a time. That person grew up to be me, your author. Here is my story, from the beginning.

On December 5, 1928, a boy was born to Gertrude W. and Arch C. Luther at the Children's Hospital in Philadelphia, PA. He was named Arch Clinton Luther, Jr. (me) after his father. After the customary 4 or 5 days in the hospital (at that time), mother and baby came home to Wedgwood Walk in Merchantville, NJ. Wedgwood Walk was a courtyard sided by small town houses. Because there were now two people named "Arch" in the family, I became known as Archie to avoid confusion.

Everything went well with the new family and in two years and two weeks, I was joined by a brother—William Emery Luther (Bill). At that point, Wedgwood Walk started feeling too small and the family moved to a larger (rented) single-family house at 1922 Hillcrest Avenue in Pennsauken, NJ. Pennsauken is adjacent to Merchantville; the Hillcrest address is 1.5 miles as the crow flies from the Wedgwood Walk address.

A few years after the move to Pennsauken, the family gained two more people: my mother's younger sister, Helen Larkin, and her son Tommy. Tommy was three years younger than Bill (five years younger than I). Aunt Helen had married Thomas F Larkin in 1930. They had one son, Thomas, Jr. Soon after the birth of Tommy, the elder Thomas became ill, and had to go to a convalescent home. He lived for 25 more years, but never came out of the home. Helen worked as an executive secretary for a local firm, and had to support Thomas in the home and Tommy with her. She couldn't afford to have her own house, so she and Tommy came to live with us. My family now consisted of three boys, two mothers, and one father. Aunt

Helen shared the mothering tasks for the three boys with Gertrude. Aunt Helen had a much more easygoing personality than my mother; in a way they complemented each other. We boys really liked Aunt Helen; with her we could get away with a lot of things my mother would never have tolerated.

At the time of my birth, my father was a reporter for the Philadelphia Public Ledger. Somewhat later the Ledger merged with the Philadelphia Inquirer, a larger newspaper. At the Inquirer, he eventually became Sunday Editor, responsible for the Sunday supplements to the daily paper. He also became editor of the Inquirer's Today magazine, one of the first Sunday supplement magazines in the country.

My father grew up in western Pennsylvania. His father died of pneumonia before my father was born. His mother remarried and she and the stepfather placed my father in a Catholic home for children, where he completed his early years. When he reached maturity, he apprenticed as a carpenter for several years and drove an ambulance in Europe during World War I, before entering the University of Pennsylvania in Philadelphia. There, he studied journalism and eventually got the job at the Ledger.

My father retained his interest in carpentry (woodworking) as a hobby. When the family moved to the Hillcrest Ave. house, there was a garage, which immediately became a woodworking shop. During the 1930s, he equipped this shop with all the woodworking equipment that could possibly fit into a garage built for one 1920-size small car. (see Figure 1). For a project of any size, he had to open the garage doors and do much of the work outside. During my father's life, he did many woodworking projects; in his later years he specialized in period reproduction pieces and he especially liked the hand carved items (see Figure 2).

These two interests of my father: journalism and woodworking, also took hold of me at an early age and became threads throughout my life.

Grade School

I began my schooling in the first grade at Longfellow School in Pennsauken. I did well from the first, except that I was very shy and had a hard time making friends. After some years in the same school and the same

Figure 1 My father's workshop at Hillcrest Ave.

classmates, I managed to fit into the community. I learned that schoolwork was very easy for me; I especially liked tests!

With my shyness, I was generally reluctant to volunteer to answer questions in class unless I was *sure* I had the correct answer. I would never put my hand up on a guess. This behavior got me the reputation of always having the correct answer. That wasn't true, of course; I was just very selective about when I would volunteer an answer.

I liked most subjects, but it was soon clear that math and science were the favorites. I liked to draw and I learned to use a typewriter almost as soon as I learned handwriting. Since I did not have formal training in typing, I figured out my own system using two or three fingers on each hand. I got very good at it and have used that method to this day. My father had a typewriter at home that he let me use. In the sixth grade, with his typewriter and carbon paper, I published a small newspaper for the school, making 5 or 6 copies at a time. I also included drawings that I made through the carbon paper, and I sometimes colored them individually

Figure 2 Examples of my father's woodworking

on each sheet. *Unfortunately, none of these papers have survived. Today no one would think of producing a newspaper with a typewriter and carbon paper. Kids today can quickly and easily produce publications of any kind using computers.*

At home, I enjoyed watching my father work in his shop, although those occasions were limited because he worked nights during many of my grade school years. He would be gone when I got home from school and didn't return until after we all were in bed. When possible, I would sit on a stool in the shop and he would describe to me what he was doing. Later, he began letting me do some projects myself under close supervision. Thus, I learned the basics of woodworking at an early age.

I also liked to take things apart to see what was in them and how they worked. I was especially interested in mechanical devices at this time.

Taking apart was one thing I was good at, but putting them back together was something else.

Working for Grandfather

At age 10 or so, I began working on weekends and in summers for my maternal grandfather, Frank Leroy Wilson, who had a somewhat unusual business in East Camden, adjacent to Pennsauken. My grandfather had always been an entrepreneur and had tried a variety of businesses. For example, one of his businesses was making potato chips in his kitchen to sell on the street. At the time I worked for him, his business was repackaging and marketing various substances that he bought in bulk.

He had a factory on Lois Avenue, in East Camden. It was about 1.8 miles from the Hillcrest Avenue house to my grandfather's factory (note that putting in details like this, which you may feel are unnecessary to the story, is an engineer's trait--it is difficult for me to avoid saying such things.) I would ride my bicycle to go to work there. Sometimes, I even went there after school. The most interesting thing about his factory building was that it had a large still prominently displayed on the roof. The still was nonworking, but it sure got a lot of attention.

The business at the time I worked there consisted of buying barrel-quantities of vinegar, mustard, bleach, and other products, and then filling smaller bottles or jars for distribution to local stores. The bottles were used — he had a group of people who picked them up on the street for a few pennies a bottle. Beer bottles (brown) were especially good.

To reclaim the bottles, we had a large tub of water that was heated by passing steam through it. There was a gas-fired boiler in the factory that produced the steam. There were lots of steam pipes going around the building; it was fascinating to listen to the stereophonic pipe symphony when the steam system was started up in the morning. Also, the steam going through the cold water made an interesting cracking noise.

The bottles were washed in this steaming tub of water. After drying, they were filled with one of the products being dispensed, capped, and labeled. The labels were printed in his factory — yes, he had a printing press there. I quickly learned how to use that and took over the printing of the labels. I learned to set type and handle the ink and run the press. This was

Figure 3 Kelsey printing press

a Kelsey printing press, which was popular in those days for small printing jobs. I later got a small Kelsey press to do my own printing at home.

The Kelsey press was an interesting device. The press was a V-shaped cast-iron mechanism that sat on a table (see Figure 3). It had a handle that one pushed down to cause the V to close up. On the left side of the V was a place to mount the frame containing the type to print from. Above the type frame was a round steel plate on which one put the ink. The ink was like stiff jelly, and had to be spread on the round plate. Finally, there was a roller mounted on an arm that held the roller at the top of the round plate when the press was opened. When the press was closing, the roller passed over the ink plate and then over the type. On the right side of the V was a place where a sheet of paper was placed to align with the type on the other side when the press was closed. Closing the press printed on the paper. The press was then opened, and the printed paper was removed. To make multiple copies, one simply loaded each sheet of paper and closed the press.

Printing is sort of a sub-thread to journalism, which includes (by my definition), the acts of writing and publishing. Printing is part of publishing (the other part is distribution). The entire process of journalism is massively enhanced by today's computers compared to what it was like in the 1940s, which is the time period I am talking about here.

Summer Camp

Another summertime activity during my years from age 7 until age 14 was the YMCA summer camp, Camp Ockanickon, near Medford, NJ. The name, Ockanickon, is that of a chief of the Delaware Indians who conveyed the land of Bucks County, PA to William Penn in 1682. South Jersey has a lot of pine and cedar forests, growing in sandy soil. In the forests there are many streams, which have been dammed to make chains of small lakes. The needles falling from the cedar trees contain iron and tannin; this gives the water in these streams and lakes a transparent brown color, known as "cedar water". Much of the cedar water region is a resort area. The camp was (and still is) for boys, age 7 to 16. We stayed overnight in canvas-sided bunk-bed cabins, 7 boys to a cabin with a counselor, who was age 14 or older.

This was a wonderful experience for me and I would have stayed all summer if my family could have afforded it. I did manage to stay anywhere from two to six weeks each summer. The attraction for me was that the camp activities were much more interesting to me than those at school, which consisted of competitive, physical contact sports (baseball, basketball, football). At the camp, things such as swimming, canoeing, nature studies, hiking, archery, and photography were subjects that blew me away. In my last year at the camp, I was a counselor. This camp still exists; you can find out more at www.ycamp.org/ockanickon.htm. The Ockanickon experience was the start of two more threads in my life: boating and photography.

Longfellow School only went up to the sixth grade. For seventh grade, I went to Pennsauken Junior High School. This turned out to be a very bad experience. Longfellow was a small school where I had been for six years and everyone knew and respected each other, and were friends. PJH was a much larger and very competitive school and, coming in at the bottom, I knew no one. I was only there one year, which was not enough time for me, in my shy way, to find my place in that school.

Moving to Merchantville

In early 1941, war clouds were swirling in Europe and everyone in the US could see that we were headed to join the conflict somehow. This environment caused our landlord at Hillcrest Avenue to decide he wanted to sell that property. We were offered a buy-out, but my parents decided they didn't want to buy that place. If they had to buy, they wanted something better. The real estate market had already become tight because of the prospects of war, but they found a place in Merchantville that was of interest and was for rent. Feeling that there weren't many other choice, my parents rented it. (Later, after the War, my parents bought this house.) We moved in the summer of 1941, a distance of 1.7 miles. I was at the YMCA camp during the move. I went to camp from one house and came back to a different one. I missed most of the work and excitement of the move.

Figure 4 The house at 207 Westminster Ave, Merchantville, NJ

The Merchantville house (see Figure 4) was on Westminster Avenue, a street of medium-sized custom-built individual houses. Our house was built by a developer from Florida, who didn't believe insulating a house was necessary. One of the first things my father did was to have the roofs insulated. This building, (*which stayed in the family for 56 years*), was built of cement blocks, partly two-stories, with flat roofs. The cement-block walls couldn't be insulated without tearing out the interior, which we didn't do. It's prime feature was a domed-ceiling livingroom 15' x 30' and 13' high. During WW II, we closed off that large room to save heating oil. There was also a "sun room", which had French doors on two sides. In the Florida tradition, the sun room once had a fountain in its center. This had been removed, but the plumbing was still there. The sun room was our family room, which was a new concept in small residences at that time. The lot was 90' x 100', level, pretty well filled by the house. As we soon learned, the remaining land was not much good for gardening because of shading on the west, north, and east sides, and too much sun on the south side — it reflected off the light-colored two-story side of the house and burnt up almost anything you tried to plant there. Gardening would be another thread in my life.

The Merchantville house had a two-car detached garage, so my father expanded his woodworking shop into there. I know the car never got into the garage. With the larger space, he could buy more tools, make bigger projects, and generally increase his woodworking capability. The garage did have one problem — it was located at the low point of the block, and we occasionally had a flood there. Not bad, just a few inches in the shop, but we had to be sure to get stuff off the floor if heavy rain was expected.

Much later in my life, I stored many of my archives (papers) in that garage. A considerable number of file boxes were lost in one of these floods. These were resources that would have helped me in writing this book.

Having moved to this house in the summer of 1941, of course we were there on Sunday, December 7, 1941. My father was home that day and we learned of the Pearl Harbor attack when he was called to his office to help get out special editions of the newspaper.

When I went back to school in the eighth grade, it was at Merchantville School, which had a K – 8 grade school and a 9 – 12 high school in the same building. Of course, I was a newcomer to this environment, but the climate was like Longfellow, and I adapted more readily than at PJH, even though most of the other kids had been in this same school since kindergarten and I didn't know any of them at first.

I had always been interested in music — listening, that is. Merchantville school had music classes, and for some unknown reason, I took up the clarinet as my instrument. This did not go well, particularly because I had trouble with my lips and the reed. I dropped this as soon as I could. But music still became a thread for me.

I also found two new friends who had similar interests to mine. These were the Dischert brothers – Bill and Bob, who lived about three blocks from my house on the way to the school. Bill Dischert was in my class and Bob Dischert was one year behind. Their father, George Dischert, was a buyer at the Samuel M Langston Company in Camden NJ, a manufacturer of corrugated papermaking machinery. George had thoroughly infused his boys with an intense interest in all kinds of machinery. There was always some kind of project going on at the Dischert house.

Another New Thread

About the time we moved to Merchantville, I found a new thread. This was electronics, in the form of radio. I didn't know it then, but it was the thread that would become my career. I started by building crystal radio sets, which were radio receivers that used a crystal such as galena (lead sulfide) as the detecting element. One connected an outside antenna to a receiver that consisted of the crystal with a probe that touched the crystal, a tuning coil, and a set of headphones. There was no power source except the energy of the radio signal itself. The challenge was to optimize the components to get the best possible signal from the greatest distance. For example, one needed to find the exact best place to locate the probe on the galena crystal. The set could receive the local AM radio stations, especially station WCAU, which had a 50,000-watt transmitter about four miles from Merchantville. This station was so powerful that, if you were within a mile or two from the transmitter, you might even hear the programs being detected by the fillings in your teeth, or by the wires on a fence.

The other challenge to crystal sets was to find materials other than galena that had the same capability to detect radio signals. One had to buy galena, but I found some local rocks that would work almost as well. Another challenge was to receive signals from far away. My best effort was to receive station WCKY in Cincinnati, OH. For more information, go to http://en.wikipedia.org/wiki/Crystal_radio_receiver.

My crystal radios rapidly grew into full-scale receivers made with vacuum tubes and loudspeakers instead of headphones. With the help of the Discherts, I began acquiring old radios. It was surprising how easily some of them were fixed simply by exchanging a few parts. I found the local sources to buy radio parts and used all my money to acquire a supply of parts and, as was my style even at that age, a library of books and pamphlets on the subject. I taught myself the basics of electronics. I also learned how to solder, which was how you connected the parts then.

Looking back at this period, and comparing the difficulties of finding electronic parts and information then with how it is today, I can see how easy it is for kids today to get into electronics. They just go to the Internet or down to Radio Shack and it is all there.

Bob Dischert was also interested in electronics, but Bill was not. He was mostly interested in machinery and cars. The Dischert family introduced me to something that I had rejected in my own house. That was drinking coffee. Mrs. Dischert (they called her Bess, but her real name was Dorothy) made a large pot of coffee every morning. This was kept warm on the stove all day long. For some reason, this coffee tasted good to me, especially late in the day. At home, my parents and Aunt Helen drank coffee, but it was always made fresh. They could never understand why I liked stale coffee.

The Discherts had a very different philosophy about the durable items that most people would simply go to a store and buy, things such as appliances, cars, or other things. Instead, they would look around for a used item that they could fix. So they bought junk cars and restored them, or they found appliances on the curb that someone had left for the trash collector, brought it home and fixed whatever was wrong with it. Sometimes the fix that was needed was extremely simple and they had things running in only a few minutes.

My family bought everything new. I did, too. I have had 17 cars in my life — all bought new except the most recent one. I have made the choice to not spend my time fixing used things. When something breaks seriously, I get a new one; I don't fix it. The Discherts looked at this differently: Save your money by acquiring used items and fixing them. When they needed a house, they built it themselves. They also never went into debt. I was always in debt. There are certainly advantages to their life style. However, I'm still happy with what I did. In general, whatever choices I made in life, good or bad, I don't carry regrets. One's past is the way it is; you can't do anything about it, so why regret?

Another interest I had from about age 10 to 14 or so was model-building. I tried some of the kits that were available in the stores for model planes, or buildings, etc. That was OK, but I wanted to do elaborate ones, and I soon learned that I just didn't have the patience to complete them. However, I did manage to complete one project that I made without a kit. That was to make a model of our Merchantville house (see Figure 5). This was done to scale. Although the real house was built of masonry with stucco exterior, my model had a wooden frame. I covered the frame with

Figure 5 The model of the Merchantville house. Bill is on the left and I am on the right.

cardboard and then stuccoed it with a mixture I made that looked like stucco. The result was very effective. I entered the model in a national contest held by Lionel Trains (yes we had model trains — how could a family with three boys not have trains?) I won second prize, which was a Lionel bascule bridge for our O-gauge train set. But the model-building thing never became a thread because of the patience issue.

Yet Another New Thread

Merchantville School had a theater program in all grades; in the high school part of the building, there was a completely equipped auditorium with a (somewhat small) theatrical stage. Some of the eighth-grade boys were allowed to join the stage crew that handled scenery and lighting for the stage productions. I volunteered for that, but I was crushed when the teacher in charge said I was too small. At the time I was only about 5′ 2″ and slight. So I did without the stage crew in the eighth grade. However, when I came back from a summer at the YMCA camp between eighth and ninth grades (the start of high school), I had had a growth spurt of about 6 to 7 inches. I was now taller than the teacher who had said I was too small. I joined the stage crew, which was one of my activities for the rest of high school; theater became another of my threads. *This thread contributed to my efforts at business presentations and meetings in my future.*

Summers at the Beach

In the summers before the War my parents rented a house in Surf City, NJ for the whole summer. This was a beach community on Long Beach Island, a barrier island off the coast of NJ. This house, a cape cod with an attic, was on the Bay side of the island (Bay meaning Barnegat Bay), but it was only about four blocks to the ocean beach on the other side of the island. Since these were the same years I went to the YMCA camp, it was a conflict for me. The beach was nice, but I felt the camp was better because it had more interesting activities. So I still went to camp while the rest of the family was at Surf City. When the War came, gas rationing ended the all-summer beach rental, because there wasn't enough gas for repeated trips to the shore on top of the essential driving.

Merchantville High School (MHS)

I started at MHS in the 9th grade. It was simply a matter of walking to the other end of the same building where I had attended 8th grade in the previous year.

MHS not only served the students advancing from the local eighth grade, but it also took students from Pennsauken and several other adjoining communities. So some of my Longfellow friends joined me in high school. I had no trouble becoming a fully involved member of my class this time. I jumped at many extracurricular activities, so long as they were not sports. I was never interested in sports—I didn't want to do things that had no tangible output. Besides, I wasn't good at sports; I only wanted to do things I could be good at. My initial extracurricular choices were: Print Club, Camera Club, Biology Club, Spanish Club.

The print club was most interesting. In the basement of the school there was a locked room that contained a complete print shop: press, type, paper supplies, etc. This facility was used to print announcements, notices, and tickets for school events. The members of the Print Club had access to this room and did most of the work there. It was also a unique place in the school where the print club members could hang out privately during

Figure 6 MHS

school hours, right in the school. There were about six members. Many "study" hours were spent there. It was a better studying place than the study hall — if you wanted to study, which I seldom did.

My experience with printing gave me an unusual capability. I demonstrated this one day in Latin class. The teacher asked me to come to the front of the class and read from a Latin textbook. I went up to the front and began. Soon, the rest of the class began giggling. The teacher didn't know what was going on, but the rest of us did. I was holding the book upside-down while I was reading. This ability comes from setting type for printing. You set type upside-down in the printing frame. This is because you want to begin setting type from the top of the printed page (just like you would read it), but if you tried this right-side up, there would be no way to make the type stay in the printing frame. It would fall out. So a typesetter learns to read text upside-down (*see* Figure 7). *This is something I can still do.*

During high school, I continued to grow slowly in stature up to 6-ft, but I didn't increase much in width. The name for this was a "beanpole". *Later in life, I overcame this characteristic and grew to normal weight, if not slightly heavy, for my height.*

Teaching Math

Mr. Elder was the high school math teacher, and he was also the basketball coach. In the latter mode, he was most interested in recruiting all the tall boys for the basketball team. I was one of the ones he was after, but as I have already said, I wasn't about to spend any of my time on a new thread that was a competitive sport. However, Mr. Elder and I reached a compromise. Since I was very good at math and, as he said, I knew more about math than he did, he would let me teach the math classes and he then could spend that time in the gym. I did this many times, which some

Figure 7 Type case overlaid with a typesetter's composing stick.
Note that the type in the stick is upside-down.

of my classmates were not too happy about. But what it did for me was to help me overcome some of my shyness, at least in front of a class of my peers.

The 60-watt Amplifier

During high school, I did a number of electronic projects to build high-power audio amplifiers. The culmination of this was a 60-watt amplifier that became a fixture at school parties and meetings. It was about an 18" cube that weighed 100 pounds. Combined with microphones, turntables, and speakers, this was quite a load to carry around. The system was used to play recorded music (records) or to do public-address with microphones, or DJ service. The latter mode, I didn't usually do myself. The amplifier system was another way I participated in social activities but didn't necessarily have to interact on a social level with the other people. I wouldn't say that I was antisocial, but I limited my social interactions to "business".

More about Photography

Although my interest in photography was sparked at the YMCA camp, where they had classes in photography, it wasn't until I got a real camera of my own that I could pursue it seriously. That happened at Christmas

1942, when I asked for a camera. My father was very anxious to help me with my interests as long as he could see that it was serious, and that it related to his interest, too. I got a 4 x 5 Speed Graphic camera with flash and all the accessories that Christmas. Cameras were not readily available during the War, but my father used his contacts at the newspaper to get this camera, which was the same type of camera used by most newspaper reporters at that time. The impressiveness of this camera probably helped me get accepted as the official school photographer.

This camera used 4" x 5" sheet film that you had to load into magazines in a darkroom for use in the camera. Each magazine carried two sheets of film, one on each side. To shoot, you had to put the magazine into the back of the camera and then pull out a slide that protected the film from light. After one shot, you replaced the slide and removed the magazine, turned it over, put it back in the camera, and shot the other side. To tell whether a particular magazine slide had been exposed, you flipped the slide over after shooting; the handle of the slide was painted black on one side and the other side was plain metal. *Pretty awkward and error-prone compared to what we have today!*

The other major problem of photography in those days was getting your films developed and prints made. If you were using a roll-film camera, you could send the films out to be developed; they would come back in a matter of days or a week. However, with sheet-film as my camera used, the only place you could get them developed was at a professional photo lab. The nearest one of those to me was in Philadelphia, which meant going there, dropping off the films, and coming back another day to pick up the negatives or prints. It wasn't cheap, either.

The solution, of course, was to have your own darkroom. Besides, for a budding technical person, that was very cool. So I worked on my father about that, too. I needed all the equipment: an enlarger, chemicals, printing paper, and a place that could be darkened for these activities. Eventually, these goals were all achieved. I got an old (even for that time) Elwood 5 x 7 enlarger (my films were only 4 x 5, but it didn't matter if the enlarger was bigger.) The Elwood was a monster, six feet tall, and made mostly of wood. It had a column up the back on which slid the enlarging head with a bright light, film carrier, bellows, and lens. The image was projected on the floor (or a low table, which is what my father made).

My father and I built the darkroom in the basement of the Merchantville house. The windows were permanently covered, so darkness was not a problem. The darkroom had two tables, the low one (about 12" high for the enlarger, whose enlarging head went up between the joists of the ceiling for the largest enlargement), and a worktable at waist height to hold the three trays needed for the chemicals. We also plumbed a sink and drain in

Figure 8 My Speed Graphic camera

there so that water and a drain were available without going out of the darkroom. During my high school years, thousands of negatives and prints went through that darkroom. *By the way, I still have all those negatives, 60+ years later.*

So I became the high school photographer. I had no competition for this task. I went everywhere the school had activities and took pictures. I took yearbook photos of people. I took pictures at the school plays. I went to all the sporting events. At a football game, I would shoot during the first half and then go home and develop the pictures and bring back prints before the game was over. That impressed everyone.

Photography was my way of socializing. I didn't have to say anything except "line up here", "say cheese", and things like that. It made me a member of the crowd, and I didn't have to play sports or anything else to get attention.

Theater at MHS

My theater thread continued to get my attention throughout high school. As I already explained I got on the stage crew in 9th grade. My interest was mostly in lighting, although I also participated in some set building. When we did our class plays in the junior and senior years, I became stage manager and also took a small acting part in each play. We did "Snafu" and "Out of the Frying Pan." Bill Dischert also was on the stage crew.

During high school, I and the Discherts also joined a community theater group in Merchantville, called the "Merchantville Playcrafters". This was an adult group, but they welcomed us because we were interested in doing lighting for their plays. Their theater was on the second floor of an historic brick building on the main street of Merchantville that housed the offices of a lumber yard on the first floor. This theater had a small stage with rather crude lighting facilities, which we later rebuilt to provide more complete capabilities.

Chemistry Class

I had a lot of fun with the chemistry class. This class had classroom sessions and lab sessions. In the lab we worked with actual chemicals and instruments. The chemistry teacher's name was Mrs. Croker (like the fish). At one point I made a logo for her using the letters of her name arranged in the shape of a fish. She was very good-natured about this. Chemistry was an interesting class, but of course all the boys wanted was to blow things up or make smoke.

Class Yearbooks

Because of my interest in journalism, photography, and printing, it is natural that I would get involved in the class yearbook production process. I did some of the photography for the two class yearbooks ahead of me. For my own graduation year's yearbook (1946), I did less of the photography, because I was the editor of the yearbook. That was my first experience with leadership. It meant getting involved in all aspects of yearbook production, including some things I didn't like to do, such as advertising sales.

The yearbook was my first appreciation of the fact that as a leader, you sometimes have to do things you don't like. For example, I didn't want to have anything to do with selling ads for the yearbook. I'll have a lot more to say about my attitude toward leadership, but I'll save that for later when I got into leadership in my career.

Learning to Drive a Car

In those days, you could get a permit to learn to drive a car at age sixteen

Figure 9 The 1946 yearbook staff. From left: Arch Luther (editor), William Murphy, Louisa Hofstetter, Miss Rasmussen (advisor), Eleanor Holman

and one-half. Of course, I did that as soon as I reached that age. My father wanted to teach me to drive, but he didn't want to risk his own car to my inexperience (it was a Hudson). So we used Aunt Helen's car, which was a 1937 Plymouth 2-door. We called that car the "auntmobile". It was a stick shift (the only type there was in 1937 cars). I mastered that along with the rest of driving and got my license promptly when I turned 17. There were no mishaps while I was learning. The Discherts already had cars and knew how to drive from much earlier ages, although they didn't go on the road until they were 17 and had their licenses.

Summer Job during High School

During my high school years, I had an after-school and summer job for J. Harold Wells, who ran a glassware-marketing business from a plant several blocks from my house in Merchantville. The basis of his business was to buy hand-blown glass items from the glass blowers who were (*are*) ubiquitous in South Jersey around Millville and Vineland. I started out helping him make modifications and improvements to the plant and cutting

Figure 10 Swanee Barometer

and grinding glass mirrors that were used underneath the Swanee barometer, which was his signature product.

The Swanee was a hand-blown glass swan with a long neck (see Figure 10). It was filled with a colored liquid that came partially up the neck. Depending on the barometric pressure, the liquid would move up or down in the neck. So it was a barometer of sorts: high liquid would mean low barometric pressure and low liquid would mean high pressure. For more about the Swanee, see

http://www.ccel.org/music/scheer/swanee/swanee.html.

The Swanee was one of the items that sat on a mirror. The mirrors were cut from large sheets of mirror and the cut edges were ground so that they were not sharp. This was done on a vertical belt grinder with water lubricant.

I learned to do all of the processing for the mirrors. I first had to master glass cutting to cut the large sheets of mirror into the sizes required by the swans. This was easy, and it is a skill that I have used many times since then.

The glass grinding, particularly, was tedious, and my lack of patience made me find ways to make it quicker and easier. I learned a two-handed method where I picked up a mirror with my left hand and ground the first two edges by flipping the mirror in my left hand. Then I would pass the mirror to my right hand and do the same procedure with my right hand to complete the grinding of that mirror. As soon as I had passed the mirror to my right hand, I would pick up another mirror with my left hand and start grinding it (the belt was wide enough to do this); I was effectively doing two mirrors at once. After I got into the rhythm of this process, I could produce each completely ground mirror in about three seconds. Since we usually needed only a few hundred mirrors at a time, I never spent enough time at this work to get bored with it. This was a case where my lack of patience made me find a better way to do a tedious and potentially boring task. Mr. Wells and everyone else there were amazed at this. *This demonstrates that there are many motives for creativity.*

Once I got my driver's license, I began driving Mr. Wells' truck, which was a 1932 Diamond-T. This truck was of a type that was very familiar around South Jersey, because it was used by Lit Brothers department store in Philadelphia. Its most distinctive feature was a vertical, flat windshield that must have been at least four feet high. You could stand up in the cab of that truck and still see through the windshield. I started driving his weekly route down Delsea Drive in New Jersey to Millville and Vineland to pick up glassware directly from the glass blowers. These rides produced many interesting incidents. For example, some of the glassblowing places were associated with certain activities that required armed guards or other sinister people. You had to be careful you didn't go in the wrong place. Bill Dischert also drove this truck route some times.

Mr. Wells had a summer house on the Rancocas Creek. This creek ran off from some of the cedar lakes that I mentioned earlier, and emptied into the Delaware River. His place was called "Cactus Point". The Rancocas was navigable for small craft, although you had to know the sand bars and sunken trees to survive on it. Mr. Wells had a boat, a 17-ft varnished mahogany speedboat with a Ford Model-A engine (boating thread). I learned how to run the boat and to navigate the creek. I also worked on the engine to keep it going. In good weather, I would take a bus after school out on Route 38 to Jake Adam's boatyard on the Rancocas where the boat was kept when not in use at the cabin. I could take the boat and run it a couple of miles down the creek to Cactus Point. There, I often did work for Mr. Wells around the property. Just before dark, I would drive the boat back upstream and tie it up in the boatyard, and take the bus back home. This substantially advanced my boating thread.

MHS Class Trip

In the spring of 1946, we went on the traditional (for MHS) class trip to Washington, D.C. In preparation for this, I had assembled an amplifier and music player that ran from a car battery, which I took on the bus to entertain my classmates. Such a system was unusual at this time; the power source was constructed from war surplus parts.

Graduation from MHS

When one has enjoyed, or endured, or some of both, all that high school offers, you come to graduation. My graduation occured on June 20, 1946, along with 179 other class members. I was third-ranked in the class, which meant that I escaped by one rank from having to make a speech at the graduation. I also got a number of awards, including the Bausch & Lomb Honorary Science Medal, the Class of 1939 Service Cup Award, and probably others which I no longer seem to have a record of except that people signing my yearbook congratulated me for "all those awards".

I never have liked large meetings, and I guess the graduation ceremony was one of these. Anyway, I endured and afterwards I felt a certain degree of freedom — to be short-lived, because college was in the offing.

Chapter 2

College Years

Long before my senior year in high school, it was clear that I would go to college and that I would study engineering. *How did I decide that? This is my analysis today of the situation: I have reported many of these factors in the previous chapter; I'll summarize them here. First of all, I have had a lifetime interest in machinery, equipment, and how things worked. Second, I enjoyed and did well in math and science classes in school. Third, I wanted to design and make things (that's what an engineer does). Fourth, I wanted to apply my skills to things that would eventually be used by many people and would benefit mankind in general.*

Applying for College

When the time came in my senior year at MHS to decide which colleges to apply to, I had to make a list of engineering colleges and then plan to visit them before applying. My short list was Lehigh University (LU), in Bethlehem, PA; Massachusetts Institute of Technology (MIT) in Cambridge, MA; and Rensselaer Polytechnic Institute (RPI) in Troy, NY.

My parents and I took a trip to visit them all, starting with LU and ending with MIT. The result of this was that MIT was the hands-down winner for me. That was because of its location (Boston area), the campus, the buildings, and especially the technical facilities, faculty, and curriculum.

When I got back home and announced this to my college advisor at MHS, he said: "No one from Merchantville has ever gotten into MIT. I don't think your chances are very good." I applied to MIT and LU (second choice). I was accepted at both. So I began preparing to go to MIT. Over the summer after MHS graduation, I continued to work for Mr. Wells and had many adventures with the Dischert brothers.

One day that summer, Bob Dischert and I went to Philadelphia to go to Herbach & Rademan, an electronics store that had a lot of surplus material. When we got there, we found that they were cleaning out their warehouse and putting lots of surplus stuff out on the curb. We rooted through it and collected all that we could carry and began walking down Market Street to take the subway back to Camden where our car was parked. As we were walking, we heard a horn blowing behind us; we looked and it was Bill Dischert in Wells' truck. He had made some deliveries west of Philadelphia and was on his way home. Bob and I jumped into the truck and we turned around and went back to H&R. Suffice to say, a lot more electronic parts went home with us in that truck.

Getting to MIT

In early September, I packed up all my stuff and my parents drove me to MIT. 1946 was the year most of the veterans came back from the War, and MIT had made an effort to accomodate as many of them as possible under the GI bill, while still taking the usual number of high school graduates, like me. That left no regular dorm rooms for freshmen. Instead, they had converted a WW 2 laboratory building into a dormitory for the newcomers. (We called it "the barracks".) I landed in one of these. The barracks was Building 22 (See figure 1).

MIT is located on the banks of the Charles River, across from downtown Boston. Massachusetts Avenue, running through the center of the campus, crosses the river on Harvard Bridge. Harvard University is a couple of miles up Mass. Avenue. The bridge got its name because Harvard was there long before MIT. Harvard was established in 1636; MIT was established in 1865.

The barracks room I was in was set up for 16 students, typical for this building. Each group had a sleeping room with bunk beds, a study room across the hall with a small desk for each person in a kind of cubicle, and a large bathroom with showers. For eating, we went to the campus dining hall, which was about a block away. It was located in the Walker Memorial building.

There was only one other student coming directly from high school in my barracks room besides me; the rest were veterans. They were typically five or more years older than me, and vastly more worldly. I was initially worried about this, but we were all in this together and the

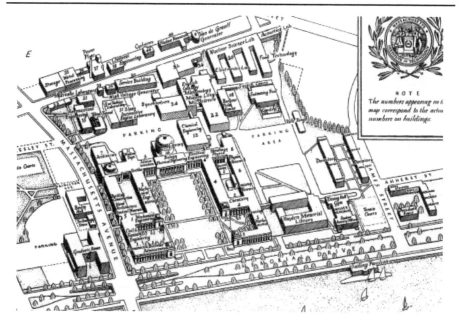

Figure 1 Map of part of the MIT campus in 1949.

cooperation was wonderful. They had been out of high school for five or six years and had forgotten a lot of the stuff that MIT demanded you know before coming there—things like trigonometry. You could say they were "rusty" about school. I could help them with that and they weren't hesitant to ask. What I needed was to learn the college environment and also the surrounding area.

Compared to any school I had ever been in, MIT was huge, both physically and in terms of students. My class had 1800 students—ten times larges than MHS. I was initially overwhelmed by the size, but I made an effort to find my way around and soon became comfortable with it. However, I was still intimidated by the large number of students and so many of them being much older than me. I never got as involved in the activities at MIT as I did at MHS.

First Year Courses

The curriculim at MIT emphasizes the fundamentals of science and math. There were few courses about practical applications of those fundamentals.

I was initially disappointed with this, but after a while, I realized that knowing the fundamentals allows you to deal with any kind of practical problem, not just what you learned in school.

Today, after nearly 60 years of experience applying my MIT education, I can say unequivocally that the fundamental approach is absolutely right. During my career, massive technology changes occurred that were not even dreamed of when I was in school. I faced them and became involved early in the changes. I had no trouble doing this because I knew the fundamentals and could easily apply that to understand the new technology. I had a considerable advantage over engineers that did not have a good fundamental background.

Because of my established interest in electronics, I enrolled in the electrical engineering (EE) course. There were two kinds of EE at that time: power engineering and electronics engineering. However, the distinction between these in the curriculum did not show up until the second or third year.

MIT courses followed the usual college format: there was a lecture session where a large number of students heard lectures by a full professor or equivalent person who introduced the course material. Typically these were held in a large lecture hall seating 100 or more students. Then, the students had "recitation" sessions, once or twice a week. These were headed by a lesser faculty member or a graduate student; class size here was about 20 students. The session leader worked closely with the students to help them grasp the material and learn it. Tests were also conducted in these sessions. Finally, in the courses where it was appropriate (like physics or chemistry), there was a laboratory session, also weekly.

The courses in the first term of the Freshman year were:
General Chemistry
Physics
Engineering Drawing
English Composition
Calculus
Military Science (ROTC)
This totaled about 26 hours per week of class time. The rule at MIT was that each hour of class time should require approximately one hour of

homework time. Thus, schoolwork will take around 52 hours of the student's time every week. Maybe that doesn't sound like a lot, but we students found that it was difficult to get all this done every week and find time for anything else other than normal living activities such as eating and sleeping.

The first-year math course was calculus, which is the basis for all engineering work, so it was strongly emphasized at MIT. Even before we ("we" here is the barracks room group) went to the first class, the Math department issued a requirement that we read and study the first three chapters of the textbook, *Analytic Geometry and Calculus, 2E,* by H. B. Phillips. This was 100 pages! Furthermore, when we tried reading it, it was rough going and essentially all the time before the first class was spent by us as a group trying to figure it out. We did not succeed very well. In the first class, we complained about the assignment and the difficulty of understanding the text. The instructor, whose name I don't remember, remarked that the text was considered to be excellent and anyone who had difficulty understanding it must be an idiot. *I still have that textbook and while writing this I got it out and skimmed over the first 100 pages. I would have to say that even now, after 60 some years, I could generally understand it, although it was tough. So, I guess the book might be considered excellent by someone who already knew the subject, but students new to the subject didn't see it that way.*

Anyway, we got past that and the math course proceeded with a normal degree of difficulty for most of us with no further controversy.

One thing made clear at the start of the math course was that it expected students to have a complete understanding of trigonometry from the start. A graduate student who was handling the recitation session I was in, offered to give a refresher course in trigonometry after hours for anyone who felt they needed it. Everyone signed up, including me, who had taught some of Mr. Elder's trig classes at MHS. The session was held in one of the large lecture halls and it was packed. The teacher went through a complete derivation of trigonometric principles, beginning with the unit circle concept. It was a wonderful presentation and everyone took copious notes. I'm sorry that I don't still have those notes. The whole course took two hours. In high school it was a full semester.

The Physics curriculum was designed to run concurrently with the math curriculum, so that as the student gained the math concepts, they would be immediately applied in the physics classes. This worked well. The initial Physics text was *"Principles of Physics"*, by F. W. Sears. I do not remember any problems with the physics classes. However, I had to wait until the second year before it got to any of the electrical subjects, and the third year before we got into electronics. The first year of Physics was spent on Mechanics, Heat, and Sound.

The initial friendship in the barracks group was based on our common need to get up to speed on the classes. Beyond that, there was a large difference between me and the veterans, because of the age gap. I was still 17 when I began at MIT. The others were in their 20s. When the work was done and we went out for fun, they wanted to go into Boston and eat, drink, and enjoy adult things. The only part of that that I could relate to was the eating. I didn't even want to go into town. I was perfectly happy to eat on the campus and walk around or read in my room.

However, I did become a close friend with one of the barracks members, Jack Mohr. Jack was from Lima, Ohio, and had been in the War before coming to MIT. Our friendship came about because of a shared interest in photography. Of course, I had my 4 x 5 Speed Graphic camera with me, and Jack had a 35-mm Argus camera at that time. Later he also got a Speed Graphic, but it was a smaller one, 2 1/4 x 2 1/4 size. *My friendship with Jack lasted throughout our time at MIT, but it faded after that because I went back to New Jersey and he got married and stayed in New England.*

A big difference to me about school in the Boston area was the winter. There was a lot more snow than in South Jersey, and it lasted longer. However, I was in a situation where I didn't have to go any distance to school, and other people shoveled the snow, so I managed to accept it. *East coast winters were one of the things that eventually got me to move to the west coast.*

Because of the distance, I came home from school only once during the year – at the Christmas holidays. I traveled by railroad, using the New Haven Railroad, the Long Island Railroad, and the Pennsylvania Railroad, arrriving at the North Philadalphia Station after a full day of traveling. My parents picked me up at the station and drove me to

Merchantville. The holidy vacation lasted about two weeks, so I felt it necessary to bring home the parts for a number of my projects with me. I did this each time I came home for a holiday, but I seldom had time at home to do much with the stuff I brought with me. There always seemed to be plenty to occupy me at home other than building electronics.

Anyway, the first year at MIT went well, even though I didn't have as many friends as at MHS, and I wasn't involved in many activities outside of my classes. My grades were good, although not as good as at MHS, and I definitely could no longer say that I never had to study.

Summer Job - 1947

Since I was not getting any new practical experience at MIT, I decided that I should have a summer job to gain some of that. For the summer of 1947, I managed to get a job in the engineering department of Philco Corporation in Philadelphia. Philco was a large manufacturer of radios and they were just beginning to manufacture television receivers.

I began at Philco doing odd jobs for a technician who handled supplies for the engineering department. One of the activities I became interested in was the transformer design department, where a couple of engineers designed transformers for all the engineering projects at Philco. For the non-technical reader, a transformer is a device consisting of a laminated iron core with two or more windings of copper wire. It is used to change the voltage of an alternating-current (AC) source higher or lower to power the components of an electronic circuit. I had been very interested in transformers because they were an important (and expensive) component of audio amplifiers such as I had built for use during high school.

I started learning the details of transformer design, which even at that time was something that could be done quite exactly using fairly simple mathematics. That summer I designed many transformers. This was something that I used many times in my career—not so much for actual design, but to be able to more effectively specify transformers or to deal with the people who did the design for me.

Philco was manufacturing a TV receiver that used a 10" round cathode-ray tube (CRT) to display the picture. The round tube wasted a lot of space, because the picture, of course, was rectangular. There were about 20 vacuum tubes in the Philco set for the rest of the receiving functions. I learned about all of these circuits, and even acquired the parts to build my own version of the Philco set at home.

I had never seen much television before going to Philco, so having my own TV set was unique in our neighborhood and all my friends and my family's friends came to see it. I had already decided that I probably would specialize in television engineering upon graduation from college.

Teaching Bob Dischert

Bob Dischert was interested in electronics, but he wasn't interested in going to college. In fact, he wasn't interested in any schooling. In high school he did not do well—deliberately. He wanted to graduate from high school, but he wanted to spend the least possible effort. It didn't matter if he was last in the class, just as long as he got through. He succeeded in that. It wasn't that Bob was not smart; his later career proved that he was brilliant. He was just against formal schooling—he wanted to learn by doing, and I was able to help him with that.

In the summers when I came home from MIT, I spent many hours with Bob teaching him what I had learned. I actually enjoyed that because Bob's intelligence was so great, his insight so piercing, that I actually learned things just by teaching him. It is well known that the real test of what you know is to try to teach it to someone else, or to a class. I certainly proved that in my experience working with Bob Dischert.

There are many stories I could tell about my college days. However, in the interest in moving this book on to the even better stories that came later after I began working, I will only tell a few here.

The first TV in the MIT Dorms

I already told you about the effect the homemade TV had in Merchantville. My second year at MIT, I moved from the barracks into a single dorm room. I installed my homemade TV in this room, along with all of my other things. I set it up so that I and a few other visitors could see it. There were only a couple of stations operating in the Boston area at that time and all television was broadcast live, because there was as yet no technology for recording TV. One easy source of live material was wrestling matches. It seems that this attracted college students like ants to a picnic. It became a real problem that kept me from doing homework or studying. and I eventually had to set some rules. I established hours when my room would be open and limited the number of people who could be in the room at any one time. That worked. However, I couldn't really control the people who gathered in the hall and looked in the door.

Now that I had my own dorm room, there was more space to lay out my electronics projects and their parts. I also learned the sources in the Boston area for electronics parts. One of my favorite places was the Radio Shack store in downtown Boston. This was the original Radio Shack store, which later grew into the worldwide chain of stores still known as RadioShacks.

The second-year courses were similar to the first year except that there was the first Electrical Engineering course — electrical circuits. This covered the fundamentals of electrical signals and circuits.

Summer Job - 1948

My summer jobs were very significant to my development as an engineer. In the second summer, I wanted to work at a TV broadcast station because the broadcasting end of TV seemed most interesting to me. My father knew that Philadelphia station WFIL-TV was owned by Triangle Publications, who also owned the Philadelphia Inquirer. He knew some people there and WFIL-TV hired me for the summer. That summer, I worked in the main studio for the station, which was located at 46th and Market Streets in Philadelphia. My duties were in the equipment repair section of the operation. My experience there was the start of my troubleshooting skills that later made me famous in RCA Broadcast. Since WFIL-TV was RCA-equipped, I also got a head start on understanding RCA cameras and other studio equipment.

My dorm room was filled with electronic equipment and parts for all the projects I was doing or planning to do. My plans far exceeded anything that I could complete in a reasonable time considering the demands of school work. *Overcommitting myself to projects has always been a problem with me and it still is.*

Back at MIT

One of the things at MIT that attracted students like myself was the reputation of Dr. Harold E. Edgerton, the inventor of the electronic strobe light such as is on practically every film or digital still-picture camera today. In those days, strobe was a big deal—by "big" I mean large, huge. The physical equipment to build a strobe light at that time was much larger than it is today, and Doc wanted to make LARGE strobes. For example, during the War he produced airborne strobe lights so powerful that he could take pictures of the ground from an aircraft. Some of this equipment became available in war surplus and he had a collection of it that he used to demonstrate unusual applications of strobe, such as other aircraft applications, underwater, etc. He used a crew of student volunteers to help handle this equipment as he took it from place to place. I was one of his volunteers.

Summer Job - 1949

During the summer of 1949, I again worked at WFIL-TV, but this time I went to the transmitter department. A radio or TV transmitter operator requires a First Class Radiotelephone Operator License from the FCC, so my first task was to get a license. I did this on June 27, 1949. I still have the certficate. I started at the WFIL-TV main transmitter, which was located on the top floor of the Widener building in downtown Philadelphia. The transmitter was an RCA TT5-A, 5,000-watt transmitter on channel 6. The antenna was on a tower at the top of that building. That antenna location gave good coverage in the city, but was not too good for broadcasting to outlying areas around Philadelphia.

While I was there, WFIL-TV moved their main transmitter from the downtown location to a broadcasting antenna farm near Roxborough, PA. That location, west of Philadelphia, was on higher ground and also allowed tall towers, so that the antenna height was much higher than downtown. That increased the coverage area. To facilitate the changeover, they installed a small RCA TV transmitter (500 watts) in a new building at Roxborough. This small transmitter would give enough coverage during the changeover because of the much better antenna at Roxborough. They also set up a microwave communications system to carry the picture and sound signals from the studio location out to Roxborough. The plan was to go on-air with the Roxborough transmitter during the overnight shutdown of transmission. Then, over a period of a week or so, the downtown transmitter would be torn down, moved to Roxborough, and set up in the location prepared for it in the new building.

I was assigned to go to Roxborough on the first day to start the transmitter and go on-air from there. I was trained on the new transmitter and I went there on the appointed day. The procedure was to first check that signals were coming in from the studio and then, about five minutes before air time, to simply switch on the transmitter. After a short warm-up, I would go through the procedure for signing-on, and then monitor and log operations for the duration of my shift.

The problem came when I went to switch on the transmitter. It wouldn't start! I was alone, so I called the main transmitter room downtown and told them of the problem. After some consultation, they said that the problem was inside the transmitter cabinet. I would have to open the cabinet and make the fix. This was simple enough, but the transmitter cabinet contained high voltage, about 1,000 volts as I remember. I had to make sure these voltages were not active before I dared enter the cabinet. There were capacitors that could store this voltage long after the power was turned off.

This problem was handled by what is called a "grounding stick", which was located just inside the cabinet door. After the door was opened, you took the grounding stick and used it to touch the hot terminals of all the capacitors. This short-circuited them to ground and removed any stored energy. Then it was safe to work inside the cabinet. The catch was, you had to know *all* the places to short out. They talked me through that over the phone. I kept the phone line open all through this procedure. Then I performed the fix they recommended (I don't remember what it was), closed up the cabinet and tried once more to start the transmitter. It worked! We were about 15 minutes late getting on-air that morning.

Electronics Lab at MIT

In my senior year, the electronics course included a laboratory session. The principal equipment in this lab was a war surplus shipboard radar system, the Navy SG radar. We learned all about this system and how to operate it. It was set up to scan over Boston and we could see radar pictures of the city and harbor. However, over in one corner of the lab was something of much more interest to me—some TV equipment. This was a war surplus airborne camera, a display, and some other equipment.

My lab instructor was Lester Smith, a graduate student at that time. He was delighted to find someone else interested in TV, and encouraged me to do a lab project in TV. I decided that I would build a unit called a "sync generator". This device is used to generate all the timing signals that go to all units in a TV system to allow them to synchronize. The name "sync" (pronounced "sink") is obviously a nickname for synchronize.

As all TV electronics at that time, a sync generator used vacuum tubes—about 100 of them. I don't remember how far we got with the project, but I learned a lot more about TV from that experience. Lester Smith became a lifelong friend. Although I think I only saw him once in person after graduating, we kept in touch with periodic phone calls or letters.

In my final year at MIT, I got bored with school and my grades were not as good as earlier. I just wanted to get through and begin designing TV equipment for RCA. I had now decided that was where I wanted to work.

College Graduation

Graduation from MIT was on June 9, 1950. My parents and Aunt Helen drove up for the ceremony and also to pick up me and all the stuff I had accumulated in my four years there. The graduation was held in the Rockwell Cage, which is normally used as a gymnasium. The class size was 1800 students, and it was quite a squeeze getting everyone in there. I graduated somewhat down from the top of my class, not like at MHS, and I didn't get any awards. But it was now over, and I had the credentials to get to work as an electrical engineer.

I went to MIT to get a technical education, which I accomplished and I really appreciated. I didn't participate in many of the social activities but kept to myself studying and building electronics. If you look at the class of 1950 yearbook, you won't even find me because I failed to show up for the picture-taking session. They did not list students for whom they had no picture. I do regret that a little.

My parents wanted me to go on to graduate school, but I turned that down because of my urgent desire to do some real work. *As I've already said, I don't usually carry regrets about my past regardless of what happened, but looking back on the graduate study decision, I think I made the right choice for the career that I planned. There was only one time during my career where an advanced degree might have made any difference, but I reached my goals anyhow. I'll explain that later on.*

Three friends and I decided to take a trip around the US after graduation. Gus Gross was the owner of the car. He got the car for his graduation and planned to drive the Pan-American Highway all the way to his home in Ecuador. We left right from school; my parents took my stuff back home without me. I don't remember the details of the trip, but we went from city to city mostly, because Gus wanted to spend his nights in cities, rather than out in the wilderness where there were no girls. Basically, we crossed the country to San Francisco, went down the coast highway to Los Angeles, and then back east to San Antonio, where the party broke up. That end point was because Gus had to connect with the Pan American Highway to go to Ecuador. He went south, I took a train back to Merchantville, and the other two went back to their homes, too. On to my first engineering job.

Chapter 3

Beginning Work

Getting a Job

Right from the beginning, I had specific requirements for a job. I wanted my engineering work to have a positive impact on the world. I wanted to do things that would benefit society in general, either directly or indirectly. I did not want to work on military machines or weapons. It became clear to me early in my college years that I wanted to work in the budding field of television.

During my senior year at MIT I decided that my first choice for where to work on television was RCA. I wanted to be in the Broadcast Systems department, where they designed and manufactured equipment for radio and TV stations. The other side of the TV business was the home receiver. RCA also manufactured TV receivers, but I chose the broadcast end because that encompassed a much broader range of technology. Broadcast equipment creates and distributes the signals that eventually reach the millions of receivers, which deliver entertainment and information to the general public. Working in TV broadcast will affect millions of people.

RCA Broadcast Systems was located in Camden, NJ, about five miles from Merchantville. I decided on RCA after getting a lot of information from friends of my parents, many of whom worked at RCA, some even in Broadcast Equipment. I also had a lot of experience with RCA TV equipment from my two summers of work at WFIL-TV.

So, as with the summer jobs, my parents started the ball rolling by telling some of their RCA friends about me; this got me an interview with RCA Broadcast engineers in Camden. The interview was a success for both of us and I was offered a job as a Class B engineer in Broadcast Engineering at a starting salary of $300 per month. I would begin work on July 1, 1950. The normal starting grade for a new graduate was Class C engineer. Most graduates also were required to take an internal RCA course about engineering at RCA. There also was a job rotation program, where new engineers spent six weeks in each of four different locations in the company. That was to help them decide where they wanted to work. With my summer job experience, personal electronics projects, and a commitment to Broadcast Equipment, I was able to skip the courses and the rotation program and

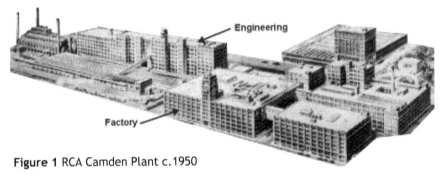

Figure 1 RCA Camden Plant c.1950

went right to work. *Engineering graduates today who do not have the experience that I had when starting at RCA would benefit greatly from such new-engineer programs, which are still offered by large companies.*

About RCA Broadcast Engineering

The broadcast industry in 1950 consisted of radio and the fledgling black and white TV. I, of course, was interested in the TV part of this. RCA was the largest of only a few suppliers of broadcast TV equipment. RCA made all the electronic equipment and supervised installation of complete TV stations. Broadcast products were manufactured at the Camden, NJ plant and the engineering department was there as well (see Figure 1). The plant was large, about 2,000,000 square feet, covering six city blocks on the Camden waterfront. Broadcast was a small part of this plant.

The factory building for Broadcast Equipment, Bldg. 17, had an enclosed water tower on it. This had lighted stained-glass windows on each side that showed the RCA dog logo (See Figure 2) The dog was called Nipper

Figure 2 Nipper window

and the tower was known as "the Nipper Tower". *This tower has been preserved as a National Historical Monument and still exists today although the rest of the plant is gone.* Another famous sign was on top of Buildings 5, 6, and 7 (not shown in Figure 1), which were located right next to the Benjamin Franklin Bridge crossing the Delaware River to Philadelphia, a couple of blocks north from the main plant. The sign was placed at bridge level and showed the complete Nipper and Victrola logo, along with the words "RCA Victor". When I first went to work, we were located in one of those buildings. After a few years we moved to 10 Building, which is where the Engineering arrow points in Figure 1. Building 5, 6, and 7 were torn down later, so that sign no longer exists.

Camden, NJ at that time was a significant industrial city. Next to RCA on both sides were buildings of the Campbell Soup Company. A major product from that plant was tomato soup, made from Jersey tomatoes, which we Jerseyians think are the best tomatos in the world. However, tomatoes took on a different view during the summer harvest season. Huge open trucks loaded with tons of tomatoes came down the street between RCA and Campbell, dripping tomato juice and generally creating an extreme tomato mess. We breathed tomato fumes all day long. Even worse, occasionally one of the tomato trucks would have an accident somewhere in the area, spilling tons of tomatoes all over the place. It was not good to think of the mess of tomatoes all over the street and then look at a can of Campbell's tomato soup.

One could look from Building 17 into the Campbell building across the street, and see overhead conveyors carrying chicken carcasses to somewhere. We wondered how these conveyored chickens ended up in the chicken soup. In spite of these experiences, I like Campbell soups.

The RCA Camden plant's largest activity was making radio and TV receivers for consumers. These products were manufactured by the millions in the same manufacturing organization that we used. The entire organization of the company and the Camden plant was focused on this mass market. On the other hand, broadcast equipment was manufactured typically in quantities of 100 units at a time. This 10,000 to 1 discrepancy in scale of manufacture created a constant battle between broadcast engineering and the manufacturing organization. Broadcast engineers called the manufacturing organization "the factory". That name will be used in the rest of this discussion.

There was a huge discrepancy between the scale of engineering required by a mass-produced consumer-product business and a professional small-quantity business. The consumer business could afford to engineer its products to a very high degree of manufacturability and low cost. In fact, that was essential. Saving a penny in the cost of a million units amounts to $10,000 in savings. That could pay an engineer's salary for a year at that time. On the other hand, a penny saved on the cost of 100-unit broadcast production is only $1.00. Not a significant saving.

The factory people were used to the consumer products level of engineering in the products they were given to build. However, in Broadcast, we could not afford to give every product that degree of engineering, and our designs gave the factory people many headaches. Broadcast engineering had a bad reputation in the factory. I don't believe this was because we did such a bad job, but it was caused by the extreme differences in the needs of these two very different businesses, which caused our relations with the factory to become quite strained.

The RCA factory was unionized. In the 50s while the consumer electronics division was still mass-producing radios and TVs at Camden, there were more than 100 classes of unionized labor. This created many complications. However, the consumer electronics division relocated its engineering and manufacturing to Indianapolis in the mid-1950s, which reduced the number of classes of labor considerably. Problems still remained because the infrastructure of job classifications and work rules did not change easily. In addition, the Government Systems Division was in Camden and had some mass production of military communications equipment. This was at lower quantities than consumer electronics, but still much higher than Broadcast production quantities. Government Systems had a much larger engineering engineering organization than we did in Broadcast. They also had additional procedures for quality and security specified by the government. In the interest of uniformity of operations in the plant, some of these government procedures affected us, too. More will be said about that situation in a later chapter

Product Design

Designing for manufacture is called "product design". Since that was the kind of work I primarily did during my early years at RCA, I should explain more about it: When engineers develop a product and make the first model of it, they can use all the capabilities of themselves and their laboratory to produce this unit, generally without regard to the cost of doing it. However, for manufacturing the unit (even in 100-quantities), the engineers must produce specifications for all the parts that go into the product. That means making engineering drawings for all parts, with sufficient detail that the purchasing department of the factory can put the item out for bidding from multiple sources. In addition, detailed drawings must be made for how the parts are assembled into the product so that the factory process engineers can develop procedures that will be suitable for factory workers (not engineers) to follow. Finally, we must specify how the factory will test the assembled product to prove that each unit works properly. This is a lot of detailed work, entailing not only the engineers, but draftsmen who create the drawings under the engineers' direction; machinists who produce sample mechanical parts; and technicians and wiremen who assemble and test the models. Depending on the nature of each particular product, other skills may be required.

When the drawings and specifications are completed, it is the job of the engineering department to produce "prototype" models from the drawings and specifications alone, without any other engineering input. This is difficult to do rigorously, but such models are important to prove the design is workable before turning it over to manufacturing. This process also adds to the schedule and cost of engineering, which means there is often temptation to skip or reduce it.

Often, the prototype models are used to introduce new products to customers at a trade show, such as the National Association of Broadcasters (NAB) annual convention. This is done even though we may still be more than a year from actual production. Customers know about this time lag, but they don't like it. Sometimes, we even have gone to the NAB with earlier engineering models. This is worse for everyone because it generates tremendous pressure on engineering and manufacturing to get the product into production in less time. Shortcuts are taken to speed up the process, often with disatrous results. There is also the issue of showing a new product prematurely, because it may shut down sales of the previous products, causing a loss of business until the new product comes out.

An engineer just coming out of college doesn't know anything about this, nor does he like it when he learns about it. Many engineers want to invent—create new things, and the product design process looks like sheer drudgery to them. It isn't drudgery and there's lots of opportunity for creativity.

Factory Follow Engineering

A further source of drudgery to the engineers is all the engineering work generated during the factory's process of purchasing materials, setting up for manufacturing, assembling, and finally testing the product. This kind of engineering activity in RCA was called "factory follow" engineering. Most engineers viewed this as the lowest kind of engineering work there was. However, most engineers also want their designs to be produced, sold, and used all over the world (I certainly felt that way), and they eventually come to the realization that factory follow work is an essential part of reaching that goal. It was still a battle to get factory follow work done, *a battle I learned a lot more about when I advanced to engineering management.*

The factory purchasing process is very important. Engineering must create drawings for every component or part in the product. Purchasing takes this information to potential suppliers to find possible sources. If a supplier is interested, he submits sample parts, which Purchasing sends to Engineering using what was called the "E-Form procedure". Engineering must qualify the parts and their supplier by testing them against the drawings. There may be more than one supplier for a part, especially important or expensive parts. Engineering has to check them all out and advise Purchasing of the acceptable ones. Purchasing will then make their choices based on other considerations such as price, delivery, supplier reputation, or support.

When a factory follow engineer solved a problem in the factory, there were often changes to be made in the factory processes or parts. The information about this was conveyed to the factory via a document called an "engineering change notice" (ECN). ECNs required approval by the top management of Broadcast Engineering, the Marketing Department, and the factory. Factory changes can quickly get expensive and cause delays that disrupt the whole system. Because of this, a factory follow engineer oftens hears this direction: "Here is a problem in the factory. Go fix it, but don't change anything." Most engineers see this as an oxymoron; it is seldom achieved. However, the real advantage comes in making changes that don't require any new parts. This avoids the delay and cost of having to go out and buy new parts.

After a product leaves the factory, there is also the need to help customers when problems occur after they receive the product. This involves a lot of telephone consultation, and sometimes field trips to the customer location. Most engineers don't like to do this either, but besides learning that his equipment doesn't work in the field, the engineer can learn a lot of other important things from customer contact. The first line of customer technical support is usually the factory follow group. However, when a large, important customer is involved, then anyone in the organization, including the Chief Engineer or even the division general manager, may become involved.

TV Terminal Engineering

My first assignment was to work with a technician who handled supplies, odd jobs, and other tasks for Broadcast Engineering. That was to help me learn the ropes of the organization. I don't remember that this phase of work lasted very long, and soon I was assigned to the TV Terminal Equipment Engineering group. Terminal equipment in a TV system includes all the units that support and connect the major studio equipment such as TV cameras. It includes sync generators, distribution amplifiers, switchers, and other units. Each of these products will be explained as we come to them later. The Terminal Equipment group at that time was headed by A. H. (Tony) Lind (See Figure 3).

Before proceeding further, I need to explain some more about 1950s-era electronic circuits. In the 1950s, circuits were built by connecting "discrete components" with wires. Discrete components were such things

Figure 3 TV Terminal Engineering Group, 1952. From left, J. L. Grever, J. P Ulasewicz, B. C. King, D. E. Warfield, H. C. Shepard, A. C. Luther, A. H. Lind, Leader

as resistors, capacitors, inductors, potentiometers (adjustable resistors), and vacuum tubes. The most important component of a circuit was the vacuum tube (see Figure 4), which was the only component that could amplify electronic signals.

The vacuum tube (usually just "tube") was invented around the turn of the twentieth century. By the time I became involved with tubes, they had been manufactured and improved for 50 years. In spite of all the improvements, tubes were by far the most unstable and unreliable electronic component. Tubes were always mounted in sockets so that they could easily be replaced when they failed during the life of a product. The simplest amplifying tube, called a "triode", had three elements: a "cathode" of special material that, when heated to a high enough temperature, emitted a stream of electrons; a "plate" that received the electron stream because it had a high positive voltage applied; and a "grid", placed between cathode and plate, on which you put a negative voltage that could control the amount of the electron stream that reached the plate. The whole structure had to be in an evacuated housing, usually a glass jar, to prevent air molecules from interfering with the electron stream. The tube is an amplifying device because the voltage applied to the grid can be very small and low power, but it is capable of controlling the much larger and powerful signal flowing to the plate. Because of this behavior, tubes are called "valves" in Europe, which is really a much more descriptive name.

There were numerous sources of instability in a tube, but the most important one was a slow degradation of electron emission from the cathode. Over a period of a few thousand hours of operation, this effect would

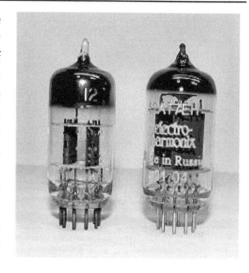

Figure 4 Vacuum tubes (dual triodes)

make the tube unusable. During that time, the circuit performance would slowly degrade; many circuit applications required a regular adjustment to compensate for the tube aging. An operator would have to do this manually. Products containing many tubes, would have many operator adjustments.

An example of this is the AM radio receiver. An AM receiver contains perhaps five or six tubes that are all in a cascade to detect and amplify the received signal from the antenna up to a power level that you can hear from a loudspeaker. If there were no adjustment, the volume out of the loudspeaker would slowly go down because of tube aging. However, a single volume control takes care of all aging, since all the tubes are doing the same thing in series. A volume control is needed in a radio anyway to set the user's preference for volume, so the user is never aware of tube aging until a tube actually fails. In a product where the tubes are doing different things, which each has to be correct for proper performance of the entire product, then there would have to be an adjustment for each tube. This is the case in a typical piece of television broadcast equipment. One of my personal objectives for anything I designed was to use circuits that would not depend so heavily on tube characteristics that change with aging, and thus would require far less operator adjustment. Few such circuits existed at that time, so I had to make several key inventions.

Another problem with tubes is that they can suddenly "burn out". Because of thermal stresses in the cathode heater from repeated cycles of heating up and cooling down, the heater can suddenly fail. The tube no longer "lights up". This is exactly the same thing that happens in an incandescent light bulb. A circuit designer can't do anything about this except to make sure that the heater voltage remains within specification, and that the tubes used are of the highest quality.

The TG-2 Sync Generator Project

Because of my experience at the MIT lab, I was immediately interested in the sync generator part of TV Terminal Engineering's charter. I studied the existing RCA sync generator, which was a design that originated at the RCA Laboratories at Princeton, NJ during development there of the television system standards that were adopted by the FCC for broadcasting. At the time of the start of RCA broadcast equipment manufacturing, broadcast engineering had far too much work to do in a short time, so they simply put the Princeton design through the product design process and shipped it to the factory to build. This was called the "TG-1", the "TG" acronym being for "Television Generator".

The TG-1 design was somewhat of a monster. It was an 80" tall cabinet full of circuits and a hundred or so controls that had to be carefully adjusted to get it to work. The whole thing weighed several hundred pounds and cost thousands of dollars. Although a sync generator is essential to a TV system, this seemed to me to be out of proportion to other parts of the system, such as the cameras, monitors, and switching equipment. I looked at this and I felt I could make it much better — smaller, lower cost, higher reliability, and far fewer adjustments. I presented these ideas to my group leader and manager and was told to go ahead and build a development model, as an "advanced development" project. That was the name given to activities done on a project prior to any commitment to product design. In fact, there were whole organizations in RCA devoted to advanced development.

A sync generator produces the pulse signals that go to each unit in a TV studio to establish synchronization between them. Synchronization is essential so that all TV signals created or processed by the system are "locked together". If this is the case, any signal can be switched to or combined with another signal with no disturbance that will be evident at the receiver. If the signals are not locked, switching between cameras or other video sources will cause receivers to momentarily fall out of synchronization, making a disturbance in the picture that may last for several seconds.

A pulse signal is a voltage that switches between two values with controlled timing. For example, sync pulses in the system normally switched between 0 volts and 4 volts. The pulse signals are standardized by an industry organization so that all equipment from all manufacturers will work together. In the case of the composite sync signal, the standard is set by the Federal Comminucations Commission (FCC), since the sync signal is part of the signal that is broadcast to all receivers. The sync pulse signal switches 15,000 times per second or more and the time accuracy of switching is specified in fractions of a microsecond (a millionth of a second).

I produced a "breadboard", which was the name we used for a model of a circuit built in the fastest and easiest way for demonstration of a concept. Breadboards were often built on a wooden board because it was easy to screw components down anywhere — thus the name. My sync generator breadboard was on a metal chassis instead of a wooden board, but we still called it a breadboard. It contained a number of unique circuits that I later patented. I'll describe two of these here.

The first is the "stabilized multivibrator", US Patent 2,857,512, "Monostable Multivibrator", October 21, 1958. A multivibrator is a circuit using two triode tubes (that are available in one glass envelope — a "dual triode" — see Figure 4), to produce one pulse of controlled duration (the time between the up and the down transitions of voltage), each time it is given a "trigger" signal. This type of behavior is called "monostable", because the circuit produces only one pulse per trigger. It is too much here to give circuit details, but anyone who is interested can look up the patent. The stabilization in the circuit is produced by adding components that make the cathode current in one of the tubes remain constant as the tube ages. Since the pulse width of the circuit depends only on the current in this tube, tube aging does not affect circuit performance.

The second circuit is used to create the "composite sync" signal required by the TV standards. This circuit is covered by US Patent 2,857,514, "Wave Generating System", October 21, 1958. The composite sync signal contains a series of pulses at the horizontal scanning frequency of 15,750 cycles per second. (The term "cycles per second" was officially changed to "Hertz" [abbreviated "Hz"] in 1960 in honor of the German physicist Heinrich Hertz. I'll make the switch to Hz when I get to 1960 in this book.) However, the composite sync signal also contains some double-frequency pulses in two different pulse durations. Previous approaches had used separate circuits to create each different pulse duration and frequency and then had additional circuits that combined the separate signals into the standard composite sync sequence. To accomplish this more simply, I designed a circuit using two stabilized multivibrators that allowed pulse width and frequency to be electronically controlled. With this one circuit, I could create the complete sync signal.

My breadboard sync generator impressed everyone in the lab. It used only about 20 tubes (compared to nearly 100 in the TG-1) to do the whole job (not including power supply). Twelve of the tubes were stabilized multivibrators. Management approved proceeding with product design.

Personnel assignments for the product design project were made. Another engineer was assigned to architect the product—this was Bob Dennison, another Class B engineer who, amazingly, started at RCA the same day that I did. An architect in an electronic design project is responsible for the overall system design configuration (sometimes called "architecture"). Bob had had a previous engineering job before joining RCA and had some real experience with product design. A mechanical engineer was also assigned to head that part of the project, which included the design of the chassis and the mounting of all the components so that they would be effective electronically and would hold up as the equipment is used or serviced. I would be the electrical designer, responsible for the circuits, and under the direction of the others. The other member of the product design team was the Product Analyst, from the Marketing department.

This was Henry "Chip" Klerx, also a relative newcomer to RCA, but not an engineer. I did not understand his role at first, but it soon became clear that he had to plan all the parts of the project other than engineering. He also had to get upper management to approve our plan for the design, and he had to determine and get approval for how many units would be built in the first run of manufacturing.

As the design progressed, there were many changes to what I had done in the breadboard, all for good reasons. Additional features were added, such as "genlock", which is a capability to synchronize the sync generator to a signal coming in from a remote location. With this capability, the remote signal could then be combined with local signals just as if it was already a local signal. This was a major addition. Another major addition was a signal generator to create some test signals that would assist testing of the other parts of the TV system. This saved the customer from having to buy and hook up another unit to get those signals.

At that time, most of our studio products were made in two versions — one for studio use: controlled indoor environment; and one for field use: where the product would be carried outside for location shooting. The field product had to be protected from the weather and other environmental extremes. For the new sync generator, this was done by putting the same chassis as designed for studio use into a field carrying cabinet that provided additional environmental protection. The ability to do this also became a requirement of the design. It meant that the studio chassis had to meet all the environmental requirements (temperature, humidity, vibration, etc.) of field operation.

The sync generator had to have its own built-in power supply, so this also was added to the design. After the entire design was laid out, the tube count had grown from approximately 20 that I had in the breadboard to 40 tubes.

This was still about 60% less than the TG-1 count. The product also became larger than my breadboard, fitting on a 21" rack-mounted chassis (see figure 5). With field use in mind, all the components were mounted on terminal boards at the rear of the chassis. That kept then from vibrating during transport and possibly breaking (see Figure 6). The new sync generator represented a vast performance improvement over the TG-1, significantly lower cost to manufacture, much easier for the user to operate and maintain, and with more operating features.

Completing this design and building prototypes to prove it out took more than a year. Once all tests were completed on the prototypes, we were ready to release the product to the factory. It took another year for the factory to source and procure all the parts, set up an assembly line for production, and start up a sample run. Again, more testing was needed before we had the first units to ship to customers. There were many ECNs during this process.

Chip Klerx and his colleagues in Marketing also worked hard during this time to create brochures, manuals, advertising, and product promotion, so all would be ready when the first units came out. They also decided that the studio product would be called the TG-2A and the field product would be the TG-12A. All of this was a new experience for me. I never realized how much was involved beyond the engineering part.

One other thing that I did not understand at first, was the pricing of the product. Marketing decided that it would be sold for the same list price

Figure 5 The TG-2A Studio Sync Generator

as the TG-1, even though the manufacturing cost was much lower. I thought: "We are not passing any of the savings on to the customer." The marketing reason for the pricing was that a sync generator represents a small part of the total cost of a TV station. Reducing the price of the sync generator would not increase how many sync generators we could sell — that was fixed based on the number of station packages we sold. The customer was still getting a good deal because of the better reliability and new features. Also, having a high-margin product like this in a station package assisted our sales people in pricing the total package attractively. In a way, we *were* giving the customer back some of the sync generator's savings in the package price. I had a lot to learn about marketing and sales.

The TG-2A was introduced to the market in 1954 and was sold for the next 10 years. Approximately 4,000 units were sold during that time, which represented nearly 90% of the market for this equipment. RCA received more than $8,000,000 in revenue from the TG-2A. What did I get of that? Just my salary. Of course, I didn't do this alone — the massive resources of

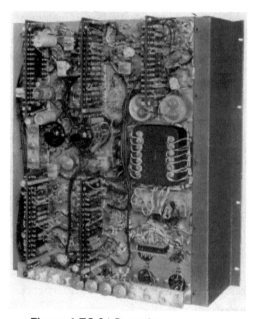

Figure 6 TG-2A Rear view

RCA made it possible for the product embodying my ideas to be brought to market.

I have been asked many times why I stayed with RCA after I developed the sync generator. Why didn't I go on my own and build that product (or other products) myself? The first (and simplest) answer is that when I joined RCA I signed a patent agreement that all engineers are required to sign. It says that everything I invent or develop at RCA becomes the property of RCA. Patents were filed by RCA and my rights to them were assigned to RCA. That answer is somewhat of a cop-out. I might have been able to make a deal with RCA to take a license for the product, maybe even have them sell it for me. I don't know, of course, because I didn't try that. However, the much more important reason was that I was simply too naive about business at the time to think of such things, let alone to be able raise the money needed to carry them out. Today, all engineers learn to think of such things, if for no other reason than that they have heard of the Silicon Valley history.

It is further interesting to see what has happened to sync generators in the intervening 50 years up to today. With the advent of solid-state circuit technology, a sync generator became a single integrated-circuit chip. What was a 50-pound unit in the TG-2A in 1956, an equivalent device is now a chip smaller than your fingernail and weighing far less than a gram. You also might note that every hand-held camcorder contains a sync generator!

Patents

I have mentioned several US patents that I acquired during this project. The Patent System was established by the US Constitution to protect inventors against others using an inventor's work without authorization. Congress has passed laws to specify exactly how the Constitution's requirement is implemented. As with other federal laws, the inventor's rights are supported by the federal courts. Thus, a patent is a legal document.

A patent is obtained by making application to the US Patent & Trademark Office (USPTO). At the USPTO, patent examiners will study the application for its originality and decide whether a patent should be issued. In doing this, they look for relevant "prior art", which is previous patents or other published work that may show that the invention has been "anticipated" by someone else. If it passes the prior art test (and several other legal requirements), a patent will be issued to the inventor.

Professional employees at RCA were required to sign an invention agreement upon joining the company. This agreement said that all inventions and patents made by the employee became the property of RCA. Any patents acquired by the employee had his or her name on it but all rights to the patent were assigned to RCA. The agreement provided for a payment to the employee for each patent. At the time I started, this payment was $1.00. *That figure increased later; some of my later patents paid $500.00.* The agreement also provided for the employee to declare any pre-existing inventions or patents that would *not* become the property of RCA.

RCA had a Patent Department that assisted RCA inventors in filing for patents. RCA had a "pool" of patents that they used to license others who needed them. The Patent Department reported in at the Corporate level and like other Corporate offices, the focus was primarily on the consumer electronics market. So the patent pool was licensed to other consumer manufacturers. Although they supported us in Broadcast in getting patents, I was not aware that there was very much licensing of our patents to other Broadcast manufacturers. *However, I'm pretty sure that our patents were a factor in the cross-licensing agreement made with Ampex in 1956-1957 (see Chapter 5).*

An engineer who had an invention worked with the Patent Department by initially filing an Invention Disclosure document. (Sometimes there would be multiple inventors for a single invention.) The disclosure was a description of the invention, signed by the inventor and a witness. It was supported by technical details that the engineer wrote in his engineering notebook. This book was very carefully witnessed and was periodically backed up on microfilm so that it was a legally acceptable document. Following the disclosure, the Patent Department would review the document, make a search for prior art, and decide whether a patent application would be filed. The Patent Department did most of the legwork of preparing the application. The engineer contributed to this and in the end, approved the application by his signature. The Patent Department filed the application with the USPTO and followed it through their processes. If the patent was issued, the engineer would get his payment.

Technical Papers

At about the time of the TG-2A, I began writing technical papers for publication or presentation at industry conferences (or both). This was the current manifestation of what I called the journalism thread in Chapter 1. *During my career, I produced about 25 papers that I presented at industry meetings, or that were published (or both). I think that was a pretty good accomplishment considering the intensity of my work during those years. Most of my writing for papers was done in my free time off the job. All of my papers are listed on my web site. People in academia produce far more papers in their careers, but they get paid for this--it is part of the job. At RCA in most cases, this kind of thing was outside the job. I wrote papers becaused I liked to write, and for the prestige it gained for me.*

Korean War — Drafted!

The Korean war began about the time I graduated from MIT. When I started at RCA, the possibility of a draft was in the air. As soon as RCA began recognizing my abilities, they took steps to protect me from the draft by having me spend a large proportion of my time on a military project for the Air Force. That was a high-resolution TV system for which I still should probably not reveal any details. When my number came up in the draft, RCA applied for a deferment for me, based on this military work. It turned out that such a deferment required "presidential" approval — Harry Truman. I'm sure he never saw it, but in this case his office took a lot of time processing it. My deferment came through the day before I was to go to Fort Dix, NJ for induction. Although I was already packed for that, I didn't go. I continued the military engineering work throughout the war. Thus, my work on broadcast products became part-time for a while. However, the military project was good experience, and I learned a lot about the limits of television technology at that time.

The First Broadcast Color Camera

During the time I was doing the other projects I have mentioned, another part of Broadcast Engineering was working on the first broadcast color camera. This was before the color TV standards had been adopted by the FCC and it was an advanced development project. I was very interested in this project, so I kept looking in on it. I helped with the troubleshooting and the testing of the first system. This system was sent to NBC in New York and installed in Studio 3H for testing in an actual broadcast environment. I had become involved enough that I was even sent to NBC to work on problems that turned up there. In the course of this, learning all about the color camera and its supporting equipment, I could already see where I could apply my design principles to make major improvements.

During the time this camera was in the lab at Camden, I was working there one day by myself, and a stranger came into the lab and began looking around. I had been instructed that any unknown people coming into the lab should be challenged, because we didn't want outsiders knowing about the project. So I mustered up my courage and asked the man: "You know, you are not supposed to be in here. This is a private lab." And he left.

A few minutes later my boss came in and said to me: "Do you know who that man you chased out of here is?" I said "No." "Well, he is General David Sarnoff, the Chairman of the Board of RCA." All I could say was "Really?" A little later General Sarnoff came back in and thanked me for being so concerned about the security of the lab. *That was the only time I saw General Sarnoff in person.*

Design of Color Cameras

The original camera design that was being tested at NBC was named the TK-40 and was put into limited production and shipped to a small number of customers. Some time after that, we started work on advanced development for a new improved camera.

At about this time (July, 1952), I was promoted to the next higher engineering grade, Class A Engineer. This made no difference in my work, and only a little difference in my salary. I suppose the most important thing to me was the prestige — it indicated I was succeeding and I was no longer a newcomer to the group.

A Color Camera Contains Three Monochrome Cameras

A monochrome TV camera at that time used a special type of vacuum tube called an "image orthicon" (IO) to pick up the image of the scene and convert it to a television electrical signal. To anyone designing circuits for, or operating it, this tube was, at best, a beast. I had had some experience with monochrome cameras previously when I was called in to consult on factory

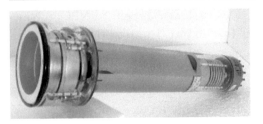

Figure 7 The RCA 5820 Image Orthicon

follow problems in the TK-10 monochrome camera. I had learned all about the IO at that time.

An IO was expensive— about $1,200 in 1950 dollars. One thought about that every time the tube was handled. However, most of the tubes we had in the lab were rejects from the factory at Lancaster, PA where the tube was manufactured, and supposedly they had no value. The IO was about 15" long (*see* Figure 7) and it had to be handled with the large end up all the time. There was danger of loose pieces inside the tube falling on the sensitive surfaces and getting lodged, which would cause a defect in the picture. The IO was mounted in the camera inside a yoke assembly of coils that created the necessary magnetic fields for the tube. It also required 12 different voltages that needed to be applied precisely for proper operation. The optical image of the scene was focused on the large end of the tube, using a lens of appropriate size. An IO had about 20 different adjustments to set up the voltages and magnetic fields for operation. Performing the setup procedure took a lot of skill, and it had to be done every time the tube was started up, and several times during the day. When set up properly, the monochrome picture was excellent.

One IO story that went around the lab involved one of the engineers, Irv Bosinoff, who one day was cradling about six IOs in his arms as he walked down the aisle. A colleague came past him and stopped, asking: "Got a light, Irv?" The expression that came on Irv's face was something to behold. After all, he was using both hands to hold $7,200 worth of IOs!

A color camera had *three* IOs, each with yokes and associated circuits. The incoming light from the lens was split with dichroic mirrors, which are mirrors having special coatings that split the light into its TV primary colors: red, blue, and green. These primary colors may surprise you. In school, you heard about the primaries "red, blue, and yellow". These are the *subtractive* primary colors used for printing and painting on white paper. The paint pigments cause those colors to be *subtracted* from the light reflected by the paper. Actually, the correct names for the subtractive primary colors are magenta, cyan, and yellow. In the case of TV, we are *adding* light to create the color picture, and equal parts of red, blue, and green light are mixed to make white. These are the *additive* primary colors. *These concepts are well known today by people who use digital cameras and color printers.*

Each color from the mirrors went to a separate IO. In order to maintain optical stability, the mirrors and IO assemblies were mounted on a heavy baseplate inside the camera, called the "optical plate". Splitting the light into three channels introduced the issue of "registration", which means that the pictures coming from all three IOs must match in position, rotation, and size when they are finally combined on a color display. If the registration is not exactly correct, color fringes will be seen on sharp edges in the picture.

The optical plate, IO yoke assembiles, and the necessary amplifiers and power circuits made the camera head quite heavy — around 300 pounds Because of this weight, the camera was mounted on a special pedestal to move it around the studio. There was no hand-holding this camera.

The studio camera pedestal weighed about 700 pounds. As seen in Figure 8, it consisted basically of a hydraulic jack mounted on a three-wheeled base. The ring just below the camera was a steering wheel — it adjusted the three wheels in the base. The camera was mounted to the pedestal with a "pan-and-tilt head", which allowed smooth adjustment of the camera angles for shooting. In spite of the size and weight, the camera on a pedestal was surprisingly agile. It took four men to mount the camera to the pedestal. In the field, cameras could be mounted to a heavy tripod instead of the pedestal, but this was difficult to move around.

The picture signals from the IOs went through separate channels of amplifiers, producing red, blue, and green signals. These signals were then sent through three large cables back to a control station where they could be monitored and adjusted. Most of the adjustments in the camera head were controlled remotely from the control station via other wires in the camera cables.

A camera system requires a lot of mechanical engineering, especially for the camera head. The optical components require extreme precision and mechanical stability; and the packaging must be able to mount all the

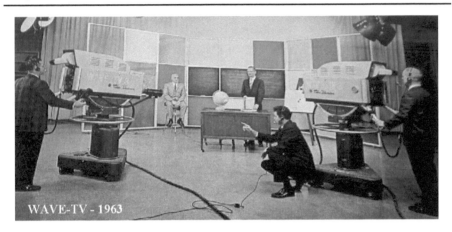

WAVE-TV - 1963

Figure 8 TK-41 cameras on studio pedestals

components in the smallest space yet make them easily accessible for servicing. Because a camera is a very visible item in the studio or field, it also must be attractively styled.

A broadcast camera system is separated physically into at least three parts. First, is the camera head — the part that goes into a studio or is mounted somewhere outside in a field application. Next is the control center, which is located in the studio control room; in the field it is in a trailer or some other type of shelter. Finally, the third part is the equipment racks, which would be in an equipment room for a studio installation, or in the trailer used in the field. There are good reasons for this arrangement. The studio location is primarily the domain of the production people — the actors, directors, and others. They want no disruption from the technical people. Normally the only technical people who work in the studio are the cameramen, who are responsible for moving and pointing the cameras. If other technical operations are required for the camera system, they should be done from a position outside of the studio. With the color camera, with its huge tail of three heavy cables, there may also be people needed to manage the cables so as to keep them from underfoot of cameras and the people in the studio. In the case of the control position, where the camera operator does his work, the reasoning is the same. That location should contain only control panels and monitors. Other parts of the system that do not require much operator attention should be out of this room. This results in the architecture I just described.

The TK-41 Color Camera

The TK-41 camera system was an improvement to the TK-40 system; the control equipment design was based on the results of my concepts and system analysis. I focused primarily on the control position and the processing equipment. All video processing equipment was built into the control console, which became possible by my circuit design, using stabilized circuits throughout. In the TK-40, the video processing equipment was located in a remote equipment rack. The new configuration simplified the control and signal interconnections, but it ran counter to the current trend to remote as much equipment as possible to equipment racks. However, the improvements in performance, operability, reliability, and cost made this configuration irresistible. The processing chassis was designed to be easily pulled out of the console for ready servicibility.

The TK41 series was introduced in 1954 and continued to be the prime color camera in the industry for more than 15 years.

In July, 1954, I was promoted to Class AA engineer, the highest working engineer category. At age 25, I was the youngest Class AA engineer in Camden. Again, the benefits of the promotion were not great salary-wise; it was mostly prestige because now I was often the lead technical person on a project. Prior to this, it was sort of ex-officio when I functioned as a technical leader. The next step up would be to a Group Leader, which was a management position. I was definitely not ready for that, a fact that I made known. More about that later.

Color Bar Signal Generator

The color bar pattern is a fundamental test signal for color TV systems, cameras and transmission equipment. The generator for a color bar signal is another pulse system like the sync generator. It is synchronized from a sync generator and produces three output pulse signals for the primary colors of red, green, and blue. These signals are fed into a color encoder to create the complete color video signal. Previous color bar generators used as many as 12 tubes to do the job. I developed a

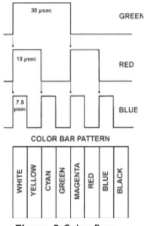

Figure 9 Color Bars

breadboard that did the same thing with only three tubes. I had to change the signal format somewhat to accomplish this, but this was no problem because no standards had been written yet for a color bar test signal. My bar generator is covered by US Patent 2,824,225, "Bar Signal Generator", February 18, 1958.

My approach to the color bar generator was to use one stabilized multivibrator to generate a green signal that filled half the width of the picture (see the top line of Figure 9). This creates a green bar on the left and a black bar on the right of the screen. Then to get the red signal, I used another stabilized multivibrator to create one half-width pulse from each edge (up and down) of the green signal. This then made a yellow bar, a green bar, and a red bar. Finally, to get the blue signal, I used a third stabilized multivibrator that put out one pulse for each edge of the red signal. This then produced the full bar pattern. The pulses are shown in Figure 9, which gives the relationships of the signals and the displayed bar pattern. Three stabilized multivibrator circuits do this. *As with the sync generator, color bars today are generated in most camcorders, using a tiny part of one of the integrated circuit chips in the camera. However, the bar pattern made by my circuit is still the one used today.*

Transistors

In 1948, the transistor was first shown by Bell Labs. This was the first solid-state amplifying device, it had no vacuum and no heater; it promised amplification at lower power, lower cost, and higher reliability than vacuum tubes. However, the first devices were "point-contact transistors", meaning that there was a critical point-contact on a piece of germanium metal, much like the crystal radio set's contact on galena. They were difficult to manufacture, short-lived, not very good at high frequencies, and very sensitive to the environment.

In the early 1950s, the "junction transistor" came out. This solved the manufacturability problem, and practical applications, particularly the transistor radio began to appear. Broadcast engineers were of course following all this, but few had the vision to see that these devices would have application to our sophisticated equipment. How wrong they were!

Fortunately, with a little prodding from myself and a few other engineers, higher management agreed that we in TV Terminal ought to begin an advanced development project to look at transistor applications in broadcast equipment. We began learning the details of using transistors, and looked for applications. Because the high-frequency capability of the early transistors was poor, we first tried using them in an audio amplifier. We built a prototype and it performed satisfactorily in low-power applications.

Meanwhile, the art of making transistors progressed rapidly. One important improvement that occurred around 1960, was the use of silicon instead of germanium in the transistor. This solved most of the environmental problems, and allowed devices of higher reliability and higher power. The theoretical lifetime of a silicon transistor is practically infinite. However, problems can come from contamination during manufacture or leaky packaging that allows environmental contaminants (such as water) to enter the device and cause it to fail. These problems were also getting solved.

As transistors improved, we began developing pulse circuits using them, looking toward making transistorized pulse amplifiers and pulse generators. It was clear that the rapid development of transistors would soon reach the capability for video circuits, too.

About this time, management saw the progress we were making and asked us to develop a course to teach our engineers about transistors, so that others could begin using them in their designs. One of the managers, Andy Inglis, told a meeting of all broadcast engineers that everyone was required to take the course or risk getting fired. He probably couldn't have actually done any firing, but it did get everyone's attention.

Another engineer in TV Terminal, Bob Hurst, and I worked on the course. I had developed my own unique approach to presenting how transistors worked and could be applied, which became the basis for the course. Most transistor books and courses at that time taught the physics of making a transistor, which we felt was something that application engineers like ourselves didn't even need to know. Only the makers of transistors needed that; we weren't going to make our own transistors. So our course focused simply on *using* transistors.

The course was designed to be taught using an overhead projector, which was the preferred method for visual presentations at that time. An overhead projector uses large transparencies to project the images. They are 8 x 10 or 8-1/2 x 11. You can even write or draw on them during the presentation. *(Overhead slides are pretty much obsolete now — you do presentations today with computers.)*

Using the overhead projector, we also decided that the course should be heavily illustrated. So there were *lots* of overhead slides. These approaches were well-received by all the participants. After the first running of the course, Bob Hurst took over all of it. It was also published as a series in Broadcast News (the Broadcast Systems' magazine) in 1958-1959, and a separate booklet was made available. *We probably could have done more with this course, such as publishing it outside of RCA, maybe as a book, but we were too busy with designing more circuits.*

In TV Terminal, we continued developing and testing other transistor applications in broadcast equipment, including video circuits. One that progressed to an actual design was a video switching system.

TS-40 Video Switching System

A video switcher is a unit that performs the selection of signals from a multiplicity of cameras to create a single continuous program. A typical TV studio has a number of cameras or other video sources, and it is necessary to be able to connect those sources to a multiplicity of output devices, such as program lines, video effects units, separate monitors (displays), etc. This switching structure may be viewed as a matrix. Arrange all the input sources as vertical lines in the matrix, and the outputs as horizontal lines, with signals coming out at the right. Each place where the lines of the matrix cross is a possible switch connection (cross-point). Earlier TV switchers accomplished the switching by placing a relay at each cross-point. A relay is a mechanical switch driven by an electrical voltage. They are slow, tend to "bounce", which is a chattering when the relay is activated, and they are not very reliable.

In our advanced development group in TV Terminal, we considered solid-state solutions using transistors and diodes, to eliminate the video switching relays. (A diode is an electronic device having two terminals; it is designed to pass signals in only one direction.) The approach we developed had a small board that was placed at each cross-point in a matrix constructed with etched-circuit boards, which at the time was a new circuit-assembly technique. Etched-circuit boards were not very applicable to vacuum-tube circuits, but they were quite suited to transistor circuits. Instead of using hand-cut and soldered wires to make a circuit, one etches the circuit pattern on an insulating board coated with a layer of copper. Holes are drilled in the board to take the wire leads of all components. After the components are inserted into the board, the board is soldered in a single operation using a "wave-solder machine", which passes the circuit boards over a wave of molten solder. This eliminates a lot of labor from the assembly.

A design for a complete switcher (which contains other features beyond the video switching cross-points that have been described) was laid out and proposed to management. Models were built of the key components such as the cross-point boards and the switcher matrix. Each output line used a transistor amplifier to receive signals from the cross-points on that line, but a tube final amplifier was necessary to drive the output line. Transistors had not yet reached the levels of bandwidth and power to drive a video line. Other features such as tally switching (controlling the on-air lights on the cameras) were planned (this still had to be done with relays).

The proposal was accepted for product design and the same group who had done the advanced development did the product design. The product was given the designation TS-40. It contained several technological firsts in the broadcast industry: It was the first use of transistors and etched wiring boards in video equipment, the first use of plug-in designs for complete switching, and the first use of solderless terminals for control wiring. Many engineers in TV Terminal Engineering had a hand in the design. Figure 10 shows a cross-point group module containing six cross-point boards being inserted into the cross-point frame. Each cross-point board represents a task equivalent to one vacuum tube (even though a

Figure 10 TS-40 cross-point frame

tube circuit would never be stable enough to do this). Compare the size of the unit in Figure 10, which has 54 cross-point boards, to the TG-2 in Figure 5, which has 40 tubes. You can see the size reduction.

TM-21 Broadcast Color Monitor

Many of the control adjustments for a color camera can be done using a monochrome monitor to view the picture. However, the final observation for picture quality should be done in color. At the beginning, this need was filled by a home-type color receiver modified to receive the signal directly from the studio rather than over-the-air. That worked, but it was far from an ideal solution. A home color receiver would not hold up very long in the continuous operation required in the studio, nor was its color performance accurate enough or stable enough for broadcast use. A color monitor in broadcast becomes the standard of picture quality for the signal that is being broadcast. The monitor must be able to be set accurately to a standard of picture quality. and maintain that over a reasonable operating period.

In about 1956, the TV Terminal Advanced Development group began work on a new 21" broadcast color monitor. This monitor would be self-contained and configured for mounting in a studio control room; it would provide the best possible color picture within the constraint of using a color CRT (kinescope) selected from the home receiver production line; and would have high reliability, easy serviceability; and, of course, reasonable cost.

Circuit development proceeded in all areas of the monitor: color decoder, video drivers, deflection and high-voltage circuits, and power supply. I was involved in several areas of the project. One of those was the problem of "dc restoration". This problem exists in home receivers as well as any other place where the color signal needs to be processed or displayed. Because of the way color signals need to be distributed, the setting of black level in the signal becomes dependent on the average brightness of the signal. A bright signal will have a lower black level that a dark signal, causing the black areas to lose detail. DC restoration is used to restore the black level to a constant value. In home receivers, dc restoration at the kinescope was usually done with a diode tube. This is only partially effective. Since a broadcast monitor is used to initially set the black level, it should have very accurate DC restoration.

I developed a circuit for this purpose, which I called a "feedback clamp" circuit. "Clamping" is a more accurate method of achieving DC restoration, but it was considered too expensive for home receivers. "Feedback" is a generalized circuit technique where a measurement is made of a value to be controlled and then compared to the desired value. The result of the comparison is then fed back to the input so as to correct the measured value. This can be very effective. My circuit is covered by US Patent 2,863,943, "Feedback Clamping Circuit Arrangements", December 9, 1958.

Another problem in a professional monitor that is operated continually is protecting the expensive kinescope from loss of signals, misadjustment, or circuit failures. This requires a means for knowing when an overload situation has occurred and then switching off the power. This circuit is covered by US Patent 2,913,621, "Protection System for Cathode Ray Tubes", November 17, 1959.

In color monitors there is the problem of providing for user adjustment of color balance as well as brightness and contrast. The color balance adjustment in home receivers is usually fixed when the receiver is installed, but that is not good enough for broadcast service. Color balance needs to be adjusted regularly to keep the monitor standardized. Sometimes, monitor adjustments interact with each other such that is is difficult to achieve adjustment of all parameters without a series of progressive repeated adjustments of the same set of controls, slowly homing in on the correct adjustment of all controls. This is unsatisfactory because it takes a lot of time, and it is tricky — some operators have trouble mastering it. I developed a circuit arrangement that solved this problem as well as several other more

Figure 11 RCA TM-21 Color Monitor

detailed issues. It is covered by US Patent 2,965,705, "Kinescope Background Control System", December 20, 1960.

The development and product design of the color monitor, now designated TM-21 was completed and production began in 1958 (see Figure 11). It proved to be a very successful product.

The Dischert Brothers Also Joined RCA

In 1954, Bob Dischert joined Broadcast Systems as a technician in the Broadcast Engineering department. He worked with us in the TV Terminal Advanced Development Group. A technician in an engineering department works in assembly and testing of equipment, but does not normally participate in design. It quickly became apparent that Bob was much more than a technician, in spite of his not having an engineering degree. His creativity showed almost immediately; he could interact with the engineers and quickly generate ideas that could improve their designs. Soon, he was submitting invention disclosures to the Patent department for filing.

Bob's approach to inventing was different. Most people approaching a problem that might require invention want to know everything that has been done before. Bob didn't want to know any of that. He felt it limited his creativity. He thought about the problem by himself and often came up with ideas that were so different and unique that everyone was surprised. Once this ability became known, he was in demand in many areas, and participated in many problem-solving exercises.This led to his being promoted to Class B engineer in a few years.

Bill Dischert joined RCA in 1956 as an engineer at the Government

Systems' Moorestown, NJ plant. He transferred to Broadcast Systems in 1972. He is a mechanical engineer.

Design Concepts

Every engineer, when approaching a design project, needs to have some goals for his work. Sometimes that is provided by the engineering organization in the form of policies or rules for design. However, in the situation I encountered at RCA in the early days, there were no such guidelines. With my experience working in a TV station and discussions with other engineers and customers, I saw that there were numerous opportunities for improvement of the then available equipment through new design practices. As I gained more experience in advanced development and product design, I identified several design objectives that were the keys to my success in new products. They were:

1. Circuits should be designed for stability against the normal effects of aging, environment, and other factors. It should not be necessary for routine operator adjustments to be required to correct for circuit instability.
2. All designs should consider the equipment operator's point of view and offer simplification of operator tasks and other convenience features.
3. The overall system should be reviewed for simplification of equipment units and interconnections.
4. Specialized features should be developed for built-in testing so that proof of performance can be shown at any time in the field.

After having implemented these ideas in a number of projects, I wrote a paper entitled *Design Trends in Color TV Studio Equipment*, which was published in "RCA Engineer" magazine in October-November 1956 (I was 28). This complete paper is available on www.archluther.com, but I have reproduced on the next page a sidebar, "About the Author", that the editors of the magazine added to my article.

These thoughts show that product design need not be a mundane process of performing a routine update on a previous design, but rather it calls for the utmost creativity and skill in producing a new design that surpasses the old design in performance, size, power usage, manufacturability, and customer convenience.

ABOUT THE AUTHOR

So that the objective of the RCA ENGINEER to publicize the achievements of RCA engineers may be accomplished, it seems in order to comment on the author of the article on "Trends in Design of Color TV Studio Equipment."

Mr. Luther received his college training at M.I.T. and has a BSEE degree. Early in his post-college experience, he participated in the technical operation and maintenance work in one of the Philadelphia stations, WFIL-TV, where he acquired practical acquaintance with equipment and with the operator's point of view. It would be difficult to visualize a more useful background for engineering development and design of studio equipment. Not every embryo engineer has an equivalent opportunity of course, but the value of such practical experience in molding the point of view cannot be overemphasized.

Coupled with this basic training, Mr. Luther has brought to his present job an unusually keen intellect, an excellent "sense of direction" in dealing with circuits, a creative attitude, and an unlimited interest in both the details of circuit performance and the broad aspects of system integration. Thus equipped, he has advanced with unusual rapidity in capability and productivity, and is in constant demand to consult on problems running the whole gamut from circuit design to system planning.

Though it is not revealed in his paper, he is responsible, probably more than any other one person in Broadcast Studio Engineering, for the adoption and expanding use of stabilized circuits in this type of equipment. The simplification of the color camera control equipment, which he has used as an example, is largely a child of his own fertile thinking. His vital interest in the broad application of such circuits has inspired many of his co-workers to enlarge their horizons along similar lines. The resulting influence on the product line has been an important factor in maintaining RCA's leadership in the field.

Mr. Luther's paper is actually a summary of his own typical thinking and planning, which led to the developments described. His achievements and recognition are an indication of the possibilities open to every RCA engineer."

Moving to Management

As mentioned earlier, I had been asked to move into a management position, but I declined. That was caused by my view at the time of what management would entail for me. Feeling that I would have less time for the creative engineering that had brought me this far, I was concerned that I might not be as good a manager as I was an engineer. I was further concerned that I would slowly lose my engineering skills from disuse, and there would be no going back to engineering. I also assessed the management people around me and wasn't sure I wanted to be like them. One manager even said to me: "I used to work next to you in the engineering lab, but when I saw what you were doing and achieving, I could never see myself matching that. So I decided to go into management when an opportunity occurred." That did not give me a good feeling to be moving into an area populated by failed engineers.

In spite of those concerns, and with my growth in confidence, I decided that the next time I was asked, I would accept the change. But my management style would be based on my engineering knowledge and skill. I would not let that lapse.

In July 1958, I advanced to Group Leader, TV Terminal Advanced Development.

In hindsight, my experience in management proved that all my concerns about moving from engineer to manager were wrong.

Chapter 4

Management at RCA

Now that I have become a Group Leader, I should say some things about what that meant to me. I was getting additional responsibilities, some that I didn't even suspect beforehand. So what did Group Leaders have to do that engineers didn't do?

As a Group Leader I was now responsible for these things regarding my group:

I must learn more about all of my people. Before becoming a Leader, I interacted with my peers regarding our projects and on an informal, personal level. As a Leader, I needed to know a lot more about each person: his skills, capabilities, and work desires. That was so I could decide what kind of projects he would do best, as I fit my manpower to the programs at hand for the group. As projects are assigned, each engineer must agree to a schedule for his part of the work. If there is a project schedule for an overall program, each Group Leader must fit his group's work into that overall schedule.

I must track the progress and performance of each engineer. At the end of the year, I must prepare a performance review for each engineer. This was done with a formal document, which was discussed with the engineer in a counseling session. At the end of such a session, the engineer signed the review document indicating agreement or if not in agreement, wrote down his concerns on the form.

I must write monthly status reports for my group. This means I must understand the overall progress of the projects and indicate whether they are on schedule or not. If the report indicates a problem, I must say what I am doing about it. If events suddenly occur that could require changes in plans or equipment, I must communicate with upper management as soon as possible — I shouldn't wait for the monthly report.

I must participate in the annual management process for deciding on programs and budgets for the coming year. This was a task that began around mid-year for planning the next year. It began with a sales forecast for the next year followed by a pro-forma profit and loss statement. This led to calculation of the total engineering budget for the new year. That was then broken down to each department in engineering and, finally, to the budget for each group. This was a give-and-take process where the Group Leader analyzed the projects that higher management decided his group should do. He may argue for more people, more support or, if he felt his group didn't have enough work, to argue for more projects or to transfer some people to another group. This process also includes the budgeting for any new equipment that the group would need to buy during the coming year.

I must be involved in the hiring of new engineers (in the years that we were hiring). Most candidates for new hiring came from the recruiting efforts of the personnel department. We gave Personnel our objectives for new hires each year and they visited colleges around the country interviewing prospective graduates. We also participated in the interviewing process. The candidates selected were hired into RCA and entered the engineering rotation program where they spent four of six-week assignments in different RCA engineering departments around the country. From that program, we got some experience with the new engineers who had chosen an interest in Broadcast Engineering.

I must participe in the annual budgeting for engineers' performance increases for the year. This was a new experience for me. Before becoming a leader, I never thought about how this worked. It began with higher management, in looking at the overall budget for all of Broadcast Systems, coming up with a percentage of total salaries that would be included in the overall Broadcast Systems' budget for personnel salary increases. Numbers like 4% come to mind. Each group gets a share of this—it might be 4% share of their salaries, or it could be a little greater or a little less, depending on higher management's view of the performance of the group as a whole. Anyway, the fixed percentage approach makes it difficult for anyone to get an increase much higher than the average because that would have to be offset by someone else getting much less to keep the overall group at the specified percentage. I had never thought about this problem before becoming a group leader. Of course, the engineers were never told about the overall percentage figure.

This became a special problem when you found that someone who was hired into your group at a low entry level but after a while is evaluated as a superstar. How do you give anyone a large increase to bring him up to a level on a par with his peers of similar performance? That happened to me personally once in my career. There must be some kind of mechanism to override the fixed-percentage limitation. I never found out what it was.

And, in addition to all that, I must technically support my engineers and their projects, doing everything I can to facilitate their success.

All these things became evident to me slowly as I started working as a Group Leader. I wondered how much of my time these new requirements were going to take. I was determined not to let being in management cause me to lose my technical skills. I would work harder if necessary to make sure that didn't happen.

Looking back, I think I kept my technical skills at a satisfactory level for a manager. I became very good in meetings at making sure I understood what I was being told about the technical status of projects, by asking probing technical questions of the presenter. I was determined that no one was going to "snow" me. This also helped me when I participated in technical brainstorming sessions.

Labor Unions

As I mentioned in Chapter 3, the Camden plant was unionized. There were several unions and each had a number of job classifications. In a union environment, job classifications are supposed to be exclusive — that is, one classification is not allowed to do any of the work of another classification. If you have one kind of work going on, and you need a little work of another class to be done, you cannot use your existing workers to do the job. You have to get a new person of the proper classification. This can add delays while you wait for the new person, and it may increase your cost for the extra person. This is a way of life in a union shop unless the job classification structure is simplified. That is possible, but it is a difficult process requiring top-level negotiation with the union. That usually happens only at contract time (every three or so years). The outcome of such change proposals is not assured, so they were avoided for long times and other means were used to get the work done.

Another aspect of a union is the procedure that is used when layoff of personnel is required by the needs of a business. This is called "bumping". It means that in a layoff, for each job classification, the lowest-seniority workers must be the ones who go out of work. Since the lowest seniority people in a classification may not be the ones in the part of the organization that is laying-off, the union contracts say that higher-seniority people who are not needed where they are, can "bump" out lower seniority people in other areas, such as Broadcast Systems. Our lower seniority people are then the ones dismissed. This concept assumes that all workers are of equal capability and that the need for on-the-job training is minimal. I don't think this is appropriate for a skilled engineering work force. However, it is what we had.

By the time I became group leader, our engineers also had joined a union. This group was called ASPEP-Association of Scientific and Professional Engineering Personnel. ASPEP had begun for RCA engineers in the Government areas of Camden back in 1944, but the Broadcast engineers were in a different part of the plant at that time and were not solicited for membership. Around 1958, there was another ASPEP recruiting effort; the Broadcast engineers voted in favor of the union. Because of my promotion just before this time, I never was in the union. I felt that a union was not appropriate in an Engineering department — it would interfere with the free-flowing activity of engineering and reduce our effectiveness substantially. Obviously, the majority of our engineers felt differently, and they voted for the union. But we found ways to live with the union rules and the situation was eventually comfortable.

The largest labor relations problem was that bumping affected us in Broadcast because at that time our engineers were classified in the same groups with the Government Systems engineers. The government business was a contract business: Engineers were hired when there were government contracts, but when a contract ended and there was not another one to replace it, everybody who was on the old contract was laid off. However, those people could bump out other lower-seniority engineers anywhere in the plant, including Broadcast Systems. The Broadcast business generally did not have layoffs like that. We planned smoothly from year to year and if this meant a growing business, we also planned on hiring a certain number of new engineers each year. By this means, our engineering organization grew.

A new engineer out of college with no prior broadcast experience usually takes about two years on the job before he is fully capable of working independently on his own projects. If a government layoff occurred during that time, our new engineers are clearly the lowest-seniority engineers in the plant and they get bumped out. Our people are replaced by higher-seniority, higher-paid ex-government engineers who also needed to be trained in broadcast before they become effective. We lost our new engineers and we lost the investment of time in training them. This was very disruptive. Obviously, we in broadcast management fought mightily when this kind of thing occurred. There was one loophole: If you could prove that a particular engineer had unique skills that could not be replaced, you might keep him from being bumped. But it was a very difficult situation.

Quite a few years later, we finally managed to get this changed in a contract negotiation and strike with ASPEP. Broadcast engineering became a separate group from Government engineering. The problem was over. Contract negotiations with unions in RCA were handled by the Personnel department (later called the Human Resources department). However, Engineering Management had to advise Personnel's negotiators of our requirements, but we did not participate directly in negotiations and the outcome was not always what we expected.

Broadcast Systems' Organization

An organization is a living thing. Not just because it has people in it, but because it constantly changes. People come and go, businesses change, philosophies change. Over the years, Broadcast Systems had many different organizations. I'll try here to boil all that down and describe a typical Broadcast organization. I won't even attempt to discuss the overall RCA organization. I don't think that is relevant here, and besides, I didn't know much about it. It isn't too unusual not to know much about what's above you in an organization, and unless the higher ranks communicate this to you, you don't have any way to know it. Sometimes the higher ranks of RCA weren't very good about communicating down the organization. Within my own organizations, it was always a challenge to decide how much downward communication was necessary or desirable.

Figure 1 is a typical organization chart for Broadcast Systems. The dotted lines show essential parts of the business that were seldom part of our organization. The most important area of these was manufacturing. Except near the end of Broadcast Systems, manufacturing always was part of a parallel organization that connected through a manager one or two levels above the Broadcast general manager. This was awkward when there were problems that we couldn't resolve via peer-to-peer involvement.

Two different organizational philosophies existed at RCA Camden. Our organization was generally of the business-oriented form. In this type, all functions related to a particular business reported to a business manager. Thus, for Studio Equipment (which consisted of TV Cameras, TV Terminal Equipment, and Projector Equipment), both engineering and product management reported to a Studio Equipment Business Manager. This was supposed to foster better focus and team spirit among the units reporting to the business manager. It seemed to work.

The other type of organization is the functional organization, where

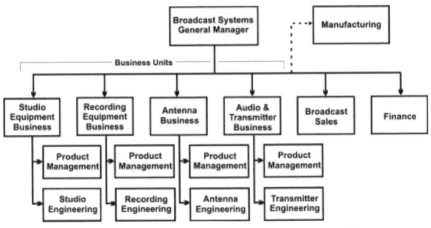

Figure 1 Broadcast systems organization chart ~ 1958

all groups of the same function (such as engineering or product management) reported to a Function Manager. This is also sometimes called a "skill center" type of organization. In the case of engineering, all engineers report to a Chief Engineer, which means that a business manager has to go through the Chief Engineer to get his engineering things done. We did not use this approach for most of my career at RCA, even when I became Chief Engineer. However, we had a functional configuration in some other parts of the Broadcast organization, such as Finance, Sales, and certain support organizations.

A variation on the functional organization is what is called a "matrix organization". Program managers are added to the organization for each program. The functional managers assign their people to the program managers as needed by each program. This gives a degree of program focus to the groups, but it means that each individual essentially has two bosses: his functional manager and his program manager. You have to have the right people for this to work. Government Systems often used a matrix organization.

Office and Laboratory Space

The buildings where engineering was located (#10 and #13) were long and narrow, with the long dimension going east to west. The typical floor plan had a corridor through the center of the building, with engineering offices on the north side where there were windows, and laboratories and shops on the south side, where most windows were closed off. The entire space was air conditioned, so there was never a need to open any windows.

The office space had a large open area with cubicles for the leaders and managers along the windows. A leader cubicle had no door, but managers got a door and a somewhat larger cubicle with walls to the ceiling. Because the buildings were originally built for manufacturing, the ceilings were 14 ft high. This was too high for an office and would make the office excessively noisy, so the offices usually had drop ceilings. There was typically a secretary's desk at each manager's door. The secretaries, however, served a manager and all the engineers in his group. As the secretarial load varied, the secretaries would distribute the work among themselves.

The drafting room was also located on the north side of the corridor. It was a large room, usually walled off from the engineering offices, and provided with better lighting than the engineers' office areas.

Financial Considerations

The financial department of RCA collected and reported costs on a program (project) basis. For this purpose, financial accounts called "shop orders" were set up for each program. The name "shop order" comes from the factory environment, where that was an appropriate name for a project. We also used shop orders in engineering. All "direct costs" such as labor charges, material purchases, or purchased help went into the shop order for the relevant project. Labor charges included not only the individual's salary or wages, but an allowance for the cost of the fringe benefits that person receives.

There are other costs, however, that apply across all projects and cannot readily be applied to the shop orders. These are things like floor space charges, heating or cooling, electricity, building services and maintenance, and management. These are called "overhead" costs. They somehow should be distributed to the program for proper accounting of the total cost of a program. This is done by establishing an "overhead rate" (a percentage) that should be added to the labor costs. In engineering, this was about 80%, which is distributed across the programs in proportion to how much labor each program used. This financial system might seem awkward, but it works, and after a while you understand it and get used to it.

The same system of direct cost and overhead applies in the factory. The factory has much a higher overhead percentage (200% or higher); that takes some more getting used to, after you first learn it. That higher overhead rate often makes an hour of factory labor appear to cost more than an hour of engineering labor.

One of the anomalies of the overhead system occurs when we made a new design that reduced the amount of factory labor needed to assemble the product. If the factory does nothing to reduce their overhead costs in proportion to the direct labor reduction, the overhead rate will go up!

Product Cost Estimating

Another financial matter is the determination of product manufacturing cost. Part of the goals for any engineering program is manufacturing cost. Thus, we have to understand how such calculations are made in order to design for best cost. In the past, engineers didn't know anything about manufacturing cost and they would complete a design before anyone really began looking at the cost. Since engineers didn't know how manufacturing costs were calculated, they had to call on the factory cost estimators to do it. Those people could not work on an estimate until a factory order was actually placed, which of course cannot happen until the design is completed and signed off. The first official cost estimate was often a tremendous surprise to the engineers.

Once I understood the cost estimating problem, one of my goals became finding ways to create good cost information while a design was still in progress. I established communication with the Cost Estimating group and got their participation with engineering at an early stage in a design program. We had to pay them for this, since their cost structure made no allowance for time spent this way. It wasn't until late in my career that this was successfully accomplished.

Engineering Management Practices

There were many things that engineering managers in RCA had to do to help plan, track, cost estimate, and review their programs. Many were developed by me and the other managers as we went along. As the business grew in the early years, these things became more important. These are just listed here; they will be covered in Chapter 6. These things are: program planning and cost estimating, budgeting, product safety, design standards, and design reviews.

Chapter 5

Electronic Recording

Background

Electronic Recording in RCA meant "Video Tape Recording". During the early 1950s, a practical video recorder of any type was the holy grail of television researchers. At the time, the primary use for television recording was thought to be for "west coast delay" — delaying a program generated on the east coast for the three-hour time difference for viewing on the west coast of the US. This assumed that an electronic means of sending the signals from east to west, such as a telephone line for video, would be available. A video-over-telephone-line system was developed and deployed across the country. It gave extremely limited bandwidth for video, but despite this, it was the best that could be done at the time.

One obvious method was to record the television picture on motion picture film. Equipment for this was built almost as soon as televison was introduced in the 1940s. The technique was to display the TV picture on a kinescope screen (a CRT television display) and photograph that screen with a film movie camera. The film would be developed and then run through a film scanning system (telecine) at a later time to get back to television. The process was called "kinescope recording"; the films made this way were called "kines". It worked, but there were lots of problems that caused the picture quality to be very poor. When television became color, this was even worse. Even so, it was the only approach available, and equipment was built for it and was widely used. Combining the horrors of kinescope recording and east-to-west video transmission by telephone line produced pictures that were barely watchable.

People with more vision realized that a practical broadcast-quality video recording system would facilitate film-style program production as is used in movie-making. In this method, individual scenes are shot separately on film. After all the scenes have been shot and developed, they are taken to an editing studio and the final program is assembled by piecing together the shots as required by the script. This is "postproduction", which has many advantages if you don't need real-time presentation of the program. The whole process of shooting individual scenes and subsequent editing is called the "production-postproduction" method of creating programs. *Today, almost all television programs and all motion pictures are produced that way. Live production is limited to sporting events or news, where the immediacy of live production is desirable or necessary.*

So the holy grail was really an *electronic* method of video recording. Research labs all over the world were working on that problem.

An obvious electronic solution to recording video was to take the magnetic recording technology that was widely used for sound recording and "simply speed it up" to record video. But it wasn't that obvious to video engineers like myself who realized that the speed-up required was approximately 300 times! Magnetic recording works by moving a magnetic tape across one or more magnetic heads. The head magnetizes the tape in a "track" along the tape in the direction of tape motion. To obtain audio bandwidth (about 15,000 cycles/second) a tape speed of 15 inches/second was used at that time. Tape mechanisms operating at that speed were well-developed, reasonable in cost, and reliable. But a 300 x speed-up was another thing — 4,500 inches/second — 255 miles/hour. Any mechanical engineer would know that was far beyond the realm of possibility. These numbers: 15 inches/second, etc. are "head-to-tape speeds", a basic parameter of magnetic tape recording.

There were three research approaches that could classify all the different magnetic video recording projects. The first was simply to speed up the tape as much as possible and then try to fit the video signal into whatever bandwidth was achieved. There was considerable potential to obtain more video bandwidth from a given head-to-tape speed by modifications to the tape and heads themselves. That would make those items more difficult to manufacture, but such problems tend to be solved in due time when needed. This approach was pursued by Dr. Harry Olson and his team at RCA Laboraties in Princeton, NJ. He built a system that was installed at NBC, New York for field testing in 1953. It had huge tape reels that gave a recording time of only 7 minutes. It took nearly the same amount of time to rewind the tape as to play it, since the rewind tape speed could be no higher than the record or play tape speed, because the play speed was already the fastest that the tape could be run.

The second approach was to split the video signal into a multiplicity of channels and then record all the channels on parallel tracks on a tape moving at a more reasonable speed. On playback, signal electronics would re-combine the channel signals to re-create the original signal. A project was started in the Advanced Development group of the Government Systems Division of RCA, which was also located in Camden. I was involved in that project as a consultant on video processing. It suffered from the problems of splitting the video signal and putting it back together. I felt these problems ultimately could be solved, but the complexity of multiple channels (we used 10) would still not be competitive with the third approach.

The third approach was basically to build a mechanism that moved *both* heads and tape in a way that the relative speed between them would be magnified. In the early 1950s we did not know of any project using such an approach. But in March, 1956, at the NAB Convention in Chicago (the National Association of Broadcasters annual convention was the primary venue for introducing new products to this industry in those days), we learned about the third approach. Ampex Corporation, a small maker of sound and instrumentation recorders in Redwood City, CA announced to the world a project that they had been working on for at least four years in secret. They had built a monochrome magnetic video recorder using four heads mounted on a wheel spinning at high speed on an axis parallel to a 2" wide tape so that the heads moved *across* the tape. The tape moved at 15 inches per second. It worked! This came to be known as the "quadruplex" technology. The industry was shocked but also pleased and responded with approximately 80 orders for the Ampex VR-1000. Ampex promised delivery in early 1957, but they did not reach quantity production until early 1958.

The first question for RCA management was: Should we enter the VTR business also and compete with Ampex? Many broadcasters had indicated to us that they wanted competition. But the industry did not need different competing technologies that weren't interchangeable with

Figure 1 Ampex VR-1000 (product)

each other. *Remember the VHS and Beta debacle at the introduction of the first consumer VTRs?* It was clear that we should use the Ampex technology.

RCA management answered the question in the affirmative, and authorized a go-ahead on development of an RCA quadruplex machine. The machine had to record color, because that was RCA's greatest advantage over Ampex at that time. A team of engineers was assembled from the technical resources of RCA. The team was headed by A. H. Lind of Broadcast Systems. (I had worked for Tony Lind for several years in TV Terminal Engineering.) The program to develop an RCA recorder using the Ampex technology was set up at Camden, with support from RCA Laboratories in Princeton, and also Government Systems Engineering in Camden. As RCA Laboratories had already developed a system for doing color recording with the Olson recorders, it could quickly be adapted to the Ampex recorder. The first working model of a color recorder was completed in early 1957.

In the meantime, it was decided that a cross-licensing agreement with Ampex was necessary. Negotiations began. The turning point was when RCA demonstrated its first machine working in color to Ampex engineers and executives. This convinced the Ampex people that RCA had mastered their technology and added the color capability as well. Any belief that Ampex's technology could not be reproduced by others was shot down. They agreed to a patent and technical aid license with RCA. RCA got the rights to use the Ampex technology with a limited degree of technical support to get started and Ampex got RCA's technology for making their recorders (which were monochrome-only) work in color.

All that happened in the first year after the Ampex announcement.

They were clearly ahead of us in the market—they shipped some recorders in 1957; we were at least a year behind that. The RCA engineering team scrambled to catch up. An RCA recorder, the TRT-1A was announced at the 1957 NAB Convention. We demonstrated a working color recorder to broadcasters in August 1957. All this happened before I was even involved in the TV tape scene.

Because of my non-involvement in TV Tape, and my relatively low position in the organization, I was not privy to most of the activity such as the design of the first RCA recorder and the licensing issues. A much better and more complete perspective on those matters is given in Andy Inglis' book, Behind the Tube.

I Move to Electronic Recording Engineering

Some time after I became a Group Leader, there was a strike of the technicians at NBC, which was a part of RCA. RCA corporate management decided to use the management resources of all of RCA to keep NBC on the air. I, as a member of RCA management having TV technical skills, was assigned to go to NBC, New York and work as a technician there until the strike was settled. I was assigned to the video tape department where I would maintain the recorders, both RCA and Ampex. Since I had not worked in video tape in Camden, I had no experience with either system. It was a quick learning experience for me. I was there for several weeks, during which time I became skilled in maintaining video tape equipment.

This is a place to talk about troubleshooting, which is a skill that I had developed for myself. I was very much in demand to troubleshoot problems for other engineers, the factory, and customers. I often went around the lab looking over shoulders and helping people solve problems on the spot. My success in this depended really on only one thing—a full and complete understanding of the equipment and how it was supposed to work. Extending this, the full understanding had to include knowing how each part in the equipment affected the overall performance. Using this knowledge, when someone gave me a problem, I went through the thought process of what would have to be wrong to make the equipment do what I was told it was doing incorrectly.

To this day, I use that approach in solving problems in equipment. If I don't understand something, I really can't troubleshoot it. The Discherts used a similar method for troubleshooting old cars and engines. I probably learned some of this from them.

When I returned from New York, I was surprised to be notified by my boss that I was being moved from Leader, TV Terminal Advanced Development to be Leader, Electronic Recording Advanced Development. It seemed to me at the time, that my assignment to video tape during the strike at NBC may have been part of a deliberate plan by my bosses to prepare me for the change they had in mind. Nevertheless, I was pleased to become part of the RCA video tape team. I had waited a long time to get my feet into that water. *I think the attraction TV tape had for me was that it included an even broader range of technologies than cameras or termninal equipment. I had a lot to learn.*

At the time I joined the Electronic Recording group, the major task was supporting the first RCA recorder, the TRT-1A, in the factory and with customers. For a while, there wasn't much time for advanced development work. However, I was still learning about the technology, so that factory and customer support was good experience and helped me build my troubleshooting skills for TV tape equipment.

The RCA TRT-1A Television Recorder

I was not involved in the original design of the TRT-1A. However, I need to describe it anyway so you can appreciate what follows. RCA was going to build video recorders in competition with Ampex, but in the interest of industry compatibility, we were going to use the same basic technology that we had licensed from Ampex. We needed ways to distinguish our products from theirs. That would be the design of the system, the packaging, convenience features, and performance and reliability improvements. We pursued all of these, but we needed a short schedule for the first design— we had to get into the market and establish our position as soon as possible. We also needed a different name for our product because Ampex had trademarked the name "Videotape" Recorder. For that, we chose "Television Tape Recorder". The TRT acronym in the RCA type numbering meant "Television Recorder, Tape", or maybe it was "Tape Recorder, TV".

Figure 2 Installation of 4 TRT-1As at NBC Burbank

I was never sure about that, but it is one of those things that is not important to an engineer.

"We" as used here, means all of RCA Broadcast, not just my group, which at the time had had nothing to do with the TRT-1A. We wanted our product to *look* different from the Ampex as well. We decided to make our first product rack-mounted, using the standard broadcast rack cabinet design. This is something that all broadcasters are familiar with and it was a very convenient and serviceable configuration. Perhaps a rack was not as elegant-looking as a console like the Ampex machine, but it was more convenient to work on rack-mounted equipment than it was to crawl around under a console. This design was so different from the Ampex machine that no one could confuse them. (Just compare Figures 1 and 2.) The resources of RCA Broadcast System and the rest of RCA Engineering were marshalled to produce a design in record time. Prototypes were working and were demonstrated to customers in only 12 months from our start — 16 months from the Ampex announcement. But a tremendous amount of work remained to get us to production status.

I should point out that a "crash" program like the first RCA Television Tape Recorder design can overstep some of the procedures that normally exist in an organization like RCA. Cost-of-engineering limitations can be relaxed, the project can get a high priority in all the service organizations that are used, and there is a lot of management attention and desire to help by giving the project every possible advantage to meet its schedule.

Quadruplex Technology

Before continuing here, I will further describe the quadruplex technology, since it occupied my full attention for the next 15 years. Referring to Figure 3, you can see how the tape and heads meet. The four heads are mounted to a wheel that rotates at 14,400 rpm, driven by an electronically-controlled motor. Such a motor drive is called a "servomechanism". I'll explain that later. The tape is held in a precision metal curved guide that has vacuum slots to draw the tape tightly into the curve of the guide. This is shown in Figure 3. In the figure, we are looking at the plane of rotation of the headwheel. The tape is shown on edge, curved into the guide. The guide moves the tape toward the spinning headwheel until the heads are actually pressed into the curve of the tape. A slot in the center of the guide provides clearance for this. The pressing of the heads into the tape causes a localized stretching of the tape that assures that the heads are tightly in contact with tape. This is essential to achieve the most possible bandwidth while recording on the tape. As the headwheel rotates the heads trace tracks across

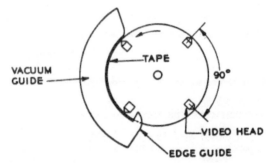

Figure 3 Quadruplex head to tape configuration

the tape. At the same time, the tape is moving slowly, causing the tracks from the heads to be spaced along the tape. This pattern is shown in Figure 4. Note that there are also tracks along the edges of the tape for audio, control and cueing.

Because the interface between the tape and the rotating heads is really that of complete physical contact and the heads are moving at about 85 miles/hour, there are serious issues of wear of both tape and heads. The materials used in both heads and tape and their manufacturing technique is very critical to obtain satisfactory wear life. Major engineering problems arise from this design. However, these are necessary for the system to work. Ampex developed this system and licensed us for the design, but we had to develop the manufacturing technology for ourselves.

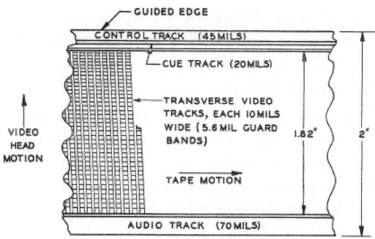

Figure 4 Quadruplex Tape Track Pattern

The life of the heads was in the range of a one or two hundred hours. That is not very long for a broadcaster; they could put that much time on their machines in a week or two. The heads must be easily replaceable by customers. Since the heads are precisely mounted to the headwheel (they must be *exactly* 90 degrees from one another) and cannot be replaced accurately enough in the field, the solution was to make the headwheel, motor, and vacuum guide into a separate removeable assembly, called the "headwheel panel". When the heads got worn, the assembly is sent back to the factory for refurbishing. Since the head life was so short, customers had to maintain a stock of headwheel panels and they were constantly going back for refurbishing. It was an expensive proposition because a refurbished headwheel panel cost about $1,000.

Headwheel Panel Refurbishing

We had to set up a manufacturing facility to perform the refurbishing process. In fact, we had to set up *two* complete manufacturing and refurbishing facilities so there would always be headwheel panels even in the event of some catastrophe at one or the other facility. One facility was located in the Camden Plant; the other was on the Isle of Jersey in the English Channel between England and France. Later we even started a third facility in Sunbury, PA. *Actually, there never was a catastrophe that completely stopped headwheel panel refurbishing, but there were many crises that almost did.*

Headwheel panel manufacturing and refurbishing required precision metalworking, with dimensions and tolerances in the millionths of an inch. (A human hair is 3,000 millionths of an inch.) We had to work on parts that could not even be seen without a microscope. This work is mechanical engineering, the fundamentals of which I had learned at MIT, but I had no practical experience with the actual kind of precision work that was required here. *At the start in Electronic Recording, I was not involved directly with the design or manufacture of headwheel panels, but later on that became part of my total responsibility and I had to learn all about the work so that I could manage it effectively. This was a requirement of my management style.*

The key component of the headwheel panel was the head itself. There were four per wheel. The key parts of the head were the "pole tips", which are the two magnetic parts that contacted the tape and picked up the magnetic signal. The pole tips are fastened together with a non-magnetic spacer of small, accurately-specified thickness. The material of the pole tips was very critical—it needed to have both good magnetic properties and good mechanical properties to withstand the stress of contacting the tape at high speed. The wear life was especially important and was always an important element of competition between RCA and Ampex. During the life of quadruplex recording, we were always doing development work on the heads. The RCA Laboratories even developed a special new magnetic material for our heads.

The pole tips were very small and very expensive. Thousands of dollars worth of them could fit in your pocket. Purchasing found a good vendor to handle the production of pole tips, but they were always on the lookout for other vendor possibilities or a better price. This caused them to build up a large supply of pole tips when the price was right. Unfortunately, Engineering wasn't always consulted before large commitments were made. We might have been working on something that would change the pole tips, making any existing inventory obsolete. In one case, we came up with a change in the tips that made a major improvement in head life, only to find that manufacturing had something like $250,000 in inventory of pole tips. Because we could not afford to scrap all those pole tips, a year of delay ensued before changing over to the new tip design.

Servomechanisms

An important aspect of any video tape recorder is the need for servomechanisms (servos). A servo is a type of electronic feedback circuit that controls a mechanical motion. For example, the headwheel motion must be synchronized with the television system so that head switching does not show in the picture. The headwheel servo performs that synchronization. It also controls the smoothness of headwheel motion, which is important to minimize time base error due to headwheel instability. For the headwheel servo, there is a tonewheel on the headwheel shaft that sends out a pulse at a specific angular position of the shaft. The timing of the tonewheel pulse is compared with a similar signal derived from the system sync pulses. The output of this comparison, which is a voltage proportional to the time difference, is fed back to the power driver of the headwheel motor such that the motor motion will be changed to reduce the position error. If the feedback is strong enough, the error will automatically reduce to a small value.

Quadruplex recorders have several other servomechanisms. Another is the tracking servo, which controls the tape motion to insure that the rotating heads exactly pass over the transverse tracks on the tape during playback. There may also be a servo on the vacuum guide position to control that parameter for optimum stretch of the tape. A further set of servos may be used on the tape reels to establish the correct tension in the tape for best operation of the tape transport (also called a tape *deck*).

Industry Standards

The marketplace expected that tapes could be freely interchanged between Ampex and RCA machines. Because of the critical dimensions and the fact that one could not directly measure the patterns on the tape with sufficient accuracy for this purpose, tape interchange was a huge problem. It took years before full tape interchangeability was achieved.

The first part of any interchange problem like this is to have a "standard", a written document that describes exactly what is required to create a standard recording. Since competing entities were involved here, we could not meet directly with Ampex to agree on a standard. That would violate anti-trust laws. Therefore, standard-setting was done in committees of an industry association that included RCA and Ampex as well as others from the industry, in full view of anyone who wanted to know what was going on. Customers had an extreme interest in this. The industry association in the United States that took on quadruplex standardization was the Society of Motion Picture and Television Engineers (SMPTE). They established the Video Recording & Reproduction committee with the charter to create standards for all video recording systems in wide use in the marketplace. At the time, quadruplex was the only recording system in widespread use.

The written standard was not the only item required for standardization. For normal operation of machines, a test tape was also necessary. This was a recording made on a machine certified by SMPTE to meet the written standard. Operators would set up their machines to correctly play the test tape, which then established that their machines would also be capable of recording to the standard. We were involved in the production of test tapes for SMPTE.

Quadruplex was a worldwide business, with customers and manufacturers around the world. Thus, a standard in the United States was not enough — an international standard was needed. Other parts of the world had different TV standards, which inherently meant that video recorders needed to be modified for these standards. The international standardizing task was undertaken by the International Electrotechnical Commission (IEC). A recording committee was set up under the auspices of the IEC for quadruplex standardization. That committee received input from other standardizing bodies like the SMPTE and developed worldwide standards. All this activity took a lot of time for many people. I was deeply involved in this work, which took much of my time and and a lot of traveling. This may seem like a long technical digression, but it is needed here so that the engineering challenges involved can be understood and appreciated.

I should comment here on traveling. When I began at RCA, I hated to travel. This may have come from the harrows of traveling to MIT during my college years. At first, I didn't want to go on business trips, but often I couldn't avoid it — for example, when I was the only one who could do what was needed at a customer site. As time went on, I learned to tolerate travel and I would go on any trip that was necessary. However, I still didn't enjoy it. Later still, after reaching management positions that had responsibilities at other locations than Camden, I had to travel regularly. I found out that when the same trip is taken regularly, the routine is learned, the airline people became familiar, and the other people doing the same thing became friends. It was a temporary environment that I almost enjoyed.

The TRT-1B TV Tape Recorder

When I arrived in Electronic Recording Engineering, the TRT-1A was in the factory, and engineers were already beginning the follow-on product, the TRT-1B. I was very interested in using our knowledge of transistor circuits to make a contribution to the art of video recorders. I set my group to work designing a transistorized servo system for the TRT-1B. We designed a completely transistorized servo unit that replaced the vacuum-tube system used previously. Besides being transistorized, this servo used a new method of controlling the headwheel motor, which we called "Pixlock". It improved the servo reliability, the smoothness of headwheel motion, saved power, and reduced the size of the unit. This was a small precursor to what we were soon to develop. Our enthusiasm about transistors grew every day, and we were now ready to tackle an *all-transistor* TV Tape Recorder!

The TR-22 Solid-State TV Tape Recorder

Transistorization of previous tube equipment (see Chapter 3, TS-40) had demonstrated large savings of power, size, and major improvement of reliability. Transistors don't burn out or degrade with use. They use vastly less power and they are many times smaller than vacuum tubes. But there were major challenges in designing transistor circuits for a quadruplex tape recorder. Such a tape recorder requires audio and video amplifiers, servomechanism circuits including power amplifiers, frequency modulator and demodulator circuits, delay circuits, and special pulse circuits. Many of these were at the leading edge for transistors. It would take a lot of good design work to put this all together in an easy-to-operate high-performance system with good service features. Those were our goals when we set out to design the "world's first solid-state TV tape recorder".

There are 100 or more major subassemblies in a quadruplex tape recorder. These include mechanical and electronic modules. To create an all-new product, all these items have to be dealt with. Altogether, there are more than 10,000 individual components in the system. Changing from tubes to transistors does not reduce this count very much. The work had to be partitioned to groups of engineers, both mechanical and electrical. The mechanical engineers first had to develop a concept for the cabinet that would house our self-contained recorder. After much discussion between all the engineers, product management, and management and some human engineering studies, a concept emerged that was eminently practical and would be a delight in the marketplace. This is shown in finished form in Figure 5.

It was felt that neither of the approaches for mounting the tape deck in the existing RCA and Ampex machines was ideal. The Ampex flat-top console was fairly convenient for loading reels and threading the tape into the tape path, but it was difficult to service the rear of the tape deck, because

Figure 5 TR-22 Front and rear views

one had to crawl into the console to get at it. The RCA upright tape deck was easy to load reels, and gave good access to the rear of the tape deck, but it wasn't very pretty. We decided that a tape deck angled back 45° at waist height would be best. We could put the heavy vacuum pump, air compressor, cooling blower, and power supplies at the bottom of the cabinet with two rows of electronic modules above that. On either side of the tape deck there would be narrow control panels, also at 45°. Above the angled tape deck would be a fluorescent light for the tape deck and control panels, and above that would be a monitoring bridge, with room for an audio monitor, monochrome or color picture monitor, and an oscilloscope for testing.

As a result of this mechanical layout and transistorized electronics, the TR-22 measured 55" wide, 71" high, and 26.5" deep. It was totally self-contained, but was not quite a lightweight at 1400 pounds.

Meanwhile, the electrical engineers were hard at work designing the necessary transistor circuits. These were packaged into 44 modules that were arranged in two rows just below the tape deck. The modules contained etched-wiring boards for all circuits, which contributed to simpler assembly, higher reliability and lower cost of the electronics. The modules would be accessed for servicing from the front, using an extender module for testing. (See Figure 6.)

The TR-22 was introduced at the 1961 NAB convention. As was usual

Figure 6 TR-22 Electronics module extended for testing

for a first introduction of a new RCA product, we burned a lot of midnight oil getting to the convention with something that worked, and still more work to keep it going during the show. It represented such an advance that customers were cautious about whether it would really work in their stations without all the RCA engineers hovering around, and we got only a modest number of orders during the show. However, the advantages of the product were very compelling and orders began coming in soon after the show.

Although there were many problems we faced at NAB, one stands out. The air compressor in the bottom of the machine had a pressure-relief valve that occasionally released excess air. During the setup period, we realized when the bottom of the machine was all closed up (which had never been done during the testing at Camden), the pressure relief took on an unusual sound, a kind of resonant watery bubbling. Someone observed that it sounded like a f--t in a bathtub. It became known as the FIB effect. We couldn't completely solve the problem while at NAB, but we did find ways to minimize its occurrence. After we got back home, the mechanical engineers worked to eliminate the FIB effect.

We returned from the NAB show pleased with the reception we got, and relieved that we could finally get some sleep. However, much remained to do to get the TR-22 into the factory and out to customers. We learned lots about the design in the weeks before the show and at the show, and we now had to turn that knowledge into completed and accurate drawings. We were just beginning to ship units from the factory by the time of the 1962 NAB convention.

The TR-22 was the start of wholesale replacement of tubes with transistors. *Tube equipment no longer exists today except in extreme high-power, high-frequency applications. However, there are some niche markets where tube equipment is still manufactured and marketed, such as in high-fidelity audio equipment. People in that market feel that solid-state and digital audio equipment as manufactured today does not equal the performance of old-fashioned analog equipment using tubes.*

In 1962 I was promoted to Manager, Television Tape Recorder

Engineering, an entire department of about 70 people. *Unlike promotions while I was an engineer, where there was little change in the work I did; promotion to a higher level of management entailed more management work. This comes naturally from the fact that a higher-level manager generally has more people under his command. He may not have more people actually reporting directly to him, in fact, he should not have too many people in direct report. For an engineering manager, I think having 7 or 8 direct reports is the maximum. Beyond that, there is just not enough time to spend with each of them, considering the amount of administrative work also required of a manager. One thing learned quickly from a higher-level assignment, is that many tasks must be delegated--tasks that you might have handled yourself in a previous, smaller, assignment. If this is not done, the manager will fail. As I moved up in management, I also found it essential to have administrative help to handle the paperwork details of the job.*

Time Base Correctors

One aspect of video tape recorders that has not yet been touched on is time base error. The television system depends on very precise control of the frequency of the video signals. TV receivers have to synchronize with the sync portion of the signal to produce a stable picture. To prevent noise in the reception of the broadcasted signal causing instability in the picture, the receiver synchronization is deliberately made slow to respond to changes in the sync. If the sync frequency changes more rapidly than the receiver synchronization circuits can follow, the displayed picture will have "jitter", which is random movement of the picture from side to side. Early quadruplex recorders had a frequency output that depended directly on the mechanical stability of the headwheel motion, the position of the vacuum guide, and to some extent, the motion of the tape. All of these parameters had to be as accurate as possible just to get a stable picture. There was no margin for error.

Most of us realized that there was a need for an electronic means to automatically correct these errors that come from the mechanical components. Ampex saw this too and developed a unit called the Amtec (AMpex Timebase Error Corrector). It used a unique electronically-variable delay line to do the job. Again, we had to play catch-up. We developed a

Figure 7 RCA TR-4

Figure 8 RCA TR-5

competing unit for our machines. It was built with TR-22 style modules, so it could be fit into all our machines based on those modules. Earlier, we had developed the Pixlock high-performance headwheel servo system to reduce timebase errors from that source. This was still needed, but the delay line method gave still better performance because it could deal with timebase errors from *all* sources. A further timebase error corrector was still required to correct all the errors that showed up in a color signal. Ampex also developed this first, but we made our own version of it. Later quad machines contained all three types of error correction.

The TR-4 Series of Products

Once the TR-22 was moving smoothy into the hands of customers, we began working on an enhancement to our TV recording product line. That was a packaging project to assemble the TR-22 components into three different configurations. The TR-4 (Figure 7) was an upright configuration of a complete machine, but significantly smaller, lighter, and lower cost than the TR-22. The TR-3 was a playback-only configuration that eliminated the left-hand equipment rack from the TR-4, making the whole machine only about 26" wide. The last member of the series was the TR-5, a portable record-only machine on wheels (Figure 8) .

In 1966, my title changed to Manager, Tape Equipment, Projector, and Scientific Instruments Engineering. "Tape Equipment" in the title refers to the same department I had been previously heading: Electronic Recording Engineering. Projector Engineering was a Broadcast Systems group that designed film projectors for playing motion picture films on TV, using a telecine TV camera. A special projector is required to show film to a TV system because the frame rate of film is 24 frames/second and the frame rate of TV is 30 frames/second.

Scientific Instruments was an engineering group that was new to Broadcast Systems, but it actually had started in the 1940s to design electron microscopes, which had been developed by RCA Laboratories. The Scientific Instruments business had been part of a different RCA organization that disbanded, so it was transferred to Broadcast Systems. Both the electron microscope and the TV projectors were heavily mechanical products; they reported to Bruno Melchionni, a mechanical manager, who reported to me. My role in these products was mostly administrative and I continued to spend most of my time on Electronic Recording.

The TR-70 Program

While we were developing the TR-4 series machines, Ampex was doing something different, which turned out to be much more important in the marketplace. They introduced the VR-2000, which had an improved quadruplex recording technique that provided much higher picture quality; so much that it was now possible to do "multiple-generation" recording.

What started out as a market for recorders that were used primarily for TV program delay, was now becoming a program production market. That meant that our customers were not only TV stations and networks, but also TV "production houses", who produced programs but did not themselves broadcast the programs. Production work had many special requirements for recorders. They wanted to be able to make recordings of a program one scene at a time and then assemble the program by editing the scenes together, just as is done in motion picture film production (the production-postproduction method, described earrlier in this chapter). After editing, the complete program is recorded again for presentation or broadcasting. This required re-recording the scene material on the finished program tape. Since the signals then had gone through the recording system twice, this is called a "second-generation" recording. The future of TV recording was clearly tied to multiple generations.

Our existing recorders, the TR-22, TR-3, TR-4, and TR-5 still used the original recording technique introduced by Ampex in 1956. They made an acceptable picture when playing back an original recording, but the picture quality degraded seriously when re-recording the signal from the original recording. The new Ampex technique overcame this problem and their new recorders could do up to five or six generations without noticable degradation of the pictures as seen by a normal viewer. They called their new method "highband" recording. We had scooped Ampex with the all solid-state TR-22, and now they were doing it to us with highband. Because we had not done anything about improving the fundamental performance of our recorders, we were in catch-up mode again.

Unfortunately for us, changing to highband recording required a total redesign of the signal system of our recorders. That represented more than half of the modules in the TR-22 and our other recorders. Furthermore, it required redesign of the video heads on the headwheel, a new tape, and improvements in the servo system. It was a major project, comparable to the original design of our recorders.

Multiple generations is a problem because the video signal system is analog and in analog circuits, distortion, noise, or degradation occurs to some degree in every circuit. (Analog signals are continuouly variable, and distortions, interference, or noise added to the signal will be visible if they become large enough.) A further issue with analog circuits is that, in a series of circuits, the degradation of each circuit accumulates on the signal passing through the series. Video tape recorders have many circuits in series. That means each circuit has to be designed to much tighter standards of signal quality, so that when circuits are placed in series, there won't be too much accumulated degradation.

This caused us many problems, because we had to find circuit testing equipment and methods that were sensitive enough to measure very small distortions, things that our previous testing approaches couldn't even see. When looking at a picture on a monitor coming from one circuit or a number of circuits, the acceptable degree of distortion had to be invisible. Only after looking at the output of three or four machines running in cascade, could there be any visible distortion, and even then it should be minimal. Where we often used to test by the eyeball looking at pictures, we now had to test with extremely sensitive test equipment.

As Manager, Tape Equipment Engineering, I was responsible for the entire department. The TR-70 project was only one of the projects for which I was responsible. I had been working under a budget that did not foresee anything like the scope of redesign needed for highband. We struggled to do the design with the funds and personnel we had, but it soon became clear to everyone, including my bosses, that we weren't making much progress. Something had to change.

At this time, Broadcast Systems was in the same management group as Government Systems, called Government and Commercial Systems (G&CS), and Irving Kessler, the Executive Vice President of that group put Harry Woll, Vice President of Engineering for the G&CS group, and his staff on the problem of helping Broadcast Engineering. There is a story behind how this came about.

We in the Broadcast Systems Tape Equipment had been struggling with the problem of how we could design a totally new recorder within the budget constraints we had. Our superiors didn't know how to do that either, and they bumped the problem up to their superior, Irv Kessler. Irv called a meeting at the RCA Moorestown plant, where Irv's office was located. I was to make the major presentation about the technical problems.

I and my staff and our superiors worked hard on that presentation, but before the meeting occurred, I got a call from Harry Woll telling me to come early for the meeting and to stop in his office before going to the meeting. I did that and Harry told me that Irv was going to interrupt my presentation and, "when that happens, I should not say anything in response to whatever Irv says". I went to the meeting, and in due course I began my presentation. A few sentences into the presentation, before I had really said anything, Irv stopped me. He stood up and then delivered a tirade against me, my department, and my superiors in Broadcast Systems. Laced with profanity and personal slurs, he told us we were incompetent in our jobs for letting anything like this happen, and he did not think we had done a proper job of planning for recovering from the situation. This happened even before I had presented the plan, so clearly he had been given a preview by someone. Irv ended his tirade by closing the meeting and directing all of us in Broadcast Systems to immediately meet with Harry Woll, who would direct us in detail about how to make a satisfactory plan.

Obviously, this whole event was staged to "get our attention" about the seriousness of the problem we had, and to spur us into extra effort to find a solution. I had no trouble not replying to Irv's interruption of my presentation because I always was comfortable with saying nothing. Besides, his comments were so terrible, they didn't deserve a reply.

Harry Woll was used to dealing with engineering projects that got into trouble and he sent his best troubleshooter, Clarence Gunther to help us with the new plan. Clarence was about 60 at the time and I was 38. Clarence's reputation preceded him: he was known as an aggressive leader who made everyone work until they dropped to solve the problem as fast as possible. Because he had white hair, he was known as the "white tornado."

I didn't think I was ready for any "white tornado", and I approached my first meeting with Clarence with considerable trepidation. He came into my office and we began talking about the TR-70 project. It was quickly clear to both of us that Clarence didn't know much about the quadruplex technology we were dealing with. I was surprised to find that soon we were in the mode where I was teaching him about the technology. He was also interested in knowing all about my organization and all the people. I presented my views about this, too.

Clarence wanted to know all about the highband problem and what it would take to solve it. He wanted action. His first objective was to make a plan for the project and then an estimate of the manpower required and what that would cost. Throughout this, he relied on my technical knowledge to guide him. Whenever a technical issue came up, he would always check with me before he took any action. He did make me work harder and acquire a greater sense of urgency that I had before, but I felt that this was going to be good.

He set up the regimen that he would come in early and meet with me in my office before everyone else arrived. We started at 7:00 AM; everyone else didn't come in until 8:00. By the time they arrived, Clarence and I had planned the day for each of us and then we worked independently with our tasks. He worked directly with the people just as I would. The department essentially had two leaders. At 4:30 PM (½ hour before the normal quitting time), we would again meet in my office to review the progress of the day. These sessions would often last well past 5:00.

The plan that we came up with required doubling the staff of Electronic Recording Engineering, and it would cost about three times as much as my previous budget. Clarence had such credibility with upper management that the plan was approved immediately. I could never have achieved that. Now we faced the problem of where the people would come from. We discussed all the people I knew anywhere in RCA who knew anything about the technology. Clarence went to their managements and tried to get them assigned to this project for the duration. This was successful in some cases, but not enough to fill all of our needs. Clarence felt we should look at people who were good engineers but didn't know anything about Broadcast technology. I was concerned about this, because I felt that an engineer inexperienced with Broadcast would need maybe a year to get up to speed. Training them would also take up time of our experienced broadcast engineers. Clarence convinced me to go ahead. (I'm not sure I had a choice.) We didn't have time to discuss it any more.

Clarence's solution to the training problem was to throw management at it—namely Arch Luther. He was so impressed with my teaching him the technology in a matter of days that he felt I could do that with anyone we hired. So we brought in a number of highly rated senior engineers from Government Systems and I had the job of getting them up to speed. I must say that my teaching was not always accepted with the interest and grace that Clarence had. But we did get the team together, about 50 engineers plus their support, and everyone went ahead diligently with the plan.

We continued the daily meeting regime, and we usually worked Saturdays and some nights. I don't remember how long it took, but we kept to schedule and eventually introduced the TR-70 and released it to production. Clarence stayed with us until the product was started in the factory, although I could see he was now doing other jobs, too. The TR-70 was a success in the marketplace and re-established our position vs. Ampex. I learned a great deal about management from Clarence and we continued to be friends long after this episode.

Market Research

One thing I felt was very important was for all my engineers to know as much as possible about the customers' use of our equipment. How could anyone design successful equipment without knowing the customers? To this end, I encouraged customer visits whenever possible, and did not hesitate to send engineers into the field on troubleshooting assignments, knowing that they couldn't help picking up some knowledge from the customer. I also required complete written reports of any trips, including any customer comments, observations, or suggestions that occurred. These were distributed to all engineers.

In the mid 1960s, Chip Klerx, who was now Manager, Product Management for Electronic Recording, and I planned a series of customer visits for ourselves, to gain information on one particular application for TV recorders that we had seen growing in broadcast customer's installations. This was the use of TV recorders to play a number of commercials during station break periods, which were usually two minutes long. This was impossible to do with one machine because of the time it took to change tapes and restart after stopping the first playback. This time, even with a very agile operator was one minute or more. Obviously, in a two-minute period, no more than one commercial could be played.

Many stations solved the problem by assigning multiple recorders to station breaks — one per commercial to be played. Each machine had its own operator and the station switching system did the starting of machines and switching signals on cue. This worked, but it was an expensive use of equipment and manpower to a task that occurred repeatedly all day long. They would have to have enough equipment and manpower to dedicate to playing commercials.

Some stations got around this by editing all their commercials for a particular break onto one reel of tape. Then, that tape was simply played continuously to air the break. However, this limited the flexibility — all breaks would be the same. If one needed to mix up commercials, as some advertisers wanted done, you had to edit a different reel of tape for nearly every break. One would be editing all the time. I and some of my engineers visualized a different solution — a special machine for playing commercials that could play as many as anyone would want back-to-back, with no operator intervention. We had done only a little work on this and we wanted to know what kind of customer interest there might be for the idea before we dedicated more work to it.

So Chip and I flew around the country visiting 12 installations (both stations and production houses) to test out the idea. Of course, the interest was there, but the first question after they understood our idea, "How much will it cost?" We were ready for that and gave a figure of $50,000, which turned out to be very low. However, there seemed to be a lot of interest in the idea and we were encouraged to work on it.

We went back to the engineers and told them to work further on the idea and, particularly to make some kind of breadboard that would demonstrate the feasibility of the mechanical system that would be required. This led to

Figure 9 Threading breadboard

building a baling-wire and duct tape model (see Figure 9) that showed how we could make a tape deck that would automatically thread up a tape. (Note that threading a quadruplex tape deck is quite tricky because of the need to slip the tape between the vacuum guide and the headwheel.) This was long before anyone else had attemped anything like it. Armed with the results of the market research and the breadboard model, we approached Broadcast Systems management to get approval for an advanced development project. After a number of meetings, it was agreed that we could proceed with advanced development.

To further explain the idea of this system, which we called the "Tape Cartridge Recorder", we envisioned a "cartridge" that contained a short length of 2" quadruplex tape (200 feet, about 2.5 minutes worth) permanently wound between two reels (see Figure 10). There would be places in the machine to put a number of these cartridges, positioned so that they could be presented to either of two tape decks. The two tape decks would have separate electronics so that the signals from each could be sent to an automatic switcher in the machine that would select either signal for output. Additionally, the tape decks would automatically thread tape from the cartridges using the method we had demonstrated in the breadboard. Thus, one deck could play to air while the other deck threaded

Figure 10 TCR-100 Final Design Cartridge-open

the next commercial. At the end of the first playback, a control logic system (like a computer but it wasn't, because small computers didn't exist yet—this was 1966) would tell the second tape deck to start playing the second commercial, and so on.

Everybody in engineering, product management, and general management were excited about the concept. The only question was "Could we actually do it?" Of course we in engineering, being optimists, had no doubts about that—it was a simply a question of time and money.

The Television Cartridge Recorder

The design concept for the overall machine evolved through a number of stages before settling on two vertically-mounted automatic-threading transports. In front of them was a cartridge magazine, which was an articulated belt moving in a flattened-oval path and carrying up to 22 cartridges. A transfer mechanism on each transport could move cartridges from the magazine to the transport for loading and playing. Below this main mechanical assembly was an electronics bay containing all the servo and signal electronics. Below that was the power supply and pumps for the machine. Above the transport and belt assenbly was a control panel; behind that was the control electronics.

Except for the signal system, which used TR-70 modules, the electronics

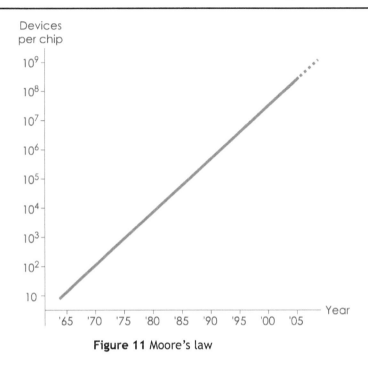

Figure 11 Moore's law

were all new, embodying the latest in transistor and integrated circuits (ICs). ICs had recently come out — they were single-chips that incorporated multiple circuits to perform many logic functions. This was another step along the path in reducing the size, lowering the power, increasing reliability, and reducing the cost of solid-state electronics.

Solid-state devices were following a curve of steady improvement that had been postulated first by Gordon Moore of Intel Corporation in 1965. Dr. Moore at that time had said that the number of transistors on a single IC chip would increase at a rate of doubling every eighteen to twenty-four months. This became known as "Moore's Law" (see Figure 11), and it has been roughly followed by the industry for more than four decades since then. This steady improvement in numbers of transistors equates to increases in chip performance, power savings, and size reduction. This is the reason for the explosion of ever more powerful and smaller electronic devices that has occurred over the years and is still going on now.

The cartridge machine control system that triggered all the sequences of mechanical operations of the machine used digital logic ICs to create a "hard-wired" computer. This is a computer that is designed to do just one thing — it is permanently wired for that task, rather than programmed for it as today's computers are. Small programmable computers that might have done this task still were five or more years into the future.

I should stop here to point out something about the control system. It was made with *digital logic chips*. That was our first instance of using a technology that would overtake almost all of electronics in the years to come. It was the start of another sea change in electronic technology. I will cover this technology in more detail in Chapter 9.

The cartridge itself evolved into the design shown by Figure 10. It had two reels with a captive tape held in a molded plastic case. For protection of the tape when the cartridges were outside of the machine, the cartridge had two doors that were opened by the machine as the cartridge was transferred into one of the transports.

Design work on the cartridge system began at the start of 1968 as a number of advanced development tasks, but formal management approval of the overall project did not happen until September 1, 1968. This included a commitment for the first engineering model to be shown at the 1969 NAB in April of that year. That was only seven months away! It was a very short cycle for such an innovative and complex equipment.

The main console of the cartridge machine was not a complete system. It relied on an external unit for the video signal processing. This could be either a separate rack specifically designed to do this task, or it could be connected to a TR-70's signal processing capability. In this latter configuration, where the cartridge machine is called a "slave", it would be possible to quickly switch between the reel-to-reel transport of the TR-70 or either of the transports in the slave.

An all-day concept design review was held on October 29, 1968 (see discussion of design reviews in Chapter 6). Sixteen people participated; five were from Electronic Recording Engineering (the presenters), and the rest were from outside our organization. Eight of these came from other RCA locations. Since there were so many people from outside our organization, it was important to give a comprehensive introduction to provide the background for the project and get the outsiders up to speed. I gave the introduction speech. In the box to the right are the first three

---

INTRODUCTION (1968)

At the present time there are nearly 5,000 television tape recorders in use in broadcasting stations throughout the world. Recent surveys of the application of these recorders have revealed that a very high percentage of recorder usage is for the playing of short recordings (less than two minutes). In the United States these short recordings consist almost entirely of commercial material, promotional material, or station identification material. Some surveys have indicated that as much as 90% of tape recorder usage is for this purpose.

All of the broadcast recorders now in service are of the quadruplex type, utilizing 2 inch wide magnetic tape transversely scanned by a rotating headwheel. This recording format is rather thoroughly standardized at this point by the SMPTE in the United States and by the EBU and CCIR internationally. All of the recorders currently available for this format are of the reel-to-reel, manually threaded type. Since it is quite common for a number of the short recordings to be played sequentially during a station break period, one will often see two or three video recorders set up with individual short recordings waiting to be played at the next station break. In many stations where a lot of tape commercials are handled, it is common for two or three video recorders to be completely used up in the playing of commercials for station breaks. Since a present-day highband color quadruplex recorder involves a capital investment of the order of $100,000, this represents rather poor utilization of extremely expensive facilities.

In addition to the expensive facilities, present-day quadruplex recorders require a lot of skilled operators to thread, cue up, and run the recorders. This is true even when the other activities of the television station have been automated. It is readily seen, therefore, that a major market need exists for a system which would completely automate the handling and playing of short recordings in the broadcast station. The cartridge video recorder described here is intended to meet that need.

---

paragraphs — the part about the market need. *You might compare that writing which was written 39 years ago, with the writing in this book.* Many comments and suggestions were collected at the meeting; the ensuing design program would consider them and decide which ones would be implemented.

There were many sleepless nights leading up to the 1969 NAB convention showing, and many problems to be solved, worked around, or simply endured during the show. At that point, the actions of the machine were far from reliable. At the last minute, we decided that someone should be behind the machine at all times during the show to watch the mechanical action for any hangup and assist the mechanism through the problem. Lee Hedlund, the Group Leader who handled system integration on the project, volunteered for this task. He had recently broken a leg in a ski accident

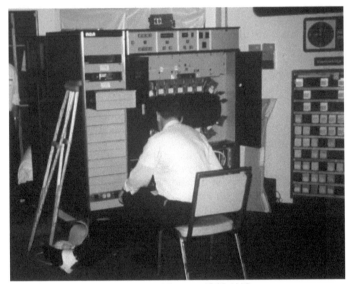

Figure 12 Cartridge machine at 1969 NAB

and had a leg cast, so he wasn't very mobile. During the show, he sat on a stool in the back with his leg propped up and goosed the machine whenever it was needed (see Figure 12). Our later objective was to improve the design to the point that every machine didn't need to have a person in it!

In spite of that, the machine was the hit of the 1969 NAB. We got lots of publicity and the future looked promising — if we could successfully complete product design and ship machines before everyone got tired of waiting.

Product design commenced right after NAB. Almost everything was redone, including a completely new cabinet layout and design. A limited run of ten units was built, two were the engineering prototypes and the others were built as a special run in the factory. The first one of the prototypes went to the 1970 NAB, where it was again well received. The machine then went to WDCA-TV in Washington, DC for field testing after the show. Six of the remaining eight machines went to other field-test locations and the last two stayed in Engineering. The product design machine is shown in Figure 13.

Figure 13 TCR-100 Final Product

After the 1970 NAB showing, work in Camden concentrated on completing the design and releasing it for production. The machine was now dubbed the TCR-100. The first delivery date for production was December, 1970. Again, a very short cycle, which we didn't meet. The first machines from production came out in April, 1971.

But there were problems. We were following all machines in the field very closely and, by July 1971 when there were 8 machines in the field, we could see that the reliability of operation was not anywhere near our objective, which was to have less than one failure (requiring human intervention) in 1000 cycles of machine operation. This equated to about a week of operation in a typical TV station. The decision was then made to hold all further shipments and embark on a crash program to improve

111

reliability.

Clarence Gunther again joined us to help organize and manage the reliability program. He had a lot of experience in reliability improvement in many government engineering programs and his help was very welcome. His first recommendation was that we get more failure data. A program was set up to log all failures from the machines in the field. Daily phone calls were made to collect data, and field men were sent out to help the customers with the problems. The customer machines were averaging about 100 cycles per day. Four additional machines were set up in a private area of the factory and cycled pretty much continuously. They could log 200 to 350 cycles per day. Analysis was done on all failures and a comprehensive list of failures was kept. This list was studied, prioritized, and tasks assigned to various engineers for solution. The entire Electronic Recording department staff was put on this project. Of course, the resulting changes had to be installed in the test machines to see if improvement was being made. It was.

In the middle of all this, I received a promotion to Manager, Broadcast Engineering, which gave me responsibility for all engineering in Broadcast Systems. I physically moved out of my office in Electronic Recording Engineering, to an office in a different building until space could be made for me back in the same building. I'll come back to my new job in the next chapter. Norm Hobson, who was currently in TV Camera Engineering and who had been involved in the original tape project in 1956 before I joined that program, took over Electronic Recording Engineering. Meanwhile, there's more to say here about Electronic Recording.

In due course, the target failure rate for the TCR-100 was achieved and shipments to customers resumed. We had 40 backorders at the time and many more customers were waiting for us to solve the problems and begin shipping before they would order. During its product life, the TCR-100 sold over $100,000,000 in products and held about 60% share of the market.

Ampex designed a competitor to the TCR-100, called the ACR-25. It used a different cartridge design and a very different method of threading the tape into tape decks. There was no effort to standardize between the two systems; it really wasn't necessary.

In 1974, RCA received an Emmy award for the development of the TCR-100. The Emmy went to RCA, not me or any other one person. However, my wife and I went to Los Angeles for the award ceremony, which was a very interesting time. Figure 14 shows Chip Klerx and I with the Emmy.

Figure 14 Chip Klerx and I with Emmy

I know from talking to many people about the TCR-100 over the years, that the average person will say "Why did you do that? Why did you make it easy for the stations to show more commercials?" My only answer was "Someone else would have done it. Why shouldn't we be the first?"

In 1969, RCA Corporation changed the corporate logo from the round form that I had known since I first heard of RCA, to a Cyrillic-looking three letters as shown in Figure 15. This change went across the board, from product labeling, to business cards, to stationery, and even to the Nipper tower in Camden. The beautiful stained-glass Nipper windows in the tower were covered up with the letters RCA.

Figure 15 Change of RCA logo

Other Projects

In the period from 1968 to 1973, the TCR-100 wasn't the only thing being done in Electronic Recording Engineering. There were improvements to be made in the TR-70 and there was the problem of having a low-cost reel-to-reel highband recorder. This need led us to upgrade the TR-4 concept to an all-new highband recorder based on the TR-70 electronics modules. This

Figure 16 TR-600 Recorder

was called the TR-50. A further upgrade became the TR-60.

An all-new console machine was introduced in 1972—the TR-600 (see Figure 16). It was also based on TR-70 electronics, but the console was smaller and the system cost substantially less than the TR-70, which remained the top-of-the-line offering.

In 1976, upper management decided that we should show off some high technology at the 1977 NAB convention. Their choice was to demonstrate an optical-disc recorder, based on an RCA Laboratories breadboard. Lee Hedlund was put in charge of this project for Broadcast Systems. The challenge was to do this in the nine months before the 1977 NAB, which took a tremendous amount of effort for all parties involved. The challenge was met. However, we never did any more with this.

The TR-600 turned out to be our last all-new quadruplex design, because a challenger was coming forward.

Helical Scanning

Since about 1961, various companies (including RCA, but a different division) had been showing recorders at NABs that were based on helical-scanning formats. The helical scanning principle was not new--it had been invented and worked on even before the Ampex VR-1000 was introduced in 1956. However, most helical recorders were directed at lower-cost markets, where the performance goals were too low to suit broadcast needs.

That was because achieving the high performance required by broadcast and production was still a challenge for the helical scan format.

In helical scan recording, the tape tracks are long tracks that are at a shallow angle to the edges of the tape. This was done by mounting the head (or heads) on a large rotating drum that the tape wrapped around. The longer tracks eliminate the complexity of multiple heads that have to be switched during one scan of the picture. Because of the track pattern appearance, helical recorders are sometimes called "slant track" systems. A helical recorder can actually be made with only one video head. However, most systems use more video heads to solve other problems.

Over the years, performance of helical recorders was steadily improved; it was only a matter of time before full broadcast performance would be achieved. Quadruplex performance was now excellent, which was a tough target for helical-scan recording. We in Broadcast Systems had not spent any of our engineering resources on helical-scan, although the issue came up in every planning session. The answer was always: "No money for that yet." We in engineering had become so used to the "no money" response from upper management that we accepted it as necessary. However we did carefully watch what others were doing, especially in Japan. I and others from Broadcast made regular trips to Japan to visit companies developing helical recorders.

My first trip to Japan was in 1966. I went with Tom Collins from the Broadcast Systems' Staff and Koichi Sadashige from my organization. Koichi was Japanese and had come to the US after World War II. He became an American citizen and completed his engineering studies in the US. He was our interpreter. The principal purpose of this trip was to review what Japan Victor Company (JVC) was doing with helical scan recorders. JVC and RCA had something in common: JVC was one of several companies worldwide who had licensed the "Victor" name and the "His Master's Voice" (Nipper) logo. They used the name and logo freely on their products. They gave us several personal gifts, which is the custom in Japan. I was given a battery-powered transistor AM radio, which I still have and it still works 42 years later! It is about 6" long. See Figure 17. On the way back, we stopped in Hawaii. That was my first visit to that part of the US.

In late 1977, Lee Hedlund became the Manager of Electronic Recording

Figure 17 JVC Transistor Radio (1966)

Engineering. By this time, it had become clear that helical scanning would be the future of broadcast video recording. Because we hadn't worked on the technology at all, we (in engineering) were behind the curve. Lee had the challenge to deal with the next catch-up we faced. Management did not want to wait for us to complete our own design; we should go to Japan and get marketing rights for a Japanese product that we could sell outside of Japan right away. We all felt that Sony was the best choice. The strategy of selling a Sony product branded with the RCA logo would be a stop-gap approach to the market while we designed our own all-RCA machine. We introduced the Sony BVH-1000 as an RCA product in 1978. Of course, no one was fooled by this. Some Sony machines were sold this way, and we found that there were many problems with them in the field. We worked closely with Sony in solving (their) problems. *Sony had not sold equipment to the broadcast market in the US before. They gained a lot of experience from the machines we sold for them. This helped them become recognized in the US as an excellent supplier of broadcast equipment. As almost anyone in the industry could predict, they later became an across-the-board competitor to RCA, which played a factor in our demise.*

Meanwhile, we pushed our own design program. As we had with the original Ampex agreement, we licensed the design from Sony, but not the manufacturing technology. Also, as with the Ampex situation, we had many problems manufacturing the machine and achieving interchangeability with Sony. The machine was called the TR-800 (see Figure 18).

Of course, Ampex was not standing still with helical. They had built a lot of helical machines for other markets, and they had mastered the manufacturing technology. They designed a helical machine to compete with Sony, using similar, but not exactly the same, technology. Their machine was called the VPR-1. So we were facing *two* competitors in helical recording. A standards activity was mounted to get all three manufacturers to be compatible, which was accomplished. It was named the "Type C format" by the SMPTE Standards Committee.

Because of the helical format and the use of 1-in tape, Type C machines were less expensive than quad and easier and lower-cost to operate. There were also other features that come with helical such as stop-action and slow-motion playback. The cost and features advantages caused a landslide in new purchases—new quad

Figure 18 TR-800 Helical Recorder

machines could no longer be sold. Of course, quad machines still worked and customers continued to use them for many years because they had invested in them. But new sales were all helical. We never achieved the competitive position in helical that we had in quadruplex.

Comments

You probably have noticed that in this chapter the personal pronouns have changed from "I", "me", and "my" to "we", "us", and "our". That is a direct result of the change of my status from working engineer to manager. I was now separated from the working level by two layers of management. My job was not to do the work any more, but to organize it, review it, encourage it, and support it. Everything that was accomplished by my group was truly a group effort. I was getting fewer patents, and the ones

117

that I did get were generally joint patents with other people. I still had ideas, but many times, I passed my ideas on to someone else to implement and perfect them.

I also was concerned with building a first-class group of engineers, and to optimize their assignments to get the best possible results from them. "We" is the right pronoun to be using now.

My years in Electronic Recording Engineering (1958 to 1971) were tremendously rewarding. During those years under my leadership we introduced two major industry-changing innovations — the TR-22 Transistorized Television Recorder, the first transistorized major equipment in the broadcast industry; and the TCR-100 Television Cartridge Recorder, a recording system that totally changed the way broadcasters used video recording equipment. We also accomplished many smaller innovations that allowed us to succeed on many fronts of a very competitive high-technology business.

The scope of technology in Electronic Recording equipment is very broad. It ranged from almost all types of electronic circuits — low-power, high-power, high frequency, digital, to mechanical packaging, to electro-mechanical mechanism, to exotic materials and micro fabrication such as are used in magnetic heads, and elaborate control systems. All of these areas contained major challenges. It was a great experience to manage such a multi-disciplinary engineering department.

I left direct involvement with Electronic Recording in 1971, except that it would still be a part of my broader responsibility. However, the technology of video recording did not stand still. The digital era was upon us. Today, video recording is a computer technology; involving tape recording, optical recording (DVD, Blu-Ray), solid-state memory, and many other technologies. I would have been happy staying in that field, but the opportunities for my advancement were elsewhere.

Now on to my new position.

Chapter 6

Chief Engineer, Broadcast Systems

I had been promoted to Manager, Broadcast Engineering, and I was told that this was a trial position before being named Chief Engineer. I assumed upper management wanted to test me before giving me the permanent title. There hadn't been anyone in such a position for many years, so my boss and I had to create a new job description. In doing that, the paragraph below was the guidance we began with.

> **Chief Engineer, Broadcast Systems.** Responsible for technical planning and direction of all engineering and advanced development programs for Broadcast Systems, including video recording equipment; television and radio studio equipment; antennas; and television and radio transmitting equipment.

Organizationally, this was a staff position, rather than a line position. That meant the engineering departments would not report to me. However, I would have some service activities reporting directly to me. The organization chart at this time (1971) is shown in Figure 1. It uses a concept that had been part of Broadcast Systems for some time. That was the organizational combination of Engineering and Product Management under a Business Manager for each product area. This was intended to foster

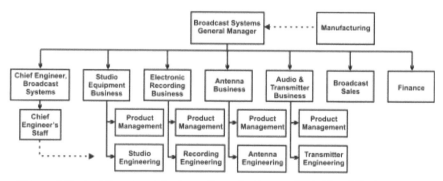

Figure 1 Typical Broadcast Systems Organization c. 1971 (simplified)

cooperation between engineering and product management and it gave each of the Business managers full control of the resources for new product development for his business. Some years of operating this way had proven that this kind of organization worked well for Broadcast Systems. It relieved the line managers of the concern about priorities between the different businesses.

The list of businesses for which I would oversee engineering included Studio Equipment and Electronic Recording, located in Camden; TV Transmitters, which was located in Meadow Lands, PA (30 mils south of Pittsburgh, PA), and TV Antennas, located in Gibbsboro, NJ (about 20 miles from Camden).

Broadcast TV Transmitter Business

Over-the-air TV broadcasting requires a high-power transmitter, an antenna, a transmission line system to connect transmitter and antenna together, and a tower to support the antenna. RCA Broadcast Systems manufactured transmitters and antennas, and we worked with specialty companies on towers and systems.

TV transmitters range in power from 5-kilowatts to 500-kilowatts, depending on the channel frequency and the needs of each customer situation. Until I became Chief Engineer, I had nothing to do with transmitters. My only experience with transmitters was working in the WFIL-TV transmitter room one summer while I was in college (see Chapter 2). Because of the large power levels and high frequencies, transmitters involve many different technologies than TV recorders, cameras, or terminal equipment. However, the basic engineering management techniques discussed in this chapter still apply. Management was the main thrust of my involvement in transmitters.

Transmitters are typically custom-manufactured for each customer. However, they are assembled from a catalog of components, cabinets, and power equipment that are manufactured in quantity. This reduces the product and engineering cost required to meet all the different customer needs. The catalog of sub-assemblies was called a "Line" in the Transmitter business. At the time I was Chief Engineer, we were designing the "G-Line" of transmitters. I conducted design reviews for the G-Line and supported the transmitter engineering department with the other things I and my staff provided to all engineering departments.

Broadcast TV Antenna Business

The TV antenna business involves many engineering challenges and much custom design work. Because an antenna has to be built to dimensions that match the channel frequency it will use, the original design of a new antenna produces a set of parameters to allow building the antenna for any channel in its range of application. Some designs are very old, like the "superturnstile" antenna, that stems from original work done by Dr. George H. Brown of RCA in 1935. Many other configurations have been developed since then.

However, the antenna configuration is just the beginning. Antennas are usually installed on tall towers, or on a tower on top of a tall building. Design considerations encompass the environmental issues at such altitudes and locations, the mechanical structure of the antenna, its support or tower, earthquake protection, getting the high-power signals up to the antenna, etc. This even goes further when customers want several antennas to share the same mounting structure, which is difficult to design, but can result in considerable cost savings when completed satisfactorily.

Antennas and towers often involve political and legal considerations associated with their location and multiple users of the site. All of this is beyond the scope of this book. Over the years, RCA Broadcast has done many antenna projects. One example that was completed while I was Chief Engineer, was the Mt. Sutro multiple antenna tower in San Francisco, shown in Figure 2. I must admit that I had little to do with this project except for financial overview of the engineering work.

Traveling to Meadow Lands, PA

Traveling to Meadow Lands where TV transmitter engineering was located, required an air trip of about 300 miles. The principal airline serving Pittsburgh from Philadelphia at that time was Allegheny Airlines, which later became part of US Airways. Allegheny was a short-trip airline serving that area of the East Coast. At the time I was traveling, they flew DC-9 planes or the BAC-1-11, which was a slightly smaller copy of the DC-9, that carried 89 passengers. Most trips were only one day — I would go out early

Figure 2 Sutro Tower

in the morning (a 1-hour flight), rent a car at Pittsburgh airport, and drive to our plant in Meadow Lands. With a sufficiently early start, I could be at the plant by 10:00 AM. At the end of the day, I would take a 6:00 PM flight and could be back home by 9:00 or so. A long day, which I did about twice a month all the time I was Chief Engineer. Regular flying like that leads to quite a collection of stories, of which this is one:

Most problems with flights to or from Meadow Lands occurred in the winter. There was one incident where a winter storm had passed through during the day while I was at the Meadow Lands plant. When I got to the airport to go home that evening, the flight to Philadelphia was ready and we took off. Once in the air, the pilot announced that there might be a problem landing at Philadelphia because the earlier storm was now moving in there. A little later, he announced that Phila. airport was closed and we were going back to Pittsburgh. Later still, we were told that Pittsburgh was closed and the plane was going to Cleveland. Before we got to Cleveland, Pittsburgh re-opened and the pilot decided to go back and land there. So after more than three hours of flying, I was back where I started and it was 10:00 at night. Allegheny Airlines said they would pay for my lodging at Pittsburgh, but unfortunately, there were no rooms available near the airport. Rather than go into the city, I decided to go back to Car Rental and pick up a car and drive back to Meadow Lands. Now I was back to where I *really* started from, 12:00 at night. I went to the hotel where I usually stayed over at Meadow Lands. They had a room; I checked in and immediately went to sleep. The next morning, I went to the airport and got home with no further trouble. Of course, I didn't go to work that day. My only concern through all that was: Did they have enough fuel in the plane for all the unexpected flying? Obviously they did.

Working as a Staff Person

A staff person with responsibility that crosses organizational lines, as I was now becoming, depends on the *respect* given to the staff person by the managers in the organization. This means that I had to build good relations with the business managers, the product managers, and the engineering managers. I started off with a good measure of this already, and I hoped to gain more by my approach to being a staff person.

Some staff people come into an organization and make recommendations without involving the people in the organization in the decision process. Then, they simply say "you do it" and walk away. My approach was to involve all the people in my study and my conclusions, then convince all the managers in the organization on my recommendations. Further, I offered to assist in the implementation of the recommendations. To help me do this, I needed to have a few of my own people to assist the engineering departments to carry out my recommendations.

At the outset, I had direct responsibility for the Camden Drafting department, a service group for all the Broadcast Systems engineers in Camden. But it was a resource that I could also use for staff work. My department would have to pay for that work, so I also needed a budget to pay for resources that I called on for staff work. I also had the Instruction Book (IB) writing group and the Packing Design group for all of Broadcast Systems. None of this gave me any great power, but it did take some of the management load off the other engineering managers.

I also kept a few engineers in the position of Staff Engineer, typically senior people with a lot of Broadcast experience, who could assist me technically. These people changed from time to time as we shifted engineers between responsibilities in the various engineering departments. Many engineers enjoyed this kind of position outside of the product design melee, but only for a while. It was a break in the routine that helped them decide where they would go next. They also got broader experience with other parts of Broadcast Systems, and more contact with other parts of RCA.

Improving the Engineering Process

Before I became Chief Engineer, the engineering departments had worked independently in their own areas for many years, without overall guidance for procedures, factory interface, or quality of work. I read into my charter that "direction" meant to institute improvements in these areas. It was certainly fertile ground for my abilities. I have always been an organized person, often to the dismay of people around me. Now I had the opportunity to apply this to an environment of hundreds of engineers. I was ready to present my ideas to all the broadcast engineers ahd help them make the needed changes. If people did not accept my new disciplines directly from me, then I would have to go to my boss and convince him to use his power to get my changes made. That would not be good for me.

GE&D Planning

GE&D stands for "General Engineering and Development", which in RCA was the name for the engineering budget. I mentioned in Chapter 4 about the overall budgeting process for engineering projects. This is how it was done: At budgeting time (midyear), the Broadcast Systems staff (all the people reporting to the General Manager) began discussions about next year's engineering projects. The overall Broadcast Systems financial budget process also began. Assuming that the engineering projects already underway were completed on schedule, a sales forecast was prepared. It must be understood that only projects that had been completed in the current year or earlier could affect the next year's sales. The lead time from start of engineering to sales is just too long to have any effect on the same year's sales.

By taking the revenue expected for next year and accounting for all the other expenses, a goal figure for the overall Broadcast Systems GE&D budget was developed. While this was going on, each business unit was conducting its own planning to determine how much funding would be needed to complete existing projects, support ongoing things like factory follow, and any new projects they would like to do. The GE&D budget was then broken down for each engineering department. At this point, each engineering manager had a target budget for the new year. This is where it got difficult. The business unit's desired budget and the trial budget developed from the "top-down" approach were usually far apart. Everybody wanted more engineering funds than were likely to be available.

The general manager and his staff then began a series of meetings that were termed "prioritization" meetings. I chaired these meetings. This became an iterative process where the departments and the general manager were involved in give and take to bring the proposed department GE&D budgets in line with the proposed overall figure.

In these meetings, we reviewed all product lines for their current market status and their likely projection for the future. Every year, there would be product lines where we didn't have a good market position and, rather than invest in that product line to help it improve in the market, we often decided to deliberately *underinvest* in that line. This allowed us to focus our GE&D investment on the strongest product areas. Of course, everyone knew that such a choice would be the death knell for any line that got underinvested. Over years of doing this, the breadth of products we sold slowly decreased. No one except engineers, who saw it clearly, seemed to care what would be the end result of doing that every year. In the meetings we were directed to consider only the need to meet the GE&D spending limits imposed by higher management. This was happening because of corporate management deliberately holding us to a lower level of GE&D investment than was needed to keep the businesses intact.

One of our general managers, Neil (Van) Vander Dussen, instituted another planning feature that seemed good from his point of view but very bad for engineering management. After the budgets were complete, Van would ask us to arbitrarily cut the engineering spending by 10% (or some other amount) below budget for the first half of the year. This provided a hedge against the possibility that the actual sales in the first half might run below the budgeted amount. If the sales did materialize, we could ramp up spending in the second half and still spend the budgeted amount.

A fine idea from Van's view, but very difficult to implement in Engineering. Since engineering expense is largely caused by the labor cost of the engineers, it is difficult to cut expense without cutting some of the staff. Van's answer to that was to lay off the lowest-performing engineers at the beginning of the year, to improve the overall performance of our staff. Do you remember the discussion about unions in Chapter 4? It said that in a layoff situation, the union contract may force an engineering manager to lay off his lowest *seniority* engineers, not lowest *performance* people. Anyway, there is an even more difficult problem with this strategy —

in the case where the first-half sales are good and we are allowed to ramp up spending, where do we find broadcast-experienced engineers to add to our staff? To fit the plan, we need people who can immediately go to work and be productive. Hard to find.

The result of this strategy was that we tried to cut expenses in other areas than engineers, such as materials and purchased support. That way, we could keep our staff intact but still manage the expense in the way the boss wanted. This was somewhat effective, but if we ran short of something, programs could be delayed until we had the funds to buy what we needed. However we played it, this was a difficult environment for engineering management.

Project Cost Estimating

An important element of GE&D planning was estimating the *cost* of the projects we planned to do in the planning year. If no work has already been done on a project, there is not much basis for estimating how much it will cost to do the project. The best way to know what it will take to design a product is to do advanced development on it first. The objective of any advanced development program is to do enough work on an idea to know whether the idea is feasible and what it will take to do a complete product design on it. If this is done well, then estimating the cost of a design project should be manageable. However, the necessary amount of advanced development can take as much as a year, with considerable expense itself. This delays the availability of the new product, where management was always pushing for shortening the time to product availability. Thus, we were often in the situation of trying to estimate the cost of a project without sufficient advanced development having been completed.

As I mentioned previously, the largest part of the cost of an engineering project is the cost of personnel. Knowing what goes into a product, one can break the design tasks down to the single-person level. The amount of work (man-months) for each task can also be estimated (guessed, probably). If all this labor is priced out, the total labor cost can be estimated. Then, material costs and outside support costs have to be estimated. Adding everything up, we have the total project cost. However, this does not determine the *schedule* for the project, unless the estimator simply divides the total man-months by the number of people, giving a schedule in months. Such a calculation is an average, and does not take into the acccount of how actual people having specific skills can be assigned to tasks of varying length to make everything come out in the estimated time. To take this into account requires something like the PERT planning that we use after a project is begun. I will discuss that in the next section. Suffice to say here that such detailed planning is impractical to do before the project is ready to begin.

Program Planning

A procedure that we had taken up from our sister division, Government Systems, was PERT planning. PERT (Program Evaluation and Review Technique) is a method of detailed planning that shows the logic of program activities and application of manpower. It is required by the government on all their engineering programs. At the urging of the VP of both divisions, Broadcast Systems began using PERT several years before I became Chief Engineer. It was a lot of work for the engineering managers, but it did help them in their management and it made the project clearer to higher management. It was very good for showing incipient problems and the possibilities for overcoming them.

In PERT, a diagram was made, called a PERT Chart, for the project. It shows completion milestones for individual activities with estimated time durations for each. Lines in the chart connect the activities in series as they follow each other in completing the project. This is a kind of network diagram. Once the diagram is finished, either manually or with a computer, the time duration can be calculated for every possible path through the network. The path that takes the longest time is called the "critical path". This is the path that will determine the projected end date for the entire project. Other paths that take less time are said to have "slack time" or "float", which means that they could become delayed by as much as their float time without affecting the overall program end date. Other views of the project can also be calculated from the chart. For example, a chart of manpower loading vs. time can be calculated. This could indicate points of manpower overload during the project. The work in PERT is making the original chart(s), and then keeping them updated as the project progresses. If changes are made to the ongoing plan to work around problems, the project PERT logic may also have to modified.

I believed in PERT, but also felt that the task could be made easier for the engineering managers if they had the right kind of support. I learned that Government Systems engineering groups all had administrators who did most of the leg work in implementing PERT. One of these administrators was brought in on loan from Government Systems to see if that would work for us. It did. The administrator, Ed Haugh, did a great job for us and he became in such demand with the engineering managers that I fought for years to transfer him to us. Government Systems fought back and we never could transfer Ed. But the loan situation went on for many years.

PERT charts and the results of PERT calculations were always a part of the GE&D reviews.

GE&D Reporting

Once we were into the new year and were carrying out the spending plan, we needed to have regular reports of progress. This was done through quarterly meetings called GE&D Reviews. I was responsible for scheduling and conducting these meetings, which were done separately for each business area. I had plenty of previous experience with these meetings as manager of the Electronic Recording Engineering department. I learned lots of things that I thought should be done differently. My new position gave me the chance to try out some of those ideas.

One problem was that the financial tracking system used by the finance department to report our financial performance did not agree with the formats that we used in the GE&D review. The engineering managers had to do a lot of extra work to process figures from the financial report into the GE&D review format. One or the other had to change. I undertook the task of working with the finance department and the general manager to get a format that would suit the GM and could be easily prepared from the financial data. That was accomplished over several years.

The GE&D format called for a series of charts for each project that showed project spending and design progress. PERT charts were usually included in this documentation. The objective was to as clearly as possibly show the general manager and his staff how the project was performing to schedule and cost goals. Much discussion always ensued while presenting the information, and recommendations were often made. It was important to record the recommendations for inclusion in the meeting report. I and my staff were usually responsible for the reports.

Design Reviews

It was another of my responsibilities as Chief Engineer to plan, schedule, and conduct design reviews for all new product programs in Broadcast Systems. Design reviews were meetings where a project was reviewed by knowledgeable people who were not part of the project. They provided an "outside look" at the technical work done on the project. At least two reviews were required for any new product program. The first was the "concept" review. This was held as soon in the program as the overall concept of the design was available. The earlier the better, because that would make it easier for the design people to consider any recommendations that came out of the design review. The second review was the final review, held when drawings were complete, but before release to production.

Once the time and subject for a review was determined, we could go ahead to select the reviewers to attend the meeting. The ground rule here was to achieve the broadest range of reviewers, without letting the meeting become too large. For a major system, 10 to 12 reviewers would be best, but often we had more than that. The reviewers have to be asked to attend. I had some funds to pay for reviewers who came from outside of Broadcast Systems. For an important reviewer, we might have to go to his or her management to get permission for spending the time for us.

Having the reviewers in place, we then faced the problem of getting everyone prepared for the meeting. An agenda needed to be created, and all the presenters from the project staff had to prepare slides and text for the meeting. This had to be done carefully so as to not take up too much of the meeting time for presentations, leaving little for discussion by the reviewers. A person was also designated to take notes at the meeting, which were used after the meeting to prepare an action list for the project people. Not all suggestions necessarily were implemented. It was up to the project staff and their related business people to decide about that. Generally I also participated in that decision-making. My staff and I tried to help the project people as much as possible in the preparations and the note-taking at the meeting.

The design review action lists often included things that the project group had not planned on doing. Engineering improvement requires such tasks, but they won't be an improvement if they take too much manpower away from the actual designing. Engineers and their managers are very sensitive to that issue, and will balk if given too much extra work. They will start calling it "red tape", or "busy work"; which means we haven't done a good enough job in helping them handle the work, and in convincing them that the extra work is worth it in improving their product designs.

Design Standards

The four engineering departments in Camden all used the same factory and the same purchasing department. Our production quantities were small — typically in the hundreds at most. If each engineering department independently chose the components they used and did all their designs accordingly, we missed any advantages of quantity savings in the material we bought. We also were spending engineering money in each department for engineering and drafting work that might have been done only once for items that could be common between all the departments.. These are the advantage of an engineering standards program. Setting up a standards program to do this was one of the objectives of the Chief Engineer position.

Using my knowledge of the various products, it was fairly easy to create an action list for standards-making. Besides the common electronic components such as transistors, integrated circuits, resistors, capacitors, etc.; there were electronic modules, PC boards, and other subassemblies that also might be candidates for standards. A standards committee was formed with representatives from each engineering department, drafting, and the Chief Engineer's staff. This group enthusiastically began researching components, choosing items to be standardized, and making new drawings for them. That was only the beginning.

The only practical way to introduce new standards is in new designs. Then it takes several years for new designs to appear in production and produce any savings. We had to publicize the standards system and its use. For this purpose, we instituted a Broadcast Standards Engineering Manual and distributed it to all engineering departments. The Manuals were updated quarterly. A lot of work, and I expected my department to do most of the leg work.

Ad-hoc Program Reviews

Sometimes, Engineering and Product Management would decide that a particular program should be reviewed separately from the design review process. They would ask me to conduct such a review personally. Usually, these reviews involved all the parts of a program in one review. I would conduct such a review by first interviewing the program people and their management. I would then do outside research about some of the questions I had. Then, I would present this to all participants in a comprehensive report that outlined what I did to collect information, what my observations were, and what recommendations I wanted to make. It was up to the program management to decide what to do after that.

I always gave such reviews a lot of my time and tried to produce a valuable report. In a sense, it was something I needed to do to justify my existence as a technical manager, which would gain me more acceptance and prestige in my position. These reviews were generally accepted well and many of my recommendations did get adopted. So I contributed to the product designs without actually being involved in them.

The reports for these reviews were occasions for me to exercise my writing (journalism) skills. That was something I wanted to keep up just like my technical skills. I have always felt that writing a report for a meeting gives the writer a degree of power. He gets the chance to express in his own way the actions and conclusions from the meeting. Other participants must review the report, of course, but the writer gets to say it first. Anyone wanting to express things differently, has to take the initiative to challenge the writer. I often volunteered to write the report for a meeting.

CCD Task Force

Around 1976, it was becoming clear to some of us in Broadcast Systems that the "charge-coupled device" (CCD) solid-state imaging devices that were being developed by RCA and several other companies for surveillance video cameras and other less-demanding video applications had potential for broadcast portable cameras.

The CCD is a type of integrated circuit that has a two-dimensional array of optical sensing devices. By scanning the array in television fashion, a video signal can be produced of whatever image is projected onto the surface of the array. Such devices are called "imagers". Because these are solid-state devices, they have the same advantage over vacuum-tube pickup devices — greater stability, reliability and longer life.

The original imagers had 512 x 320 (H x V) sensing cells in the array, which meant the video produced had a resolution (sharpness) that would be marginal for broadcast use. There were other limitations in the early designs besides resolution, such as motion smearing, overload characteristics, blue sensiivity, and overall image freedom from defects. However, being a solid-state device, the CCD is subject to the steady improvement predicted by Moore's Law, and one could not assume that it would be forever stuck at this performance. Different architectures will help, and as more sensing cells can be packed onto an IC chip, imager resolution was going to improve. It was not too soon to get ready for the coming improvements.

RCA Laboratories in Princeton, NJ was where many of the principles of CCDs were invented and they had continuing research programs in that field. RCA Broadcast Systems was a leading supplier of TV cameras for our market, RCA Electro-Optical Systems Division (EOSD), Lancaster PA, already were manufacturing and marketing surveillance CCDs and cameras, and RCA Government Systems Division also had major interest in CCD cameras for various military applications.

I was appointed chairman of a corporate-wide task force to manage this multi-divisional development program. The objective was to achieve a broadcast-quality CCD camera using RCA-manufactured CCDs. This program went on for several years and resulted in the world's first CCD broadcast portable camera, prototype displayed at NAB 1980, production models introduced in 1983. The first CCD camera was named "Hawkeye HC-2". (The original RCA Hawkeye was a camera/recorder that used tube-type sensors and was introduced in 1981.)

Product Safety

As the broadcast industry became more mature and more attention was being given to product safety, we needed to formalize our handling of this important matter in our designs. One of my staff, Floyd McNicol was appointed the product safety czar for broadcast. After researching the subject, we drafted a set of product safety design guidelines, which were eventually published in the Broadcast Standards manual.

Drafting

Drafting is the department within Engineering where the drawings are made for our products and all their parts. This is a complex job and the success of manufacturing depends critically on the quality of work done by the drafting department. There were often nearly as many people working in drafting as there were in the engineering departments they supported. It is a very labor-intensive task.

I brought in Bill Sepich from Government Systems to manage the drafting, packing design, and instruction book writing departments. Bill was an engineer and did a good job managing those activities for us. As an engineer, he also was valuable doing some of the Staff Engineer work as well.

Over the years, Broadcast Systems in Camden generated tens of thousands of drawings. These were kept in paper files of the original tracings. When someone wanted to look at a drawing, he ordered a print made from the tracing. The tracings never left the drafting room except to go to a draftsman's work table for changes or updating. The place for storage of the tracings is called the library.

In the 1970s, we installed an Applicon computer-aided design (CAD) system and library. A central computer system stored all the drawings made by the system, and the draftsmen worked at computer workstations to create or change drawings. This was early in the game of such systems and it was expensive and difficult to learn to operate. The results were worthwhile in terms of drawing quality, but not easily justified financially.

Technical Papers and Patents

Another realm of the Chief Engineer's office was managing technical papers, presentations, and patents made by our engineers. Technical papers are documents written to be presented at a conference and/or to be published ina technical journal. The pressure of the daily job was enough on the engineers that they had difficulty finding time for such activities. Even though papers and patents were valuable for an engineer's professional standing and prestige, we often had to encourage the activity and help them to find time for it, or even to find ways to help with some of the actual work.

Broadcast Systems Engineering Conference

To further foster cooperation between engineering, product management, and manufacturing, we decided that we should conduct an annual meeting of all the people in these three groups who were involved with Broadcast Systems work. We got approval to do this for the first time in 1973. We had a meeting for all our people in Camden and Gibbsboro (which totaled about 320 people), and a separate meeting at Meadow Lands. These meetings were conducted off-site, at a hotel having meeting facilities for a large group. The meetings began in the early afternoon; presentations were made about the engineering projects until dinnertime. They were followed by cocktails and dinner and an after-dinner speaker. Everything usually finished before 9:00 PM.The first meeting was called the Broadcast Systems Technology Seminar, but in subsequent years it became the Broadcast Systems Engineering Conference.

Each meeting had a theme, and the agenda contained an introduction by me that presented this theme, and the other speakers were encouraged to reinforce the theme in their presentations. At the end of the meeting, we gave awards to people in all organizations who made significant accomplishments during the previous year. There were both team awards and individual awards each year.

One activity that we added to the agenda in the third year was a session where we divided the participants into ten groups who discussed and brainstormed on ten pre-determined subjects that related to improvement of our activities or their interaction. (Brainstorming is a type of activity where a group of people try to generate as many ideas as they can think of about a subject. During brainstorming, all ideas are recorded and no critiquing or evaluation of ideas is allowed in the discussion.) The subjects were announced in advance and each participant was asked to give three choices for what session he or she would like to join. Just before the meeting, we went through the responses and worked out who would attend which session. The subjects for the third meeting are shown below.

A. **How to make our new products more innovative** Consider factors affecting innovation such as amount of advanced development, schedules, personnel management, market research, attitudes, incentives, etc.

B. **How to improve the efficiency of the total design and manufacturing process** Considering the engineering and manufacturing of new products as a total process - how do we make it more effective? That is, how do we produce better performing, lower cost products with less non-recurring cost for engineering design and manu-facturing start-up?

C. **Electronic recording products** Consider all aspects of the recording equipment product line including planning, competition, marketing, market research, new product ideas, problem solving, possibilities for expansion of the line, etc.

D. **Camera and projector products** Consider all aspects of the camera and projector product line including planning, competition, marketing, market research, new product ideas, problem solving, possibilities for expansion of the line, etc.

E. **Antenna product line** Consider all aspects of the antenna product line including planning, competition, marketing, market research, new product ideas, problem solving, possibilities for expansion of the line, etc.

F. **Control equipment product line** Consider all aspects of the control equipment product line including planning, competition, marketing, market research, new product ideas, problem solving, possibilities for expansion of the line, etc.

G. **How to learn more about what the customer needs** Consider the problem of finding out what are the important future needs for equipment. How do we recognize needs that might be filled by new equipments that do not now exist in the market?

H. **How to improve information transfer between engineering and manufacturing** Consider the relationship between engineering and manufacturing during the first production of a new product. Typical items are drawing releases, drawing format, computerization, planning, ECP's, first piece approvals, test information, problem solving, manufacturability, etc.

I. **Exploring new market opportunities** Consider the possibilities for extension of the market for Broadcast Systems products or related items. Consider new uses for our products, new customers for them, or new products.

135

J.   The **broadcast television system** Consider the overall broadcast station and its total equipment requirement (without regard to present equipment or product lines) - what are the possi-bilities for more effective system configurations? This subject can also include systems for special purposes such as electronic newsgathering or teleproduction.

As you can see, these subjects were not things that working engineers or factory people would normally discuss among their peers, nor would the subjects be areas that they would hear much about from their superiors. It turned out that these sessions were the highlight of the meeting, as expressed by many participants. The results of the sessions were tabulated and given to the most responsible people for each subject.

I and my staff carefully planned each meeting and worked with all speakers to rehearse and critique their talks. With everything planned so carefully, the meetings went smoothly and were enthusiastically received by all participants. In many ways, I viewed these meetings as theatrical events — we were putting on a show. This was probably a manifestation of my interest in theater stemming from my school days.

I have always believed that the most important personal technique is to be _prepared_ for whatever you do. I apply this practice rigorously for anything that I can plan in advance. Of course, I cannot plan ahead for something that happens unexpectedly. The Engineering Conference meetings were a prime example of the value of such planning.

# # #

In early 1973, I was given the title of Chief Engineer, Broadcast Systems. There was no change in what I was doing, because I had already been acting as Chief Engineer for two years.

In the summer of 1973, I attended a two-week course at MIT on "Management of Research, Development & Technology-Based Innovation". (This was the first time I had been back to MIT since I graduated in 1950.) It was an excellent course and gave me many ideas that I could implement at RCA. I wrote a three-page report of what I learned at that course. Some of the items that I found important were:

1.   Medium-size innovations ($10-200M market value) that are successful are predominately caused by invention pursued as a result of a market _need._

Only the major breakthroughs (i.e., the transistor) occur as a result of pure technological investigation, and any company looking for one of these to base its future on will probably go broke before it happens! Therefore, it is vital to provide close coupling of R&D with the marketplace. It is desirable for a business to spend money to figure out what to invent. The needs and desires of the marketplace should be systematically and carefully explored, analyzed, and displayed. Definite efforts should be made to develop an information base to support R&D product decisions — there is never enough such information.

2. Studies have shown that much of the innovation that an R&D group produces comes as a result of information or ideas actually originating outside of the R&D group. Certain people in the group function substantially more than others as "technological gatekeepers," that is, they serve to bring information into the group. These people are usually senior, more experienced, and more productive; they have many outside contacts in the industry, they are more active in watching the literature, and they are able to interpret what they see and hear. On an informal basis, the other group members have learned who these sources of information are and they use them as needed. Management should recognize this activity by these people and encourage it, but it should not be formalized. (Such people in Broadcast Systems are myself, Bob Hurst, Larry Thorpe, Sid Bendell, etc.).

3. The subject of technological forecasting is one that I intend to explore further. TF refers to the task of trying to predict when or how a particular technological development will occur. (When will CCD's enter the broadcast market? Will helical scan replace quadruplex?) Much methodology has been developed by researchers in the TF field; the course only scratched the surface. Some of the techniques are Delphi, trend extrapolation, trend correlation, growth analogy, substitution analysis, etc.In Bob Hurst's group and in my own personal work we are doing TF all the time and I'm sure we can benefit by learning more about how others do it. I've ordered some books to go deeper into this subject.

4. Data was presented to demonstrate that significant technological innovations on the average take seven or eight years to come to the marketplace. Because of this length of the technology development cycle, it is desirable for a company to examine its strategies up to ten years out, and to develop a technology plan which is not limited to the usual five-year business planning cycle. This certainly applies to our planning of video disc, which may not fit in a five-year plan.

5. Organizational functions such as R&D, production, marketing and sales, need to be different and to operate in different environments. The necessary differences should be accepted and appropriate mechanisms should be developed to achieve communication and cooperation in spite of the differences It is wrong to try to eliminate the differences. Typical (integrating) mechanisms that are used are coordinating individuals or groups, project management offices, project teams, task forces, etc. An integrating individual is most effective when his reputation is based on technical competence (for the project) and not on pure authority.

6. It is always cheaper to buy an existing technology than to develop it yourself. If the technology you need is available anywhere in the world, you should consider

license or technical aid agreements first before pursuing an in-house development of the same thing. This approach has been used most successfully in today's marketplace by Japan.

Looking at that report now, I still can see the value of the ideas, but I don't think they had much effect on RCA Broadcast Systems. Probably because other things were going on that were planting the seeds of our demise. These were various implementations of Number 6 above. They will be covered in the next chapter.

Awards

During the period of this chapter, I received several industry awards. They are listed here.

1969 — Fellow of the SMPTE. This is the highest grade of membership in the SMPTE. Someone has to nominate you and a selection committee chooses from the nominees the ones who will get the awards (there are a number of them each year).

1973 — SMPTE David Sarnoff Gold Medal for Meritorious Achievement in Television Engineering. This was another nomination award. A citation went with this: "For major contributions to the field of magnetic video recording including development of the broadcast industry's first quadruplex video tape cartridge recording system, and for contributions to the national and international standardization of quadruplex recording."

1974 — Fellow of the IEEE (Institute of Electronic and Electrical Engineers). Another nomination award. Multiple awards are given each year. The citation was: "For engineering contributions to the design of color television cameras and video tape recorders."

1974 — Emmy award from the National Academy of Television Arts and Sciences, presented to RCA for the TCR-100 development, for which I was the principal engineering manager.

1975 — RCA David Sarnoff Gold Medal for Outstanding Technical Achievement. Nomination for Individual Award. Citation reads: "In recognition of his outstanding technical contributions to the development of Commercial Broadcast Equipment and in enhancing RCA's reputation as a leading supporter of Television Systems." Note: I was given a copy of the nomination letter for this award, which was written by Neil Vander Dussen, Division Vice President and General Manager, Broadcast Systems, my boss at the time. In his nomination document, he showed that Broadcast

Systems' products I had a major contribution to had grossed $332,000,000 for RCA. *The significance of that number is that I had achieved my goal for my engineering work that I stated at the beginning of Chapter 3. The products I contibuted to were being sold to TV stations all over the world, creating and delivering TV signals to many millions of viewers. That is certainly a "positive impact on the world."*

1976—Certificate of Appreciation from the NAB on the occasion of the twentieth anniversary of the introduction of quadruplex recording. Citation reads: "In recognition of untiring efforts and numerous contributions in pioneering the development and introduction of Video Tape Recording to the television broadcasting industry."

Lots of recognition. I had become well known and respected in the industry. On May 18, 1978, another promotion: to Chief Engineer, Commercial Communications Systems Division. A larger responsibility.

Chapter 7

Chief Engineer, CCSD

CCSD

Commercial Communications Systems Division (CCSD) was the next-level organizational unit in RCA above Broadcast Systems. The otherCCSD divisions were Avionics Systems, Van Nuys, CA; Mobile Communications Systems, Meadow Lands, PA; Film Recording Systems, Burbank, CA; and Cablevision Systems, North Hollywood, CA.

This was again a staff position. However, the scope of technology was much greater and the diversity of locations involved a lot more travel. The total engineering population of all the units (including Broadcast Systems) was around 300 engineers. The charters for the various CCSD units were:

> **Avionics Systems**, located at Van Nuys, CA in the Los Angeles area. Avionics equipment, particularly communication radios and weather radar for aircraft cockpit use was designed and manufactured by this unit.
>
> **Mobile Communications Systems**, co-located at Meadow Lands, PA with the Broadcast Systems' Transmission Equipment unit. Two-way radio equipment for police, businesses, and taxicabs was designed and manufactured by this unit.
>
> **Film Recording Systems,** located at Burbank, CA in the Los Angeles area. Sound recording equipment for use in connection with motion-picture film editing was designed and manufactured by this unit.
>
> **Cablevision Systems**, located at North Hollywood, CA in the Los Angeles area. Equipment for cable television systems was designed and manufactured by this unit.

My responsibilities for engineering at all these units were added to what I did for the various units of Broadcast Systems.

It was decided that I should immediately move my office from the Broadcast Systems' engineering area to the executive offices for CCSD, which were on the seventh floor of Building 2 (2-7). This was to expand my previous focus on Broadcast Systems to include the other units of CCSD and to improve communications between me and the rest of the

Figure 1 Building 2 (1916)

CCSD staff.

Building 2 was built in 1916 as the headquarters for the Victor Talking Machine Company (See figure 1). The building was not the usual factory building: It was an architectural masterpiece. Floor 2-7 was elegantly furnished for the executive offices of that growing company. Individual offices surrounded a spacious hall. The southeast corner office was the President's office. It was panelled in walnut, with elaborate carvings. Adjacent to the President's office was a large conference room (the Board Room), also panelled in walnut and carvings. When RCA took over Victor in 1929, 2-7 became the executive floor for Radio Corporation of America. David Sarnoff occupied the President's office until the corporate headquarters was moved to New York City. *Building 2 still stands today.*

As the CCSD headquarters, the Vice President and General Manager of CCSD, Andy Inglis, occupied the President's office. Other members of his staff occupied the other rooms around the center hall. My office was a large room across the hall from the conference room. It had an entry room where my secretary sat and guarded the entrance to my inner office.

My office in 2-7

One major feature of my new office was that I would get all-new furniture. In Engineering, everyone had metal desks, which were handed down from one person to the next. There was no way to tell how old they were. Now I was able to select new furniture from a catalog. The approved possibilities were all wood furniture, in different styles. I chose a collection of mahogany furniture in a traditional style, which was quite elegant compared to anything in Engineering. This included a conference-style desk, which had a 3' x 6' top that overhung the base below. That provided space for a group of three or four people to gather around the desk for a small meeting. I used this feature often.

The rest of the furniture consisted of a large credenza, a leather couch, coffee table, and four leather side chairs. Larger meetings could be conducted around the coffee table. For still larger meetings, I could schedule the board room across the hall. I was told that my furniture cost $20,000. The first time any of my colleagues from Engineering visited me in 2-7, there was quite a reaction with comments about all this elegance. At first I was embarrassed, but I soon got over it.

Learning about the New Business Units

Since I now had responsibility for engineering oversight of four new units, all located away from Camden, I made a trip to each unit to meet the people and see the facilities. I was just as new to them as they were to me, but we were all engineers and there was not much trouble communicating. I had to convey my management style to them: I am a person who listens, I don't jump to conclusions, I want to see all the available information before coming to any decision, and I wanted to understand the technology. I didn't want to be in a position that anyone could "snow" me about the technology.

There was much to learn about besides the technology. I needed to know about their markets and customers, and to understand their management styles. I had no intention of imposing my own management practices, unless I felt that theirs was lacking. Then, I would have to sell them and their management on my own methods where applicable.

All this went well. After about six months, I was comfortable working in any of the CCSD business areas. However, my assignment areas dealt mostly with manpower, business planning and budgeting, and project reviews. There wasn't much time to keep up on technology. I relied mostly on the chief engineer in each area to keep me up on technology changes.

Personnel Review at Van Nuys

The Avionics Systems unit in Van Nuys, CA was co-located with the RCA Electromagnetics and Aviation Systems Division, a division of RCA Government Systems Division. GSD decided to close that unit and lay off all the people. That would leave Avionics with the entire plant, which was too large, but the more immediate concern was the upheaval in the local engineering community. At the time, Andy Inglis was the head of CCSD and he asked me to go to Van Nuys to interview the entire engineering staff, both government and commercial, to help decide who should remain for Avionics Systems and who should go. This was before I became the Chief Engineer of CCSD. *This may have been part of a test to see if I was ready to be promoted.*

Since Andy was going to spend a lot of time there during the transition, he had rented an appartment nearby in Van Nuys so there was a convenient place to stay while he was there. I traveled to Van Nuys several times with Andy to begin the process of interviews. Then I made several more trips by myself. On these trips, I stayed in Andy's apartment when he was not there. I completed all the interviews after several weeks and made my report to Andy. In the course of this I got to know all the people who would be in Avionics Systems after the transition.

Woodworking Techniques from California

While staying in the apartment, I had a lot of spare time after work and weekends. I used this to go around the Los Angeles area looking for things relevant to my woodworking interests. I was interested in finding pieces of west coast wood that would be different from what we had in the East. I found a number of sources for such items and picked up pieces that I took back East on the plane. I often carried pieces of wood onto the plane, which I'm sure amused the other passengers. But no one ever asked me what I was doing with the wood.

Although the wood itself was interesting, even more interesting was a process I learned about for finishing wood with a perfectly smooth extremely glossy surface. I had seen surfaces like that, but I had no idea of how they were achieved. The secret was to use polyester resin for the finish with a mylar mold for the surface.

Polyester resin is a clear thermoplastic, which means that it is cured by heat. In this application, curing is initiated by mixing the resin (a liquid) with a catalyst. That causes curing in a few minutes, depending on the ambient temperature. The surface to be treated is usually coated with several layers of resin, spread or brushed on and allowed to cure. Then a sheet of mylar plastic is stretched on a wooden frame so it will stay flat.

The sheet is slightly larger than the piece being finished. For the finish, a final coat of catalyzed resin is applied to the surface and the mylar sheet in the frame is immediately placed on top of it. After squeegeeing out all the air bubbles, the resin cures. After curing, the mylar is simply lifted off the surface--it does not stick. The glossy surface of the mylar has been replicated on the cured plastic surface. Very impressive.

Figure 2 shows an example of a piece of California buckeye burl finished this way. The monochrome photo cannot show the characteristics of the finish, but it does show something else that can be done with a polyester resin finish. The wood piece had a large hole at the top (shows dark in the photo). I embedded a pretty rock in resin to fill this hole. This is easily done in several layers (there are problems in curing a resin layer that is too thick). The resin was built up around the rock until it was up to the level of the rest of the piece. Then I finished the whole piece with mylar in one operation. I used the resin-and-mylar technique frequently back in New Jersey for several years. *Then somehow, I lost interest in it and have not used it since. That was*

Figure 2 CA buckeye burl

probably because my woodworking took a different turn: to building houses.

The Personal Computer Arrives

Personal computers (PCs) had begun to appear around 1975. By 1978, there were several systems that seemed to be more than game machines. That raised my interest enough that I decided to buy one on my own and find out what they were all about. After a fairly quick review of the field, my choices narrowed down to the Radio Shack TRS-80 or the Apple II. Although I didn't really know enough then about computers to make an intelligent choice, I finally settled on the TRS-80, primarily because I didn't think a company named "Apple" could be very serious. I also think I was influenced by the fact that the Apple at the time used a TV for its monitor, whereas the TRS-80 had an actual monitor (it was in fact, a modified TV). I knew enough about TVs to know that they would not be good computer monitors without modification.

I bought a TRS-80 and began to learn about it. There wasn't much serious software available at the time, but the TRS-80 had the BASIC language (acronym for Beginner's All-purpose Symbolic Instruction Code) built in and a good programming manual. I dived into programming and quickly mastered BASIC. After years of building hardware, I became enamored with how much easier it was to build something in software. No components are needed, no soldering or assembly--you simply sat at the computer and typed. Of course, this assumes that the hardware for what you are building is already in the computer. I did also try some hardware modifications in the computer, but this was not as much fun as the software. The TRS-80 began two more threads for me: computers and software. Working with the computer and writing software took up nearly all of my spare time; This engineering obsession was causing me to neglect my family life. *Since that time, I have done many many software projects and I am still doing them. I love programming. This is another example of being ready and able to embrace a new technology.*

Digital Technology

The PC is a example of digital technology, which was destined to take over much of electronics. This is a good point to explain digital to those readers who don't already know about it. Up until the mid-1970s, almost all of electronics was analog. As I discussed in the Chapter 5 section on the TR-70 project, analog signals and circuits are subject to various distortions, which will accumulate as signals pass through many circuits. The example in Chapter 5 was about recording and then re-recording video signals with analog tape recorders. The accumulation of distortions quickly makes video signals unusable when being re-recorded.

Digital technology is different. Rather than signals being continuously-variable as in analog, digital signals have only two levels: on and off, yes or no, 1 or 0, etc. Such a signal is called a "bit". So how can digital bits represent a multi-level signal such as video? The answer is to use several bits to represent an analog value. For example, if you team up two bits, you can represent four levels in your signal. You can represent as many levels as you wish by using more bits. Video values are commonly represented by at least 8 bits, which gives you 2^8 or 256 levels. If you think of a video signal as containing the brightness values for successive points in an image, then analog video would be replaced by a stream of values, representing the brightness of successive points in the image. To represent this digitally, you would assign 8 bits for each analog value, giving 8 times as many bits as you had points in the image. But each bit has only two values, which is good, because electronic circuits can reproduce bits with near-perfect accuracy. If that's not good enough, you can use digital error detection and correction (EDAC) to make it as good as you like.

But using 8 bits to represent a signal would seem to require 8 times as many circuits to handle the signal. That's basically correct, but that is where digital ICs come in. On an IC, circuits are cheap, far cheaper than analog circuits. Each IC chip can have hundreds, thousands, *even millions of circuits (today, not in 1978)*. Thus, once you change to digital signals, the circuits required actually get cheaper. It is win-win.

The above sounds very simple. That's because I have over-simplified it. The reality was that it took many years to change everything to digital, and it is not even finished in 2008. The growth curve of Moore's Law has made this possible.

Personal Computer Details

With that digital background, I will give an explanation of what's in a personal computer for those readers who aren't already familiar with PCs. This will help everyone to understand what I say about computers in the rest of the book. Computers, once they got hold of me in 1978, have been a major part of my life from that point on.

Figure 3 is a block diagram of the hardware components of a personal computer. All the components connect together through the system bus, which is a digital data path shared by everything in the PC. The system bus carries streams of digital bits from any unit to any other unit. A quick description of each component is in this list:

CPU (stands for central processing unit) is the actual computing device in the system. Everything else helps the CPU with its work or helps the user control and view what the CPU does. A CPU is usually a single IC chip of great complexity. With Moore's law being what it is, CPUs become more and more powerful as time goes on. *In 1978, a typical CPU had around 10,000 circuits on its chip. Today, CPUs can have more than 1,000,000,000 circuits on a chip!*

RAM (stands for random-access memory) is an array of ICs that do temporary storage of data and programs while the computer is running. When power is shut off, RAM loses all its data, a behavior known as "volatile".

ROM (read-only memory) is a set of different IC memory chips that permanently store programs for the computer. ROM is programmed at the factory and cannot be changed later by the computer. It's storage is "non-volatile".

Mass Storage is read-write types of storage that provides additional non-volatile storage; in the early days it was magnetic tape or disk media, which could also be physically removed from the machine. This allowed programs to be distributed on media to all machines, and to archive data produced by the machine. Later machines had hard disk storage, which gave more capacity and access speed. *Today, removable storage is CD or DVD or flash solid-state memory.*

Video System (consists of the video adaptor and the display) shows the results of the computer's actions to the user. In early computers, this display showed mostly text, and possibly simple graphics. *Today's computers can show high-resolution images and motion video as well as text and graphics.*

Audio System (consists of an audio adaptor and speakers) is the system that allows the computer to make sounds. Early computer had very simple sound systems that were capable of making only beeping sounds.

User Input Devices (keyboard and [later] mouse) provide the means for the user to input data and commands to the computer.

Personal computers have been in a state of continuous evolution ever since they were introduced. The IC components improved as the industry was able to follow Moore's law, and the other components had equally major improvements over the years. All these things meant that I had to continually upgrade my TRS-80s with new things like more memory, floppy disks, printers, etc. *This is still happening with computers today, 30 years later. If one doesn't get a new computer every three to five years, they are hopelessly behing the curve.*

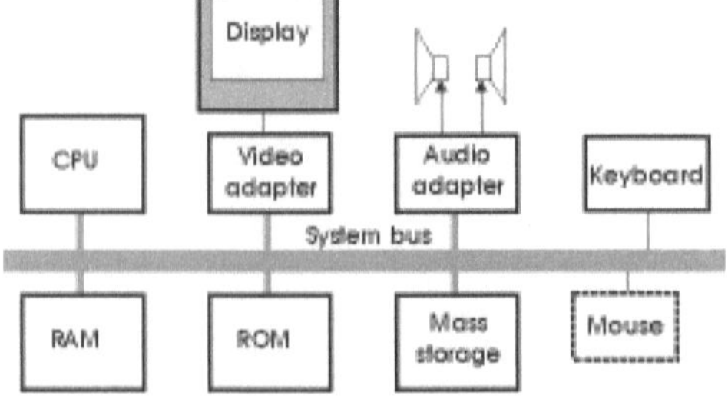

Figure 3 Personal Computer diagram (1978)

The BASIC programming language was mentioned earlier. It is a "high-level" language, because it cannot be directly run by the CPU in the computer. It must be converted into "machine code", which is the native language of the CPU. BASIC's most important feature is easy-to-learn-and-use. It was not really very appropriate for the low-powered early computers, because BASIC is an "interpreted language", which means that programs are converted into machine code at run time. This is doubly inefficient because the interpreter is itself a block of code that takes up memory space, and running the interpreter uses up a significant part of the computing capacity of these early (read: slow) machines.

It is much more efficient to have a program written directly in machine code, thus eliminating the interpreter and the computer power loss it causes. One can write directly in machine code, but it is unreasonably difficult because one has to deal with the guts of the CPU and the very arcane format of the machine code instructions. This problem is partially solved by using "assembly language" and an "assembler" program. With BASIC, each word one writes in the code is expanded by the interpreter to a number of machine-language words at run time. Some BASIC words may generate hundreds of words of machine code. With assembly language, one has to write a word for every machine instruction that will be generated, which is a lot more detail. The good part, though, is that the words one writes are easy to read and to understand what they will do. The assembler converts this into the arcane machine code.

Each time I get into technical discussion like this, I feel I have to apologize to my non-technical readers. Just bear with me. If you don't understand it, all is not lost—go ahead and you will come to more non-technical stuff soon. However, you might want to scan through the technical stuff--there are some very good stories mixed in there.

I soon learned to use assembly language and found that I could now *really* make the machine do things! I wrote my own word processor for the TRS-80, and later I even wrote a database program. That is a program that stores lists of data that can be searched for access later. I designed my database program to distribute or sell to others; it was complete with an instruction manual. However, I never had more that one other person using it besides myself. That person was Ed Gamble, who worked in Quality Control at the Camden plant. He used my software to keep the books for his church for many years, even after I had abandoned the TRS-80 for more modern computers. I moved a TRS-80 into my fancy

149

office in Camden and used it until I left there. Then it went with me to Princeton. By that time the TRS-80 had become a dinosaur, but I loved it because it used all my own software. Eventually, I had to face up to learning a new machine and its commercial software, which was far more powerful that my ancient TRS-80.

In May 1980, I was promoted to Division Vice President, Engineering, CCSD. This was the same job with a more prestigious title, and there were more perks and a little more salary. Being a V.P. also had a lot of prestige, which I thought I didn't care about, but I found I did.

Product Assurance

In July, 1981, my title again changed, to Division Vice President, Enginering and Product Assurance, CCSD. With this job, I gained the Product Assurance department of the division. That takes a little explanation. Product Assurance refers to all the things we did to assure that our products would work in the field and keep working. It was a subject that I focused on in Engineering during my time as Chief Engineer of the division. However, dealing with quality issues in Engineering was only part of the story. Ultimately, our designs would get built in the factory, and the success of that depended on the same attention to quality there as I was trying to instill in Engineering.

The Factory had an organization called Quality Control (QC), which dealt mostly with after-the-fact testing of products for quality. Having Quality Control as part of the factory was much like asking the fox to guard the henhouse. At the end of the month, when monthly quotas had to be met, there was tremendous pressure on QC to release the products for delivery. Compromises often were made to meet quotas. Now factory QC would report into my Product Assurance department. The factory would have to go through me to make any compromises at month-end. My first effort with this was to get the quality issues to be faced long before the end of the month, so we wouldn't have a quality crunch then. That helped.

Life as DVP, Engineering, CCSD

During my years as Chief Engineer, CCSD, regardless of what title I had,

I seemed to be running faster and faster and still I felt there was so much more to be done. I was traveling a lot to cover each of the business units and to participate in industry committees, trade shows, and sundry customer and vendor visits. In 1980, I made 39 trips of one day or more away from the office; in 1981 it was 14 trips, and 1982 was 29 trips. This was someone who began his career hating to travel!

Underlying my feelings at this time was the realization that something that had been brewing for years was soon to come to fruition. Broadcast Systems would go out of business. Prior to 1970 or so, there was not a lot of competition in the broadcast equipment market. However, with the rapid growth of color TV broadcasting that occurred around 1970, European and far-eastern manufacturers entered the scene. Of course, they had to prove themselves in the marketplace, but that was completed in a few years. We were finding it harder and harder to keep up. We did all right for a while because of our large and more experienced Sales department, but eventually even that was not enough.

What was also happening is that we were under-investing in engineering of new products. Anyone who studies business knows that, in a highly competitive market such as broadcast equipment had become, one had to keep engineering new products for the future or your business will surely decline. We weren't doing that. Each year, when we did the GE&D planning in our prioritization meetings, we had to cut new product programs in lesser product lines to keep going in the major areas of cameras and tape recorders. By 1980, those two businesses were all we had. We had lost our momentum and all we could see was decline.

The End is in Sight

By 1983, I began to feel that I was getting nowhere trying to keep a dead horse alive without enough resources to do it. I felt that the business no longer needed a Vice President of Engineering and I began thinking about what I should do. Obviously, if the ship was sinking, I ought to get off — go somewhere else. I was too young to retire and besides, I needed an income.

I looked at other possibilities within RCA Camden — there were none. Although I was well known in the broadcast equipment industry, I was reluctant to look outside of RCA. After 33 years with RCA Broadcast Systems, I couldn't imagine working for someone who was a competitor, no matter how much respect I might have for them.

In the end, I went to RCA Laboratories at the beginning of 1984. RCA Broadcast Systems went on without me, but at the end of 1985, they closed for good.

Why Did RCA Broadcast Go Out of Business?

I have mentioned in previous chapters several things that happened or that I thought about that were leading to the end of the business. I'll summarize them and other factors that I think (in hindsight) drove the business to destruction. Obviously, over those years, we had many leaders of the business, and at the top levels of RCA, the same thing was happening. I said many times, "If you don't like the organization or the people, wait a while and it will change." None of us wanted the business to end, so why did it?

Each leadership group has certain business and organizational philosophies they apply to their business. In Broadcast Systems, we had to meet the financial requirements that were handed down to us by RCA Corporate management. It was up to us to find ways to do that. RCA as a corporation had to meet certain performance requirements to satisfy shareholders and Wall Street. These requirements were parceled down to the Corporate businesses the same way that we in Broadcast Systems parceled our available funds to our business units. The amount of funding allocated to any particular business for product engineering, manufacturing improvement, sales development, etc. depended directly on what the Corporate leaders thought of that business. Although we were profitable for many years, we did not get to reinvest enough of those profits to improve and grow the business. Our profits often went into other RCA corporate initiatives, such as the ultimately failed computer business, or the consumer video disc program.

The "mature business" syndrome: The Corporation looked on Broadcast Systems as a "mature business", which meant they felt we were in a stable market that was growing only slowly, if at all. Investment in a mature business would not produce growth. We also were viewed as having a large market share in this stable market, so there wasn't much opportunity to grow our business faster than the market growth. In business, this kind of business is called a "cash cow." The Corporation calculated the size and growth of the market by counting TV stations, who were our principal customers at the beginning.

This methodology misses several factors: (1) The production-postproduction market for broadcast-quality equipment cannot be seen by counting TV stations, and it was growing rapidly in the late 1960s and early 1970s. The production market had the potential to become larger than the TV station market. However, it had different requirements from the stations, so some additional engineering had to be invested to meet these new requirements. This myopia at RCA about production markets was one reason we were scooped by Ampex with highband quadruplex recording. We should have been working on multiple-generation recording much sooner than we did. (2) We had not addressed the international markets very seriously. We had a small share in that market, which was potentially larger than the US market and was beginning to grow strongly. Here was a major growth opportunity. We struggled in engineering within our existing funding to design versions of our equipment for use on the international TV standards, which were different from the US. (3) In the 1960s we had almost no competition. But in the 1970s, we started having major competitors from Europe and the far East. Domestic companies, such as Ampex were broadening their product lines to compete with us in all areas. RCA's approach was to get out of businesses that became too competitive.

The improper assignment of "mature business" to Broadcast Systems caused RCA Corporation to not see the opportunities for growing the business, or more inportantly, to not see the need to invest simply to keep us where we were in the face of increasing competition.

Old-fashioned manufacturing: *I saw little change in our manufacturing methods from 1950 when I came to RCA, until the 1970s. At that time, some of the people in manufacturing and I began a campaign to upgrade our manufacturing through automated assembly techniques, computerized materials handling, and computerized testing. Some component-insertion equipment for assembly of etched-wiring boards did get installed, and we modified our circuit-board designs to accommodate it. But there was a lot more that never got done because of lack of funding for manufacturing improvement.*

Product Quality: *Industry in general began giving more attention to product quality during the 1970s, particularly in response to the Japanese manufacturers* who made quality a primary focus. The Japanese also gave a lot of attention to quality during manufacturing not only for quality of product, but as a cost-reduction technique. At RCA, we continued our practice of "make the product wrong and then fix it" before shipping. No one believed that better quality meant lower cost. This was a problem that originated in Engineering and was added-to in manufacturing. We tried to improve our designs to be more accurate and easier for manufacturing to build; many of the things that I talked about in Chapter 6 and this chapter worked toward that end. I did not succeed in getting general acceptance of the idea that investing in better quality throughout the engineering and manufacturing process would lead to lower cost. I still believe that doing it right the first time is the lowest-cost route and many companies are successful in doing that.

Engineering: I would like to think that Engineering had nothing to do with the failure of Broadcast Systems, but that was not the case. Looking at our engineering projects carefully, one sees difficulties regarding planning, scheduling, and cost that certainly affected the business over the years. These kinds of problems occurred even on our most successful programs, where the business somehow accommodated the unexpected engineering costs and schedule slips.

I described the Broadcast Systems' budgeting process in Chapter 6. In planning for new products, we had not only to come up with the concept of the new product, but we had to estimate what it was going to take in personnel and material cost to design and start manufacture of the product. An important element was also the schedule that we set for the product completion and delivery. The overall business plans for the years ahead took all this into account. The pressure was on to keep costs low and achieve a short schedule. There always was a lot of optimism. Engineers creating a new product have to be optimistic. There are so many possible pitfalls--if Engineering was not optimistic, we would never even agree to do the project. Unfortunately, the pressure of the business need and the engineering optimism often combined to cause us to underestimate project costs, which resulted in cost overruns and schedule delays. Overcoming these problems took away from some of the needs of the rest of the business, because overall funding was limited. I have to say that this affected our business performance, regardless of how great the product turned out to be when it was completed. This scenario could be seen in the TR-22, TR-70, TCR-100, and many other ultimately successful projects.

If we in engineering had not had these problems of seeing what the product design was actually going to take at the time when we made the original estimates, our *estimates of cost would have been higher and schedules longer. With the funding limitations that we were always facing, this probably would have caused us not to do some of the innovative projects, or at least delay them. It is difficult to say how much that might have helped or hindered the overall performance of Broadcast Systems. I personally believe that the business needed the innovative products to compete and grow in the market; without them, we wouldn't have done as well as we did. The funding limitations that made us try to do it for less did not take into acccount the true needs of the business. Some have said that our underestimating was a way to force the Corporation to come up with the necessary funds in the end. Whatever the case, I can guarantee that we did not deliberately underestimate. We were just too optimistic.*

Summary: *RCA Camden was an old plant, having begun as a record and record-player plant in the 1920s. Many techniques of organization, engineering, and production that began in the 1920s could still be observed in the 1970s. The organizational units were strongly parochial--interdisciplinary cooperation was extremely difficult. Getting this organization to bring itself up to date so it could compete with more modern companies was a tough fight for Broadcast Systems, and the Corporation never acknowledged the costs of doing that. After the 1960s, we never succeeded in being really competitive and it brought us down in the end.*

# # #

This chapter and the previous 4 chapters might make you think that all I did from 1950 through 1983 was to work at RCA. That's not true, and Chapter 8 will interrupt the chronology of my career and cover my life outside of work through that same period of years.

Chapter 8

Life Outside of Work (1950 to 1983)

After college, I began to work at RCA in July 1950. I lived with my parents and Aunt Helen in the family home in Merchantville. They were happy for me to be there and I was happy to be living only 5 miles from work. I didn't have my own car yet, but public transportation was available from the end of Westminster Avenue directly to downtown Camden where RCA was. I was also close to the Dischert brothers, my two best friends, who also continued to live with their parents.

Bill Dischert was working at the Frankford Arsenal in Philadelphia and taking night courses in engineering at Drexel University, also in Phila. Bob was working for a radio parts store in Phila. The following story occupied us for more than three years of spare time. It indicates a lot of naiveté, but we succeeded anyway by applying general knowledge of skills such as woodworking and engines to solve a host of problems.

Buying a Boat

My interest in boating had started while I attended Camp Ockanickon (canoeing) and grew to power boating when I worked for J Harold Wells during high school. Bill Dischert also had some participation in that. Around 1951, Bill built a 10' boat, which he would sometimes put in the water at Dredge Harbor on the Delaware River. The Discherts and I and often

Figure 1 Bill Dischert's 10' boat (1951) with a full load. From left: Bill, Ben Thompson, Ted Rommereide, Bob Dischert, Bill Luther

157

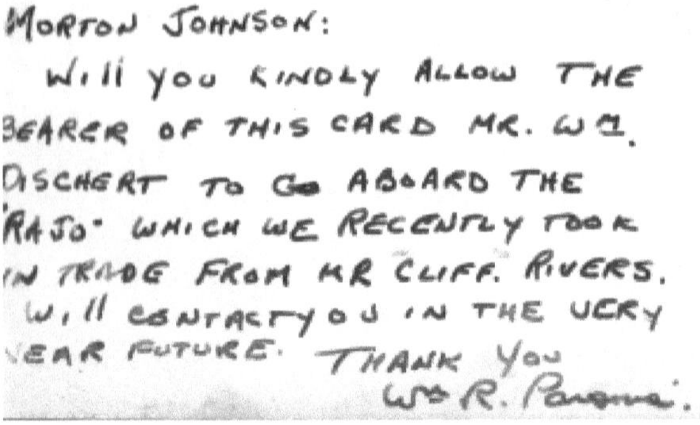

MORTON JOHNSON:

Will you kindly allow the bearer of this card Mr. W<u>a</u>. Dischert to go aboard the 'RAJO' which we recently took in trade from Mr Cliff. Rivers. Will contact you in the very near future. Thank you

Wm R. Parsons.

Figure 2 Letter of introduction to look at the RAJO.

other friends would go riding around the harbor in Bill's boat (see Figure 1). Occasion-ally we would even venture out into the Delaware. We became friendly with Bill Parsons, who was the sales manager for Dredge Harbor Yacht Basin, owned by his father and family. We let Bill Parsons know we might be interested in a larger boat-- maybe *much* larger. Later still Bill Parsons had taken a boat in trade that was out of the water at Bay Head, a boating center on the north coast of NJ. He gave Bill Dischert a note of introduction (see Figure 2) to the owner of the marina where this boat was stored, and told us to go look at it.

We were familiar with Bay Head because it was one of the places we often drove to for ice cream on summer evenings. So we went to Bay Head and looked at the boat. It was a 34-ft wooden fishing boat (all boats were wooden then) with a large deck and small cabin, up on blocks in the yard, and for sale for $250.00. The boat had the name "RAJO" on the transom. On close inspection it was clear that it had not been in the water for some time – when you looked at the hull from the inside, you could see light between the planks. The salesman said "Don't worry about that, the planks will swell up in the water and close the cracks." We speculated about what we could do if we bought it. Would it float? Would it run? Whatever happened, we felt that among us we had the skill to fix it. We decided to buy. Actually, four of us went into the deal – Ben Thompson also joined the party.

Bay Head was too far from Merchantville for convenient use of the boat, so the first task was to get the boat to the Delaware River, closer to home. We decided to put it in the water and run it around New Jersey and up the Delaware to Dredge Harbor at Riverside on the New Jersey side.

The Bay Head yard people told us to put water in the boat for a few days to swell up the planks. That seemed to help. But when we put the boat into the water, we learned that the swelling-up on land wasn't enough to stop leaks in the water. The yard people put a large pump on it and they said that it would stop leaking in a few days. It did. The next task then was to see if the engine would run. The engine was a Chrysler straight-eight car engine, modified for marine use. It was pretty rusty, but we had seen engines like that before and they still ran. The Discherts worked their magic and got it running. Of course, a marine engine uses sea water for cooling, so that might have caused a leak, too. Fortunately, everything seemed to be ok.

Bringing the Rajo Home

There were lots of things to do in preparation for the trip; I don't remember all the details, but eventually we felt that we were ready. All four owners came aboard plus George Dischert and his friend Jack McClintock. Jack brought a case of motor oil which it turned out we needed it all. We also lashed Bill Dischert's 10′ boat on the back deck.

When all was ready, we left Bay Head on a Saturday and cruised south on the intracoastal waterway, which goes through the bays behind the barrier islands along the NJ coast. It would be about a 150-mile trip. We knew enough to acquire navigation charts for the trip. They showed the way and all the buoys to follow to stay in deep water. We learned a lot about spotting buoys in the distance and which ones were the correct ones for us to follow. Talk about learning by doing...

The Rajo ran smoothly and we were quite ecstatic. We knew the trip would take two days and were prepared to stay overnight somewhere. Late in the day we pulled in at Sea Isle City, a town near the southern tip of NJ, for the night. The four owners went to a motel on shore, but George and Jack stayed the night on the boat.

The night was uneventful and the next morning we were off again; we proceeded further south to Cape May, NJ, where we followed the Cape May Canal west into the Delaware Bay.

At that latitude the Bay is about 20 miles wide, so it was pretty much open water. Our plan, however, was to stay close to the NJ side of the river so as to avoid any ship traffic in the center of the river. There are a lot of shallows near the coast in that part of the bay and we had some trouble navigating around fish nets, crab pots, and other artifacts of the fishing industry. There were lots of things out there that the charts did not show. However, we finally made our way up to Fortescue on the NJ southern coast and pulled in for gas. Continuing up the Bay from Fortescue, we entered the River itself, which at that point is only two miles wide.

Shortly after this, the engine began overheating. We looked and saw that the engine water pump had become loose so that the drive belt was no longer tight. Some jury-rigging was necessary to get it going and soon we were underway again. We continued up the Delaware, finally reaching Essington, PA, a boating community just south of Philadelphia on the west side of the river. By this time, the Rajo had begun to leak and the engine water pump was not doing too well. It appeared that we could not complete the trip that day. So we left the RAJO at Essington and came home. We would not be able to continue the trip until the following Saturday.

The next day (Monday), we got a phone call that the RAJO was leaking pretty badly and someone should come and man the pump. I was elected to go to Essington and stay with the boat. The main problem was the leaking. I had to man the pump periodically to keep the water level below the engine and the bunks in the cabin. I spent the night sleeping restlessly in the cabin with one hand over the edge of my bunk so I could tell when the water was rising. When I felt water, I had to get up and pump. The next morning I arranged for the yard to put an electric pump in the boat, and I went home, too.

We all went back to Essington on Friday night. The Discherts brought a new engine water pump and mount for it and we installed that for the rest of the trip. On Saturday, we continued going up the river and reached Dredge Harbor, which is just north of Philadelphia on the New Jersey side of the river. We pulled in there and immediately had the yard take the boat out of the water. The leaking had steadily been worsening as we came up the river, so this was the prudent thing to do. What we found upon inspecting the bottom of the boat meant that it would be out of the water for the next three years.

Rebuilding the Rajo

The inspection revealed many things. First we learned that the garboard planks on the boat had dry rot, which is deterioration of wood caused by a fungus that grows in wood that repeatedly gets wet and dries out. The planks could have easily failed during our trip and sunk us before we could do anything about it. The garboard planks are the ones next to the keel. There was also dry rot around the transom, in the keel, and in the superstructure. All of this would have to be rebuilt. Similarly, examination of the engine re-

Figure 2 Rebuilding the RAJO

vealed that the engine block had rusted out between the water passages and the cylinders. This was fatal—the engine would have to be replaced. Our confidence remained boundless that we could solve all these problems.

We first tackled the hull problems. We removed the garboard planks. Then we discovered that the deterioration had gone further and we removed several more strakes of planking. We also had to replace several of the frames (also called "ribs", the pieces that support the planks). The major learning task here was finding out how to make the cedar wood of the planks bend and twist to conform to the shape of the hull. The Rajo was carvel-planked, which means that the planks are placed edge-to-edge on the hull with caulking between them to keep the hull watertight. This requires careful fitting so there is space for the caulking between the planks, but not too much space.

We also sawed off the transom and rebuilt that structure. That action removed the name, Rajo. We spent a lot of time thinking about what we would name the boat, but we could not agree and finally we decided to keep the original name, which we had been using for two years and had

Figure 3 The almost-restored Rajo on its maiden voyage with (from left) Bob Dischert, George Dischert, my father, Bill Dischert (driving below), and Ben Thompson aboard.

learned to like it. So we painted "RAJO" on the new transom.

Then we tore down the superstructure and rebuilt decks and cabin. At this point we were saying that we had restored the Rajo by replacing everything except the shape. We kept the shape of the hull, although we changed the cabin plan.

In the course of this, we removed the old Chrysler engine. At a nearby boat engine dealer, I found a used engine that would be suitable for this boat. It was a Kermath 6-cylinder "Sea Rover" marine engine, 96 HP.

Figure 4 The Rajo when we completed it

Unlike a car engine, this was designed for heavy-duty marine use, which involves a lot of steady running under a fixed heavy load at high throttle settings. We bought it for $200.00. This engine weighed nearly a ton. Bill and Bob rebuilt it completely, and we had Dredge Harbor lower it into the boat. After everything was hooked up, we went on the maiden voyage, even before the cabin was finished (see Figure 3).

When the restoration was completed, (see Figure 4), we began going on voyages with it. We took a notable voyage down the Delaware, through the Chesapeake and Delaware Canal into the Chesapeake Bay, then down to the Potomac river and up to Washington, DC.

There were many adventures on this voyage, for example, we inadvertently cruised into a naval shooting range. This became clear when shells began landing in the water a few hundred yards from us. A quick look at the chart showed the mistake we had made, and we got out of there. Another incident involved several days waiting out a northeast storm in a place called "Ridge", just south of "Point no Point" on the Chesapeake western shore above the Potomac. A better name for this place would have been "Nowhere". Bill Dischert was even more of an optimist than I was. Every couple of hours, he would go out on deck into the storm and observe, "It's getting brighter". We were there for three days before anyone else could see it getting brighter.

However, we soon found that we could not decide on where to go with the boat as a group and no one wanted to go out by himself. Also, Ben got married, Bob got married, Bill got an airplane, and I got my own boat (see next). In 1956 or so, we decided to sell the Rajo and go our separate ways. We sold it for $2,000, which was considerably more than our out-of-pocket expense, but in no way paid for the months of time spent working on it. But it was a good experience for all of us and we have enjoyed relating the story many times.

I Buy My Own Boat

The Rajo experience triggered my boating thread in a big way. I decided that I would get my own boat and do my own things with it. In 1955, I bought a used 1948 Owens 33-ft Sedan Cruiser that was for sale at Dredge Harbor (see Figure 5). This boat was mostly all cabin, except for a small

Figure 5 1948 33' Owens Sedan Cruiser

back deck. The cabin was all on one level with glass windows all around. There was a small sleeping area with a marine toilet (called a head) under the front deck. Some people called it a "floating greenhouse". It had a 6-cylinder 125-hp Chrysler marine engine. I named it "Scope", for the nickname of the ubiquitous one-eyed test instrument (oscilloscope) used by electrical engineers to display and analyze electrical signals (see Figure 6).

Figure 6 Oscilloscope (1957)

I bought the boat in September and had only a couple of months to run it before hauling it out for the winter. I did discover one thing: because this boat had a round bottom, it tended to roll excessively in even the slightest rough water. However, I learned to tolerate this.

On haul-out in the first year, I inspected the hull and discovered dry rot in the planks and frames around the transom. This was bad. Over the winter, my father and I sawed about six inches from the back of the boat and built a new transom from two layers of mahogany. I now had a 32.5-ft Owens Sedan Cruiser! I ran this boat for two seasons before the bug hit me for a new boat.

Scope II

This time, I bought a brand new boat—a 1957 34-ft Richardson cruiser with twin engines (see Figure 7). Twin engines meant that the boat was more maneuverable in tight places, such as when docking, and it would go faster. The latter feature also meant that it would use more gas. It was built from cedar at the Richardson plant in Millville, NJ--carvel-planked like the Rajo. I went to the plant to watch the building operations before buying. The

Figure 7 1957 34' Richardson cruiser - Scope II

interior of the hull plaanking was unpainted, a requirement for planks that have to swell up in the water. When you were inside the cabin, it smelled like a cedar closet, a pleasant smell, although sometimes it would get to be too much. Again, my boat was delivered at the end of the season, so there wasn't much time for cruising before the winter. I ran this boat for two years on the Delaware and the Chesapeake Bay. During this time, I learned that my parents enjoyed boating almost as much as I did. They and their friends often went on cruises with me. This boat only slept four people, so I couldn't have many friends on an overnight cruise, but I made the most of day cruises.

The twin engines gave a faster cruising speed than I had with the Owens, but they also significantly increased the fuel consumption. That wasn't too much of a problem in those days because gasoline was only 35 cents/gallon. However it was something to think about and it became a much more significant issue when I got an even larger boat. That happened in 1959.

Scope III

It seemed that I was on a two-year cycle for getting a new boat. This was unintentional, but after about two years with the Richardson, I was again in the boat market. This time, my objective was not just a boat, but one that I could actually *live* on if I wanted. I also had decided that I wanted a Chris-

Craft. Chris-Crafts had a double-planked (two layers) mahogany hull (painted--no swelling required), and their cruisers had great interior design and construction. Dredge Harbor Yacht Basin, where I kept my boat, was a Chris-Craft dealer. I had a lot of opportunity to study their boats.

For the 1959 model year, Chris-Craft came out with a 40-ft double-cabin cruiser that I thought I could afford. A double-cabin cruiser actually had three cabins: There was a raised cabin amidships, with a large sleeping cabin with head aft and a smaller sleeping cabin and head forward. The controls for the boat were above the back of the center cabin, so the operator stood on top of the aft cabin. The double-cabin layout also provided a small cockpit behind the aft cabin. This was important for handling the lines while docking. With some creative financing, I could buy such a boat.

After studying the layout of the boat and actually going to Holland, MI to see them being built, I felt it would meet all of my live-aboard needs except that there was no shower. I saw that the aft bathroom area could be redesigned slightly to include a shower and I asked Chris-Craft to make this modification. They did once I gave them permission to use the mod in other boats.

So I made the deal and the boat was built for me. Again, I took delivery in the fall at Dredge Harbor. The first thing I felt when I saw my boat arrive on a trailer was that this boat is BIG. It was 40' long, 12.5' wide, and about 13' high when out of the water. Once it went into the water, however, it seemed much smaller. Of course, this boat became Scope III.

Scope III as I bought it had two Chris-Craft 6-cylinder marine engines of 160 hp each. The engines were in a room below the center cabin in an area about 4 ft high that I presumptuously called the "engine room". You could go down there when the boat was running and sit between the engines if you could stand the noise, which was close to the threshold of pain. Scope III is shown underway in Figure 8.

With friends and family, we cruised the Delaware River and the Chesapeake Bay. I lived aboard as much as I could. Because of the attraction of the Chesapeake as the prime cruising area, and the fact that I could live aboard, I moved the home port of the boat to Sassafras Boat Company marina at Georgetown, MD. Georgetown is on the Sassafras River, a short river near the top of the Chesapeake Bay. It was about ten miles from the

Figure 8 1959 40' Chris-Craft Conquerer double-cabin cruiser
(factory photo)

dock and you were out in the Bay.

I mentioned earlier that fuel consumption with a large boat would become a problem. Scope III at cruising speed (about 20 mph) used 20 gallons of gas an hour (1 mpg). At 35 cents/gallon this was $7.00 per hour for gas. The tanks on the boat held 200 gallons, which could run for about 10 hours, 200 miles, $70.00 to fill up. That was significant money for me in those days. *Think about those numbers today, with gas near $4.00 a gallon. Gas cost at $80.00 per hour!*

After about two years, the new-boat bug bit me again, but this time it was different. I decided to make major modifications to Scope III. This was possible because it was a wooden boat and I was a woodworker. The next-larger model of Chris-Craft was a 42' flush-deck cruiser. A friend at Gerogetown had one of these and I admired the advantages of the flush deck. I couldn't lengthen my boat, but I could make it into a flush deck. On Scope III, there were low walking decks along both sides of the aft cabin to provide access to the cockpit without going through the interior of the boat. On a flush-deck cruiser, these decks and the cockpit are raised up to the level of the top of the aft cabin. That makes the aft deck cover the entire width of the boat, making the aft cabin larger, and the larger deck is better and more convenient for operating the boat and especially for entertaining a large group of people.

Contemplating such a modification was much easier than actually doing it. It would entail tearing out the entire aft cabin, raising the sides of the hull, and building a new deck that went all the way across the width of the hull. This deck would also be extended to the transom, which needed to be raised, too. The space that was the rear cockpit would become enclosed and accessible from a hatch in the deck. That area, called a lazarette, contained the gas tanks, and I also put in a small workshop area above the tanks. I did all this myself—it took me a year of spare time. My father helped me in making many of the special wooden pieces in his shop. I began the work while I was still keeping the boat at Dredge Harbor and completed it after I moved to Georgetown. All the work was done while the boat was in the water.

While I was doing this work at Dredge Harbor, a hurricane came through New Jersey. I had just installed the hard top on top of the windshield; it was temporarily fastened and I went home for the night. The next morning I came back to do more work and the hard top was gone! It had been made of a wooden framework covered with plywood and then fiberglassed. It was a compound curved object. I looked around and finally found the hard top on the shore, at least 500 feet from where the boat was docked. It was undamaged. I reinstalled it and proceeded to complete the project. Figure 9 shows the result.

Other features that I added while doing this were the hard top over the the control station, railings all the way around, and a dinghy mount on the raised transom. These changes are also visible in Figure 9. The hard top required raising up the windshield assembly so that there would be standing height under the hard top. Another new feature that is not visible in Figure 9 was a transom platform, which is a platform made of teak wood and mounted to the transom near the water line. This is convenient for loading small boats, fishing, or just sitting there with your feet in the water. A ladder went down from the main deck to the platform.

A further major modification was to replace the original engines (a process known as repowering). The original six-cylinder engines were really a little small for the size of the boat and my modifications had made the boat somewhat heavier. To get the boat up to proper cruising stance (called planing) required running the engines near full throttle—not a good situation. Dredge Harbor happened to have a pair of Chris-Craft 275-hp

Figure 9 Scope III Flush Deck after my modifications to the Chris-Craft 40' Conqueror

V8s that a boat owner had taken out to put in diesel (a good move, but too expensive for me.) I bought the 275s, rebuilt them just to be sure and had Dredge Harbor lift them into my boat. Chris-Craft had provided a sealed hatch in the roof of the main cabin for this purpose.

The repowering was a success and Scope III perfomed much better, and because of V-8 vs. 6-cyl, it was also much quieter under way. The top speed, which I only ever used for short tests was 30 mph. However, the cruising gas consumption went up to 25 gallons/hour, and the cruising speed was closer to 25 mph. Thus, the mpg stayed around 1.

Georgetown is only about 50 miles on the highway from Merchantville or 45 miles from Camden, and I made the trip many times, coming from work on Friday evenings and getting up early on Monday to drive to work before 8:00 AM. I almost always had guests on the weekend; sometimes they stayed overnight on the boat, other times they came just for the day or they stayed in a motel on shore. My parents came almost every weekend and they often brought guests. Figure 10 shows a group of their friends in 1963 on the back deck of the boat. Scope III actually could comfortably sleep 8 people. Occasionally this capacity was tested. Once or twice in good weather, we had a few more than eight; some slept on the deck outside.

One advantage of Georgetown compared to Dredge Harbor (besides the large advantage of being in the Chesapeake rather than the Delaware) was that I could leave the boat in the water year round. The river froze in

Figure 10 Group of my parents' friends on the deck of Scope III. My father is at extreme left, third from left is my mother, and Aunt Helen is third from right. The rest are their friends.

Figure 11 Scope III frozen in the ice in the winter of 1963 at Georgetown.

the winter at Georgetown also, but they had a bubble system, which circulated warmer water from the bottom of the river up to the top to keep the ice from freezing next to the boat. Figure 11 shows Scope III in the winter of 1963. I was standing on the ice to take the picture; that's my father standing on the deck.

During the early years I was in Georgetown with Scope III, a neighboring boat belonged to Charlie Colledge, who was the General manager of RCA Broadcast Systems at the time, several levels higher than me in the organization. His boat was the Queen B, an elegant older cruiser, about 46 ft, with a large raised cabin. I would often drive to Georgetown on the weekends using one of Charlie's cars. That was so that he could carry more stuff down to his boat than would fit in one car. There were often parties on the Queen B, which I attended if I didn't have guests of my own.

Unexpected

In the late summer of 1963, Bill Dischert and I were spending a weekend on Scope III at Georgetown. We had taken the usual short trip out the Sassafrass River to Back Creek, a small cove where several boats usually anchored for swimming, fishing, crabbing, or just hanging out. This was a trip of only a few miles to a place where you were away from everything except boats. The surrounding land was farmland, so there was no disturbance from people on land. When we got back to the dock and were walking off the dock, I was walking ahead of Bill (which was not too unusual because of my long strides, Bill met Bob Sakers, who asked: "Would you like to take a ride on the *Dancer*?" Bill called me back to discuss the matter.

I knew Bob because he was the guy who painted (and gold-leafed) the names of boats on their transoms. He had done Scope III several times. He added, "My niece is out on the river in her boat, the Dancer. Would you like her to stop around when she gets back?" "Why not", I thought, so I said "Sure." A little, later a small white speedboat with an outboard motor came up to my transom platform. We introduced each other; her name was Pat Morgan. She offered to take us for a ride (one at a time, because her boat was small.) Each of us took a ride around the harbor. Following that (and some small talk), she left. This seemed like something to follow up, and Bill and I discussed that possibility. Bill wasn't too interested, but I was.

I haven't said anything about women in my life up to now. The reason is simple — there weren't any. That was not for lack of interest, but because I was so busy with "things", and "work". Also, I was still shy with women. I had had the occasional blind date, but nothing ever clicked. However, after passing age 30, I realized I was missing out on a significant piece of life, and my interest increased. So meeting Pat was a real opportunity for me. After some more talk with Bob Sakers, my matchmaker (and not actually Pat's uncle — just a family friend), I got Pat's phone number and called her. We arranged to meet at her house in Warwick, Maryland, where she lived with her mother and her real uncle on a dairy farm. She kept her own horse there. I thought living on a farm was cool.

Pat had just graduated from nursing school and was working at a local hospital. She was 21 and I was 34 at the time we met — 13 years apart. That didn't seem to be a problem to us. I kept seeing Pat over the winter and we became engaged early in 1964.

<u>Marriage</u>

Pat and I were married in Middletown, DE on June 6, 1964. Middletown is just over the Delaware line from Warwick. For our honeymoon, we drove to Grand Teton National Park in Wyoming and stayed at the Jackson Lake Lodge for a week. When we returned, we moved onto Scope III at Dredge Harbor and stayed there until winter came and it got too cold. Then we rented a small house in Merchantville that belonged to a friend of Aunt Helen at her work. We stayed there over the winter. While living on the boat, Pat got me a kitten — I had always lived with cats. This is another one of my threads. We named him "Snoopy" for the comic-strip character. Snoopy enjoyed living on a boat; he could usually be seen out on deck somewhere in good weather. He also enjoyed the fish that Pat caught, mostly catfish. She tried that on me too, but I rejected the idea until she tricked me by labeling the fish on the plate as something different. I ate it and it was ok, but I still did not think eating catfish was something I would knowingly do.

Our Own House

We were determined to have our own house as soon as possible, and I wanted it to be one designed by me. We bought a lot in Fox Hollow Woods at Cherry Hill, which is close to Merchantville. Pat and I began designing a house to fit

Figure 12 Fox Hollow House - winter 1967

that lot, which was wooded and sloped down from south to north. Our design was an upside-down house with the living areas on top and the bedrooms downstairs, down the hill. We contracted with the developer of Fox Hollow Woods to put up the shell of the house according to our design. I finished the interior myself (see Figure 12). I subsequently added a storage room addition with an

Figure 13 Fox Hollow greenhouse addition under construction—1967

attached greenhouse (see Figure 13). All this activity: new wife, new house, and RCA, left little time or money for Scope III.

Then something else hap-pened that made it clearer what to do about Scope III. Pat became pregnant. A daughter, Nicole Marie Luther, was born on our first wedding anniversary, June 6, 1965. We nicknamed her "Niki". Considering the needs and priorities of a young family, we decided to sell the boat. I put it up for sale at Dredge Harbor; it sold in the fall of 1965. After debts were paid off, we actually had a little money in the bank. But that didn't last long. Something like $50,000 had gone into my boating ventures—a lot of money considering what my salary was at that time.

173

Playing the Organ

While we were living at Fox Hollow, I decided to buy an organ and learn to play it. This was somewhat prompted by my friendship with Bob Hurst, a manager reporting to me at work, who was an accomplished organist. He played pipe organ in some of the local churches. I had always enjoyed pipe organ music. I heard him play once and was really impressed and thought that I could learn to do that, too. I bought a Wurlitzer theater organ, which was one of the first transistorized electronic organs. It had two manuals (keyboards) and a 25-pedal footboard.

I did learn to play it and found that I could handle the coordination of hands and feet reasonably well. I had learned to read music in grade school when playing the clarinet, and I was surprised that sight reading came back right away. However, for some reason I never could play without the music. I always played from printed music. My guess is that my mind was so filled with other things that I never had memory space to remember music. I'm sure that this limited my playing ability.

As was my style of collecting information about subjects I was interested in, I amassed a huge collection of music to play — almost all types. I found it quite relaxing after coming home from work to play for an hour or so. The family sometimes enjoyed this, but mostly they got bored with it and would go somewhere else in the house.

A Second House Instead of a Boat

When the Fox Hollow house was finished, we started looking around for another major project. Pat and I both wanted to get back to the Chesapeake waterfront. In 1967, we found a house for sale on the Bohemia River at Hack's Point MD. The Bohemia was the river north of the Sassafras on the Eastern Shore of the Chesapeake. It was a short river, only about 5 miles to the Bay. Hack's Point is on the south side of the river. The house we were interested in was right on the riverfront; it had a peninsula jutting out into the river from the northeast corner of the lot. The peninsula was mostly sand with grasses growing on it. The property also had two boat houses on the beach at the base of the peninsula. The rest of the lot with the house was about 20 feet above the water. The land was nearly one acre all together. We bought this property for $14,000.

Figure 14 The Hack's Point house when we
bought it in 1967

About this time, Pat became pregnant again. A second daughter, Kay
Lynn Luther, was born in October 1967. My father gave her the nickname
"Kayle", pronounced "Kay-lee".

Figure 15 The beach at the Hack's Point property when we bought it.
The building to the right is the Boathouse, the other structure was a smaller boathouse, which we removed.

Figure 16 Hack's Point house after renovation—1974

Although the Hack's Point land had several desirable features, the house on the property didn't. It was actually two separate houses, joined in the shape of a "T" (see Figures 14 and 15). The oldest part of it was a Sears, Roebuck kit house built in 1941. You could still see the part numbers on all the beams in the floor, ceiling, and attic. This house had a living room, kitchen, two bedrooms, and one bath. It was 800 square feet. The second house was added probably around 1960. It was not a kit, but it was the same size and had the same room count. Neither part of the house was in very good shape. Probably because things were pretty rough at the beginning, we named the place "The Cottage". That name stuck even after we had converted it into a real "house". We decided that everything would have to be renovated (we knew that before we bought the house) and in the process, we would convert it into a single house. We made the newer part liveable so that we could use it to live in temporarily (as a second house) while we worked on the project. We began by putting a new roof on the whole house. Then we tore off the siding and replaced that, while changing the window plan to fit our new floor plan for the inside. We then tore out the inside partitions one at a time and built new partitions according to the new floor plan. That had a total of four bedrooms, an entrance foyer, a large living-dining room, a small family room, a comfortable kitchen, and two baths. Because the house was on a hillside, there was a two-car garage underneath one end. That had a fairly low ceiling and it was too small for two cars of that era. So it became a workshop that I used while building the rest of the house. After all was done, which took about 8 years of my spare time and much of Pat's, as well as help from the Discherts and other friends, we had a very comfortable single family house on a magnificent waterfront property (see Figure 16).

Family Events

In 1970, Pat became pregnant with our third child. This one was a boy, born in November 1970, and was named Arch Clinton Luther, III. As happened with me for a while while I was very young, my son's nickname was "Clint". This name took with him, but it never worked for me; I was always Archie as a child.

Shortly after Clint's birth. my father died. He had been slowing down for some months, leading up to his going into the hospital in mid-December. He died on Christmas day, 1970. It was not a happy holiday season that year. This was my first experience of the death of a close relative — someone who had so influenced my interests in my earlier years. Daddy's death made me aware for the first time of my own mortality. I was 42, my father was 72. In the years after he retired from the newspaper, we became closer than we had ever been since my childhood. He was always interested in what I was doing at work, the technology, the products; and what I did at home, the boats, my houses, and of course, my family. His death left a hole for me that has not been completely filled after more than 35 years.

Moving our Principal Residence

Also in 1970, we decided that Fox Hollow was no longer suitable for our growing family. Cherry Hill was becoming a mega-suburb, and we didn't like that. We wanted to move to the country and have more land. We looked around further south in New Jersey and found a house that we thought could suit us with a little work (we weren't afraid of that). We made an offer on the property, which was accepted with a closing date about six months into the future. We hadn't even put the Fox Hollow house on the market. We did that immediately.

However, the six months passed and there was no sale of Fox Hollow. But on the day after the deadline, we got an acceptable offer. When we contacted the realtor for the new house, we found out that he had sold it to another party on the same day! He never contacted us. I don't know whether that was ethical or not, but it certainly gave us a problem. After consideration, we decided to go to Plan B, which was to accept the offer on Fox Hollow and move to our other house, the Cottage, in Maryland. That would be an opportunity for the family to live in a wonderful place while we looked for another property in New Jersey. It meant that I would have a 50-mile commute to work, but we agreed that I would do that only once a week, and stay during the week at my mother's.

Living at the Cottage

We enjoyed the Cottage while we were remodeling it, and even more after it was done, and when we lived there for a while, which turned out to be a year. The children loved the Cottage; they played in the water at our own private beach; they went fishing and crabbing in a small rowboat we had for that; and there was plenty of room for their indoor activities. We went there every weekend in good weather and entertained our family and friends the same way my parents and I had done on Scope III. My parents also enjoyed the Cottage.

My boating thread became active again. We bought a used 24-ft Stamas cruiser, which we moored off our beach during the summer. In winter, we pulled it out at a local marina and moved it on a trailer to our driveway for winter storage under tarps. Of course this boat was far smaller that Scope III, and we couldn't live on it or entertain very many friends. However, it was a very stable boat for its size and much more economical to run than Scope III. We enjoyed being on the water again.

The Stamas' engine was old and I became concerned about its reliability. This led to trading the Stamas in on a new Sea-Ray 24-ft cruiser with a larger cabin and a flying bridge above. This performed well, it had more space and all my family could stay overnight on it. However, the hull design was different from the Stamas and did not have quite as much stability underway. We got used to that.

As the children grew, they became interested in fishing and crabbing. Since we were on the waterfront at the Cottage, it was a perfect opportunity for this (see Figure 17). Having our own boats helped, also. The children would go out and sit in a rowboar moored off the beach and crab with a fish head on a line and a crab net. Lots of Maryland blue crabs were caught that way. Pat loved crabs and would cook them and everyone would sit down at a table covered with newspapers and pick and eat the crabs. "Everyone" wasn't quite correct because I didn't participate in these crab-picking sessions. I liked crab meat, but I couldn't stand dismembering crabs to get it myself.

There were also fish to be had off our beach. The most useful ones were perch. These were six inches long or so, and many were available. I learned how to fillet small fish like that. From a six-inch perch, you got two small fillets, each one a mouthful. pan fried, these were a delicious treat, but it took 20 or 30 fish to make a dinner from them.

On several occasions, we chartered a deep-sea fishing boat from Rock Hall, MD and went out into the Bay, usually down by the Chesapeake Bay Bridge near Annapolis. We fished for rock fish (striped

Figure 17 Kayle and Clint crabbing off our beach

bass) around the bridge piers. On one trip, we caught about 50 rock fish and bluefish five pounds and larger. When we got home late that night, we set up tables in the yard at the Cottage and everyone cleaned fish. We ended up with more than 50 pounds of cleaned and filleted fish in the freezer. On later fishing trips, we rarely caught any fish because the fishing in the Bay had become very poor.

Finding a new Location

Our search for property in NJ did not yield any existing property that we felt would do, and we eventually decided to just look for land, and we would build our dream house. We bought a 2.5-acre lot in a small custom development outside of Woodstown, NJ and began designing another house. This one ended up at 3,000 square feet, all on one level, with a full basement below, which I would eventually finish for more living space. With that in mind, I designed the basement to have a 8-foot ceiling just like the upper level of the house. This house had four bedrooms, 2 ½ baths, a living room with a separate dining room, a kitchen, an entrance foyer, and a playroom for the kids.

After completing the house design and getting approval from the County, I hired a contractor to put up the shell of the house. I would finish the interior. I don't know how I found the time to do that, but it did get

179

Figure 18 The Woodstown house—May 1973

accomplished enough that we moved back to NJ from Maryland about a year after we made the first move. Figure 18 shows this house in 1973. It was a very comfortable house for us.

I used large steel beams to support the upper level so that there were few posts in the basement. That worked, but when the house was finished, we found a minor problem. The steel beams had a metallic resonance, which was excited if someone jumped on the floor or if you dropped something heavy. The beams would ring like a bell! However, things were structurally sound and we learned to live with our built-in bells. The children thought the sound was cool.

The large basement also was finished by me. It was divided into three approximately equal-sized areas. The main one was a 30 x 30-ft family room that had a fireplace, a sitting area, a pool table, and a serving bar. This was reached by a staircase from the foyer. The second was a 1,000 square foot workshop, which had a separate entry at the back of the house for moving large projects in or out; and the remaining space was a large storage area, including a cedar closet.

The 2.5-acres of land had to be made into something other than wilderness, which it was when we bought it. The land was clear in front of the house and wooded behind the house. We landscaped around the house and enclosed a large area for a vegetable garden. We also planted evergreen trees along the road to give more privacy from the road traffic. There was more than enough opportunity to exercise my gardening thread. Behind the house, I built a large deck with a gazebo on one corner. There also were play buildings for the children and trails through the woods, which filled a ravine on the property. An A-frame play house on stilts that I built is shown in Figure 19.

I also made toys for the children. My engineer psyche kept me building things whenever and wherever I could find the opportunity. One toy that got a lot of attention was a playhouse-building set that allowed the kids to make their own structures. It was made of small wooden cubes having holes on all sides and sticks that could connect the blocks to build any kind of play house based on a series of cubes. Pat made panels

Figure 19 Children's playhouse - 1972

of colored fabric that went over the sticks to enclose the play house. This is shown in Figure 20.

Another notable project was a Halloween costume that I made for Clint when he was about seven. The Star Wars movie had just come out and Clint wanted to be R2D2. So I made him a costume, shown in Figure 21. It had flashing lights on the front, but Clint had to provide the sound effects himself. It was quite a hit.

As the children grew up past the toddler stage, we wanted take them traveling. As every parent knows, this is quite difficult until they become used to it. However, that was not the only problem we had. My building projects were using up a large part of our income, so there wasn't money left over for extensive travel with the children. We went on day trips and occasional longer trips. I don't think we met the children's requirements for the longer trips their friends were taking. We spent most of our weekends at the Cottage. This was inexpensive and we had invested in the

Figure 20 Children's house-building set.
From left, Clint, Kayle, Niki

Figure 21 Clint as R2D2

property and we felt we should use it.

We Sell the Cottage

But things were changing. Our girls were reaching teen age and they no longer wanted to go to the Cottage every weekend. They wanted to stay at home and do things with their friends in the Woodstown area. They went to school in Woodstown, so they had many local friends. Also, we had two incidents of robbery at the Cottage — people came in via water and broke into the house and took all our belongings. We were usually not there during the week; this gave them plenty of time to do their dirty work. Further, because the house was at the end of the road and did not have full-time neighbors on either side, no one else knew that we were being robbed. The insurance paid for the losses, but still, we lost confidence in the safety of the place. Another incident occurred when some local boys were out in the grass on the point, smoking, and started a fire in the grass. They couldn't control it and it burned along the point until it came to our boathouse and severely burned that. We lost a small sailboat and various other boating materials. The boathouse had to be torn down.

As I progressed at RCA, I was having to give more time to that, especially as I traveled more and more. This cut into my time with the family. Since I married late, my family was still young, whereas most of my peers in management had grown children, often in college. They could spend less time at home and fostered a hard-working environment in

Broadcast Systems' management. I didn't like that, but it was necessary if I expected to go farther in management with the Company.

The other thing that was happening was the financial stress of the 1970s – wildly high interest rates. Both of our houses were mortgaged and we suddenly found ourselves having trouble keeping up with the payments.

The obvious solution was to sell the Cottage, which we did in 1977, for $65,000. *During all the years of construction on the Cottage, I had in the back of my mind that it would be a place for my retirement. So it was a blow to that plan when we couldn't keep what we had built there. But this was probably a good thing, because I eventually got something much better.*

Figure 22 My family in 1973: Kayle, Pat holding Clint, Niki

My Situation Changes

By the late 1970s, I was spending so much time traveling for RCA, that I didn't want to go anywhere when I got home. This also limited my building projects; that was probably a good thing for the rest of the family. However, it seemed that I was becoming more distant from my family.

Pat also had changed. She had matured into a completely capable woman, not needing any support from me to do any of the tasks of running the family. During my times traveling, she handled everything for herself. But we had a lot of disagreements about things the family should do, things I should do, and more. One thing that particularly irritated her was my management style from work, which had crept into my family life, too.

At work, I had become a complete skeptic, questioning everyone and everything. I always wanted to know the details of a project and I asked probing questions to find them out. I felt this was necessary to understand things well enough that I could assess the needs of the project. This approach of probing questions did not work well at home. If I used it on Pat, she became angry. She didn't think I was giving her any credit for what she was doing. That was not my intent, but it appeared that way to her. The children felt the same way about my questions.

The result of all this is that in early 1981, Pat and I decided that we should separate. I left the family home and she stayed there with the children. Since I was spending all my income to keep up the house and family, I could not afford to establish another location for myself. My solution was to go live with my mother and Aunt Helen in the Merchantville house. They were now getting on in years and, although they did not like the reason for it, they were actually very appreciative of having me live there and help them with many of their needs and the needs of that house.

The separation, and subsequent divorce (1984), was something I never dreamed would happen. It was a very low spot for me that took a long time to get over. After the divorce, the Woodstown house was sold and Pat, Niki, and Clint moved to Antrim, NH. Pat and a friend, Shiela Hatmaker, also divorced, bought a house there together. Shiela had four children and Pat had two with her.

In early 1984, my mother passed away. It was sudden and quick. She was 80. This left Aunt Helen and I owning the Merchantville house, where we continued to live.

Kayle stayed in Woodstown with friends in order to complete high school. That was 1985. After that, Kayle went to college at American University in Washington, DC to study Communications. In the summers, she stayed with Aunt Helen and me in Merchantville. She graduated from American in June, 1990.

In subsequent chapters, I will cover personal matters along with business matters. That reflects my greater flexibility to control my personal time after leaving Broadcast Systems at the start of 1984.

Chapter 9

Research Scientist

At the end of 1983, I moved from RCA Camden to the David Sarnoff Research Center at Princeton, NJ (Known as "The Labs"), which was the central research facility for RCA. A research lab was quite different from the engineering departments we had in Broadcast Systems. The objective of Broadcast Systems' Engineering was to develop and design products for manufacture and distribution to the broadcast equipment market. The objective of the RCA research lab was to study and develop broad-based fundamental technologies, and then develop applications using those technologies (and others), for commercialization in collaboration with the business units of RCA. RCA Labs was eminently successful in its role, having contributed heavily to the development and commercialization of television, and then, especially, color television. Other fields that they were innovators in are: microlelectronics, especially the CMOS process so widely used today; lasers and LEDs; computer video technology; video displays; electronic cameras and imagers; electronic materials and processes; communications and computers; and more. *Today, the Labs is a private company known as Sarnoff Corporation. They do contract research for major worldwide companies in the fields listed above and others.* I was pleased to be able to join such a prestigious and productive organization.

I continued to live in Merchantville, which gave me a 45-mile daily commute each way. I learned to live with this commute because the Labs had flexible time, so I could leave the house at 5 or 6 in the morning and return in the afternoon, just 9 hours later. This strategy avoided rush hour traffic entirely. The roads were good most of the way, so the commute took slightly less than one hour each way. Getting up early was easy for me — I have always been an early person. There was only one problem: The 4:00 PM meeting. If I arrived at the Labs at 6 AM, I could theoretically leave at

3 PM, after putting in my 8 hours plus one hour lunch time. Many managers liked to have meetings at the end of the day, they thought 4:00 PM was a good time. If I stayed for a meeting of maybe one hour, it put me at the peak rush hour. So I would stay until 7 PM before leaving. That became a pretty long day. However, I survived with the situation.

Part of my agreement with the Labs management was that I could look at all the Labs projects and choose what I would like to do. I had been a Division Vice President at Camden, but in the Labs I was given the title of Senior Staff Scientist. That was a new title; I was the only one. I kept my previous salary, but I had to give up some of the V.P. perks. The title and the perks didn't really matter; what mattered was the opportunity to choose my own work.

The Labs Environment

The Labs facility was very different from Camden. The buildings were typically three to six stories, arranged on a landscaped campus much like a university (See Figure 1). The buildings were relatively modern compared with Camden—the first one was built about 1940 and others were more recent than that. The interior layout was much like a hotel—a series of private rooms off a main hall. The rooms varied in size, depending on the work being done, but typically a room supported one or two "members of the technical staff" (MTS), which was the equivalent title to "Engineer" in Camden. There were also associate MTSs, senior MTSs, and "fellows of the technical staff". The people in each room had everything they needed: an office area with desks and file cabinets, and a separate area for laboratory work. The room was a private space that had a door to the hall that could be closed off, if necessary. Mostly, the doors were open. This was very different from the large open office and lab areas we had in Camden, which were shared by dozens of people.

Many of the Labs projects were related to the consumer electronics business—television and other products for the consumer, which was also the major thrust of RCA. I wasn't much interested in consumer electronics, but I didn't want to work on anything related to broadcasting either. I thought that after 33 years, I should have a change. There was a group called "Digital Products Research " that was working on a project that

Figure 1 The David Sarnoff Research Center

interested me and I thought my background in video engineering would help the project. The project was digital video, specifically as it related to personal computers. Since everything else in electronics was going digital, why shouldn't video also do that? The name of the project was actually "Home Computer" (HC). It was intended to be a user-friendly computer suitable to be used by anyone, not just geeks, and it did digital color motion video (movies). That latter feature was really the only thing that was different from other computers, but that was revolutionary.

The Home Computer Project

The head of Digital Products Research was Art Kaiman, a Lab Director. Art reported to the same Labs Vice President that I did. I told my boss of my decision to join Art's project, and he agreed, but he mentioned that the HC project was not very well respected by the rest of the Labs. Many Labs people felt that RCA should not be doing anything with computers, and the HC was just a sand box project (meaning that it was just for fun). That didn't matter to me.

So I joined the HC project as a staff advisor to Art Kaiman, somewhat of a strange situation because I was organizationally at the same level that

187

Art was. However, I had faced similar strange situations in my Chief Engineer positions at Broadcast Systems, so I was ready for that.

The total staff of Digital Products Research numbered around 40. Everyone, even the technicians and secretaries had a computer terminal on their desk. These were connected to the departmental VAX minicomputer. *This was 1984, before the days of having massive computer power on a desktop as we do today.* The VAX computer had its own large room containing the computer racks and its peripheral units. Everyone had an e-mail acccount, going through the VAX. E-mail was a primary method of communication. I hadn't experienced this before because the Internet and its capabilities didn't yet exist outside of industrial situations like the Labs. I quickly became addicted to using e-mail.

I brought my TRS-80 to the Labs when I started there. It was on my desk along with the VAX terminal. Other Labs people would often ask why I had the TRS-80, since they felt the VAX would do everything and the TRS-80 was already a dinosaur. My reason was that I knew the TRS-80 and it was full of my own software, which I could make do anything I wanted. I could demonstrate that to convince anyone. The other reason was that I didn't yet know the VAX software, and I had to use what was there, I was not allowed to or able to change anything about the VAX.

The organization of HC consisted of three groups, each led by a Group Head. These were: Software Technology Research, headed by Al Korenjak; Digital Systems Research, headed by Larry Ryan; and Consumer Software Research, headed by Dave Ripley.

Shortly after I joined the group, the Apple Macintosh (Mac) computer was introduced to the world. This new computer contained most of the user-friendly features that the group was working on, except it didn't do digital color motion video. The introduction of the Mac was important to the group because it made it less likely that an RCA home computer, with a friendly user interface that was still several years from being finished, could succeed in the marketplace.

Labs management bought Mac computers for everyone on the staff. I got one, and I was expected to use it for my office work, such as word processing and drawing. I did. That was the end of the TRS-80 for me.

Change of Project Name

Since existing projects will do whatever is necessary to continue to exist, the HC project name was changed to "Compressed Digital Audio and Video" (CDAV) because that feature had been the program's main thrust all the time. It also solved one of the things that caused the rest of the Labs to have little respect for the project: many people felt that it didn't make sense for RCA to be doing another computer. (RCA Corporation had a massive business-computer program in the 1950s and 1960s , but that was dropped in 1971 with huge losses, because the market became too competitive.)

Digital Video Technology

I would like to discuss digital technology some more at this point so you can appreciate what an advance it was at that time to have digital video on a computer. In Chapter 7, I talked about how numerical values are digitized and represented as series of digital bits. Video extends that concept to very large numbers. Motion pictures are created as a series of individual pictures displayed at a rate sufficiently high that the eye sees the result as smooth motion. Each picture is called a "frame", which must be shown at a rate of 30 per second or so to achieve the desired visual effect. To see what this means digitally, we have to examine how a frame is transmitted electronically. The starting point of this is a process called "scanning". This is happening all the time as you watch television. The scene in front of the camera is focused on an image sensor, where the scanning process occurs to read out the image electronically. This is done by beginning at the upper left of the image and reading out the image data in a series of horizontal lines across the image. The geometry of this is shown in simplified form in Figure 2, which shows the face of an image sensor and how the scanning process progresses from the top left to the bottom right. The number of horizontal lines determines the "resolution" (sharpness) of the reproduced image.

A solid-state image sensor, such as a CCD (see page 131), has the line scanning pattern built into its geometry. In addition to the number of horizontal lines, it has a pattern of cells along each line, a number usually in proportion to the number of lines. The number of cells along a line

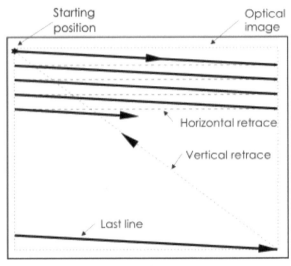

Figure 2 Scanning

determines the "horizontal resolution", and the number of lines determines the "vertical resolution". Resolution is thus expressed (for example) as 640 x 480 = H x V. The larger these numbers, the more detail can be reproduced in the image. Each of the cells in the imager is called a "pixel". Another number of interest is the total number of pixels in the imager, H * V, which for our example is 640 * 480 = 307,200 pixels. (This is approximately the best resolution that can be provided by standard NTSC analog television.) To make motion video, we have to display the total number of pixels at least 30 times per second. For the example, this means there will be a stream of 307,200*30 pixels each second, or 9,216,000 pixels per second.

To put this in terms of digital bits per second: We have to know how many bits will be needed to reproduce each pixel. For a color image, we need to produce a signal for each of the primary colors, red, blue, and green. The usual accuracy of reproduction of these signals requires 8 bits of data for each. The result is that reproducing each pixel will need 24 bits of data. Multiplying this number by the pixel rate for our example image, gives the astronomical number of 221,184,000 bits per second. This is 221 megabits per second (mega means a million).

What does this kind of data flow mean to a personal computer in 1984? It was a mind-boggling number.

The Challenge of CDAV

In 1984 when I arrived on the scene, the fastest type of removeable storage medium was the CD-ROM, a computer version of the ubiquitous audio

CD. It had a data rate of 1.5 megabits/second: about 150 times less than the video data rate we just calculated. The challenge was: how did one fit a 221 megabit/second data stream into a 1.5 megabit/second channel? The obvious answer is to *compress* the data — video compression. A video signal produced by scanning contains a lot of redundancy (repeated or unnecessary data), which could be removed without hurting the image very much. The uncompressed video stream also contains a lot of information that the human eye cannot see. If ways can be found to detect and remove all this redundant and unnecessary data, it just might be possible to get the data compressed to fit through the channel. Then all that must be done is to develop a way to decompress the video in real time on a personal computer. This assumes that one is playing pre-recorded video only. Doing compression on the personal computer could come later as Moore's Law gave us more power for that task.

This challenge was well known in research labs around the world and many proposals had been made. None so far was good enough to do the job needed here. But the Digital Products Research group felt that they had the answer. They had a theoretical approach, which they had been able to simulate on the VAX computer running overnight to produce a minute or so of video. It looked good. But this just moved the challenge to a different area — how does one get the amount of processing power needed to decompress video into a desktop computer and make it run in real time?

All this is very complex and highly sophisticated. Here are a few key parts of the solution. The current general-purpose microprocessors in 1984 as used in personal computers, were far from the power needed to do video decompression, let alone compression. However, it would be possible to design a special-purpose processor (a *co-processor*, working along with the main CPU of the computer) that could do the task. This was the approach they would take. The special processor was designed to do the basic tasks of decompression, but the exact algorithm (the formula for decompression) was *programmable* on the chip. I say "on the chip", because that was key to the speed. The internal workings of the chip were many times faster than anything done off-chip. On-chip programming was called *microcode* programming.

As the design of this progressed, it was decided that the task would require two chips — one was the microcode-programmable video processor (VDP1), and the other chip (VDP2) provided the details of coupling the video output to the display device (a CRT monitor at that time). VDP meant video display processor.

The Audio Part of CDAV

I had little to do with design in the early years of my involvement with the CDAV project. I decided to get my feet wet with actual design (which I hadn't done for about 20 years while I was a manager in Camden) in one area of the project that I observed was being neglected by the rest of the group. That was the sound for the video. Everyone was looking at the video part of the project, which was by far the greatest challenge, but no one on the project was assigned to do a sound system. All you have to do is turn off the sound on your TV to realize that a moving picture is not much without the sound. Most of the information content of a video presentation is contained in the sound; the pictures only help the sound tell the story. This is the reason that radio was so effective for all the years before we had television.

I volunteered to design the sound (audio) part of the CDAV system. Of course, CDAV was digital, so a digital sound system was needed, to create sound data that could be integrated into the video bit stream. The CD audio system already existed and was digital, but as it existed, the CD-audio system used up the entire capacity of the CD disc. We wanted to put video on the same type of disc, and the video would take all the data capacity it could get. This meant that I had to compress the sound information, similar to what was being done with the video.

Much research had already been done by others in digital audio compression. This was mostly concerned with the telephone system, which was going digital also. Researchers had studied different methods of audio compression and their effect on sound quality. I studied all this work and saw that there was a tradeoff between the complexity of the compression task and the sound quality that was eventually achieved. (This type of tradeoff was also true for video.) Higher sound quality than the telephone was needed, so I would not be able to compress as much as phone systems do. I also realized that a co-processor approach was required here, too.

Fortunately, there were already off-the-shelf chips with sufficient power to do audio compression. These were called digital signal processor (DSP) chips. I would design my sound system around one of these chips, the Texas Instruments TMS32010. This chip was programmable for any specific task, not in microcode, but in a kind of machine code that was stored in off-chip memory.

At about this time, Labs management decided that we should target the CDAV project to the IBM PC computers. So an IBM PC/AT computer was added to the desktops of all the members of the project. The PC/AT was IBM's second-generation PC, which had just come out. Now my desktop had the VAX terminal, my Mac, and the PC/AT. It was getting full. As I learned about the PC/AT, I realized that it would be my primary programming platform, since the programming of the PC/AT was accessible and I would have to learn it anyway to do the sound project.

My skill in programming that I had learned from the TRS-80 would apply to this task, and I had no concern about being able to do the entire project myself. However, the project would also require hardware in the form of a board that could be plugged into an expansion slot of the PC/AT. The video system was also being designed in this format, although the first video board was much bigger—so much so that it stuck out the top of the PC/AT by about a foot (see Figure 3).

The sound board was built with off-the-shelf integrated circuits. To breadboard this kind of circuitry, the "wire-wrap" technique was used. This started with a board that had a pattern of holes all over it. Sockets with long pins extending out the back were plugged into the holes to hold the ICs. Turning the board over, there was an array of pins sticking up; the circuit connections were made by connecting wires, which were wrapped tightly around the appropriate pins by using a special tool that did the wrapping.

I did not do the wirewrapping myself. At this time, I was assigned a technician, Sam Wood, who did this work for me. He moved into the lab area of my room during the sound board project. It turned out that Sam lived in Pennsauken, about a mile from my Merchantville house. He also commuted every day in a car pool with several other people. However, the

Figure 3 Arch at the DVI demonstration system

car pool was not for me because of my early-start schedule, and the uncertainty of when I would be able to leave after work. So I continued to commute alone.

Of course, I would have to test the board after it was built, and also use the board and the PC/AT to develop the software for the DSP chip. So my lab area then included an oscilloscope and other test equipment. I also had to write a program on the PC/AT that would control the audio board and allow all of its functions to be tested. This was written in 80286 (the CPU of the PC/AT) assembly language. I was successful in getting the whole thing to work, and Sam produced more boards to supply to others who were working with the rest of the CDAV system.

The CDAV audio project demonstrated my success of keeping up with design technology, even after nearly 20 years away from the engineer's bench. Technologies in this project that were never dreamed of when I was at college included integrated circuits, etched-wiring boards, wire-wrapping, microprocessors, software, computers and computer tools, digital circuits, and audio compression. Since new technologies seem to keep coming faster and faster, every engineer should be prepared for the inevitable new technologies that will obsolete everything he or she had been doing.

Somewhere along the way, the name of the project changed again, from CDAV to CSAV, for "Compressed and Synthetic Audio Video". This change was in recognition that the video system was also capable of *synthesizing* video; that is, it could make computer-generated video or animation. Since the new name included synthetic audio, I had to write more software for the audio board to do that, too.

A Change of Management

The CSAV project progressed well, and by April 1986, an objective was set to have the entire system, including custom chips, working by the end of 1986. I had already finished the audio boards and was available to take up other work on the project. I undertook to do the leg work on the planning for what would happen to get the system commercialized. But then, my boss, Dr. Jon Clemens decided that completing the design of VDP1 and VDP2 and getting them built was going to be the toughest part of the project to complete in time for the end of 1986 deadline. He decided that the project management should be changed to strenghten the chip effort. He put Art Kaiman, the Digital Products Lab director in charge of the chip program only, and he asked me to manage the rest of the Lab until the chips were done. I agreed.

So I became responsible for management of the hardware design, the system design and integration, and the software programs. I did this for six months, during which time all parts of the system were completed. After that was over, Jon Clemens wrote a letter to his boss, Dr. Jim Tietjen, reporting success and commending me for my contribution. The content of his letter is below:

> Six months ago, with your concurrence, I made a rather drastic temporary reorganization of the CSAV management. In order to concentrate on our number one priority of getting the VDP chip set into silicon by the end of 1986, I relieved Art Kaiman of all his Director duties except the completion of the chips. The rest of his director duties were assumed temporarily by Arch Luther. I thought it was a good idea at the time, but the people involved made it succeed beyond what I had hoped for. The chips will be in silicon before the end of the year, barring a real catastrophe, and in addition Arch did an excellent job of directing the rest of the laboratory. Arch's assignment is now over and I want to report to you that it was very well done.
>
> Coming as he did from an engineering operation, Arch brought what was needed for the success of the project at that time. He was able to focus many options into a cohesive system plan. In addition he was able to work with the group heads and improve their effectiveness. All this was done while maintaining the respect and admiration of the group heads. This was perhaps best exemplified

by the group heads themselves at the end of Arch's assignment when they took him out to dinner at their own expense for what Arch said was "the best dinner of my entire life"!

The focus on the chip project in the previous letter indicates that I should say some more about what the chip project involved. I have already briefly described the two chips: VDP1 coprocessor, and VDP2 display processor. The chips were designed by developing a block circuit diagram for each chip based on what they had to do. This was then further developed into logic diagrams that showed the internal parts of the chips and how they were connected. At that point, a tool called a "silicon compiler" was invoked to generate the actual chip layout that could be used by a "silicon foundry" company to make the chips on a silicon wafer.

The silicon compiler is special software, running on the VAX, that let the chip designers, working at computer terminals, input their logic design. After much checking by the program, it outputs the actual patterns that are used to etch the circuits on silicon. This was very sophisticated stuff, and it was the first time we had used it. These patterns, if printed large enough for the details to be seen, would cover an entire wall of the lab.

The chips were completed on time, and the first time out of the box, they worked almost flawlessly. There were just a few small bugs, which were corrected by a second run.

Commuting 90 Miles per Day

After doing the commute from Merchantville to Princeton for more than two years, I was comfortable with it—except in the winter. The commute became impossible if there was significant snow or ice. That wasn't too bad if I was at home when the storm occurred; I could simply work at home. I didn't have an audio system test setup at home, but I could do paperwork from there. There were always writing tasks that I hadn't gotten around to, or design tasks. I could also access my VAX e-mail from home. However, it was a different story if I was at the Labs when a storm occurred that made the roads impassable. In such cases, I had to stay close to Princeton.

One day, a severe storm began just after I reached the Labs in the morning. By mid-afternoon, most of the other people in the Labs had already gone home. I thought the weather had become too bad for me to try going home, so I asked my boss whether I could stay in my office overnight. He said I needed to get permission from the head of the labs, Bill Webster. I knew Dr. Webster and went to his office and asked the question. He said he had a better idea, and he gave me the keys to the Sarnoff suite.

The Sarnoff Suite was in the David Sarnoff Library part of the Labs. The Library was completed in 1967 as the central library for the Labs as well as a museum section to hold the memoriabilia of David Sarnoff. It included an office and suite for the use of David Sarnoff when he visited the Labs. After David Sarnoff's death in 1971, the Suite was kept in memory of him. I went there and found a small office, a conference room, and a bedroom. That was great. I worked at Sarnoff's desk, and slept in his bed, all only a short walk indoors from my own office. I had to catch the guards who toured the buildings at night and make sure they knew I had Dr. Webster's approval to be in there. The only problem was food. I was able to get food for my dinner from the cafeteria before they closed in the afternoon. In good weather, the cafeteria stayed open for dinner for people who worked late, but in a storm, the cafeteria workers went home, too.

During the writing of this book, I had occasion to contact Dr. Alex Magoun, the current curator of the Sarnoff Museum. I mentioned to him that I had several times stayed overnight in the Sarnoff Suite. He said that I would not want to do that now because the bed had a foam mattress, which had turned to rock in the 20-plus years since I was there! I confirmed that when I visited the Museum recently.

CSAV Software

As the development of CSAV proceeded, the system architecture was crystallized and design moved ahead on many fronts; including the video board; the video coprocessor chips; my audio board project, which had been taken over by others; and software for the system. The software task had many projects: microcode programming for the video coprocessor chip, system software for incorporating CSAV on the PC/AT, test and demonstration tools, and application software.

The application software was most interesting; it is software that runs on the complete system to make that system do a useful task. Applications that were being developed included: An educational tour of the Palenque Maya site in Yucatan, Mexico; a Sesame Street application; a flight simulator;

and a variety of demonstrations of the technology.

The Palenque project got the most attention, primarily because it involved several field trips to Mexico by the project staff, and it was the most complex application. It was also a project that the rest of the Labs often viewed as a sand box project—for fun, not a real thing. However, since all this was for demonstration, the focus was on showing an overall application plan, but only developing key parts of it. One part of Palenque was an interactive walk-through of one of the temples at Palenque. This involved shooting video on site, compressing it for demonstration, and writing software on the CSAV system to show the walk-through. Another part of Palenque was an interactive panorama, accomplished by shooting a series of still pictures with a fisheye-lens wide-angle camera pointed straight up. Such a camera gives a round image, with the horizon around the edge of the picture. With special software, the fisheye can be unwrapped and made into a 360-degree panorama in a single strip. Then, in software on the CSAV system, this can be shown an an interactive panorama that the user can move right or left, forward or back, to view it on the screen.

The demonstration and test software was also interesting. Basically, this kind of software allows the user to exercise any part of the system and view the results. At the simplest, it can send a single command at a time; however, when enhanced, it can let the user build a sequence of commands that can be stored for later playback. With sufficiently powerful software of this type, a complete presentation of slides, video, text and graphics can be built. One of the software designers, Doug Dixon, built a test and demonstration program he called "Command-Line Interface" (CLI). I learned to use this program (it took programming skill), and applied it to many demonstrations. Later, I wrote my own program of this type, which is described in Chapter 10.

Another Big Change

By early 1986, much of this work was well along, and we had made plans for its completion and possible eventual commercialization. I did a lot of the leg work in that planning. However, in August 1986, it was announced that RCA Corporation had been sold to General Electric Company. This was initially announced as a "merger", but it turned out to be a takeover and divestment of all the parts of RCA except NBC. At the Labs, we all had to make presentations to GE management about our projects. The reason for this was that GE already had a Research Lab at Schenectady, NY and they announced early on that they did not need another Lab. This threw all kind of uncertainty into the Labs staff, with people worrying about what would happen to our Labs and their jobs.

After the presentation of the CSAV project to GE, in which I participated heavily, GE announced that they did not think our project was useful to them, and we should terminate it. All the work the group had been doing for four years — down the drain. No researcher wants to face that. We decided to ask our management and GE whether we could publish papers and make a public announcement of the project before shutting down. They agreed. However, the problem was that we didn't yet have a full working system, because the VDP chips were not completed and tested. We still could only show the VAX simulations.

We decided that the best place to have a public showing, was at the Second Annual Microsoft CD-ROM Conference. That was a meeting hosted annually by Microsoft for industry presentation and discussion of CD-ROM applications and equipment. The 1987 meeting was scheduled for March 3 – 6 in Seattle, WA. The day chosen for our presentation was March 4.

Working Toward the Public Announcement

It wasn't until Dcember 1986 that we had a firm commitment that we would go to the March, 1987 CD-ROM Conference. There was still so much to be done. We had tested the first-silicon VDP chips, but a second run was going to be needed. The software for the show was next to nowhere, and the video for the show still needed to be compressed and CD-ROMs had to be pressed.

At that time, there was no such thing as a recordable CD drive like we have today. All CDs had to go through the complete replication process used for high-volume production, where a master CD is cut with a laser etcher and playable copies are made by pressing them in plastic like sound records. This process cost about $7,000 for each CD made that way. CDs have come a long way: Now you can record your own on your PC, and blank discs cost less than 20 cents!

We hired a public-relations consultant to help with the planning for the announcement. One of his first recommendations was to change the name of the program. After considerable deliberation, the name was changed to "DVI Technology". The letters D V I came from the words "Digital Video Interactive", but the use of DVI in the name of the technology was not intended to be an acronym. This name lasted until the end of the program. *Today, you will still see an acronym "DVI", but it is not the same thing. The letters now mean "Digital Video Interface" and they refer to a standard for digital video cables.*

The name change was not settled until shortly before the introduction. I have copies of the presentation script dated February 17, 1987, two weeks before the introduction, and we still had not settled the name!

The presentation was to be given by three speakers. The introduction and first showing of motion video was given by Art Kaiman. Then I spoke about the technology details, and finally, Larry Ryan spoke about the chips and their features. It was to be a real theatrical event, a show. I was very much involved in the planning and scripting of the entire presentation.

Everything was in flux during the last two weeks. It was a major task just to manage the changes so that they did not destroy everything. Everyone was working long hours, nights, weekends. A go-nogo demonstration was done on February 20 to Labs and GE management. This was successful enough that the decision was "go". All the equipment, software, and people went to Seattle on February 27, 1987.

At Seattle, everything was set up in hotel rooms, because we did not want it to be seen by anyone at the Conference until the actual presentation on March 4. Work continues on fixing system bugs. A teaser press release was sent out one week before that date, saying simply "Expect something great from GE/RCA at the CD-ROM conference next week."

At the conference, there was a booth on the exhibit floor set aside for us to use after the announcement to promote the system. Before the announcement, it contained a Microsoft exhibit. Of course, Microsoft was party to what was going on; some of their people had seen a preliminary and confidential demo at Princeton before we left for the show. The night before the announcement, we moved everything from the hotel to the meeting room stage and the booth. We were still having trouble with some parts of the show and several people worked all night to fix some of the problems.

The worst problem was that the demo system would sometimes unexpectedly crash (freeze up). The only way out of that was to reboot the system, which took 3 to 5 minutes. If that happened during the presentation, the speaker would have to hold the audience for the reboot time, hoping

Figure 4 Slides from the DVI Public Announcement show. From upper left: The opening slide; interactivity with realism on a PC; the procerss of making a CD for DVI; the VDP chip set; Warp, the ability to apply textures to line drawings; a sample of a landscaping application. All displayed on the DVI system.

201

that it would work after the reboot. Mike Keith, one of the VDP researchers, worked all night to implement a fast restart routine. He managed to achieve a restart in something like 30 seconds.

The speakers got a good night's sleep; everyone else worked as much as they could through the night.

The DVI Public Announcement

There were about 1,000 people in the meeting room. We had the first spot on the program of "Industry Announcements". Bill Gates introduced the session and, then we were on. Art Kaiman's speech began; the large screen behind him unfolded with moving video. When Art said, "What you are seeing is full-motion video stored on a CD-ROM and played by an IBM personal computer", applause erupted.

As the presentation progressed, I came to the podium and showed image and graphics capabilities from the same system — more applause. As Larry wrapped up with the story of the chips, the presentation ended. Everyone thought it went flawlessly. And then, as all three speakers stepped to the edge of the stage, applause again erupted. But this time the audience was standing. A standing ovation! What a rush of adrenaline it was to be standing there and they were applauding *you*, as well as all of our group. I can't think of anything in my life that was higher than that.

But was the presentation flawless? No. There actually had been a system crash halfway through. But Mike Keith's fix restored the continuity so fast that no one noticed, not even the speakers. Success all around. We had told the story and it was received with excitement and respect.

We were the hit of the show. Some writers said the Conference would have been boring except for the GE/RCA announcement. Our booth was jammed; the demonstration room we had in the hotel was also jammed all day. During the conference, we collected more than 1,000 contacts from people who expressed interest in knowing more. In the month following the show, we collected 1,000 more contacts. The effort had been worth all the hard work, the sleepless nights, the last-minute inventions — everything. It also had catapulted me into the limelight of DVI Technology, which was to occupy me for several more years.

Now What?

GE had said the technology was worthless. What did they know about this market anyway? They were so disinterested that only a few GE people were in the audience. However, they were enough to carry home the story. And even if that did not tell the story, we got fantastic press coverage, in trade journals as well as mass market newspapers and magazines.

GE management quickly agreed to keep the project going until they could sell it. It still did not fit their view of GE's corporate focus. So we were on the market, doing our best to attract a deep-pocketed buyer who would continue what we had started. By mid-1987, it seemed that there were buyers — both Intel and IBM wanted to buy the technology and the team. A deal was inked with Intel as the buyer with extra funding and support from IBM. A new era began.

While we were working to get to the CD-ROM Conference, GE announced that they were going to donate the RCA Laboratories to SRI International, an independent research corporation previously known as Stanford Research Institute. The Labs would continue, but considerably smaller than under RCA. After the Conference, GE withdrew the DVI project from the donation to SRI, so we did not go to them. We continued to be located at the Labs as tenants on the SRI International property. After the deal with Intel and IBM was consummated, the staff became employees of Intel, who moved them to a new building, still near Princeton. I didn't go with them. I stayed a GE employee for the rest of 1987, when I took early retirement.

GE was offering early retirement deals to many Labs employees in an effort to accomplish the staff reductions needed by the SRI change. I received an offer I could not refuse. I would leave the Labs on my birthday in 1987, when I was 59, and I would be paid *my full salary and benefits* for one full year until I was 60, when I would officially retire. During that year, I didn't have to work for anyone. Wow!

But I intended to keep working. I had a year where I could find what I would do next, but I didn't have to worry about my income while I was doing it. Several possibilities surfaced almost immediately.

Opportunity No. 1

Immediately after the CD-ROM Conference presentation, when I walked backstage to leave, I was approached by a man who introduced himself as Dr. Alan Rose, a book producer. He said, "Someone has to write a book about DVI Technology." I agreed. Even though the retirement idea had not even entered my mind, I thought, "I'll do that!" I was still a GE employee, so I would have to get their permission, but I was confident that they would give it, simply for the publicity value. So I began my first book right then as a part-time activity. My other work at the labs for the rest of that year consisted of keeping track of the market contacts we made, and conduction demonstrations in a demo room we set up at the Labs. This was good for me, because it gave me the experience to completely overcome any shyness that was left with me from my earlier years. I no longer had any trepidation about getting up before an audience of any size and speaking without notes or any help. I also did a lot of visits to potential customer and demonstrated and told the DVI story at their locations and in the demo room at the Labs.

My first book, *Digital Video in the PC Environment*, about DVI Technology, was published in early 1989 by McGraw-Hill. Alan Rose produced the book. This was the full conversion of my journalism thread to writing books.

Opportunity No. 2

As soon as I left the Labs, the DVI project found that they still needed me. I was called back as a part-time consultant. It turned out that I would be in demand for a number of years in that role. The next chapter will cover what I did after leaving the Labs at the end of 1987.

Chapter 10

Video and Audio Consulting

After leaving the Labs and GE at the end of 1987, I quickly learned some of the reasons why many people become self-employed when they get the chance. Now, I wonder why I didn't do that years ago. I had had several people approach me over the years, who suggested that I leave RCA. I should probably have taken that more seriously. But I also say I don't have any regrets.

I set up an office at home in Merchantville. This was in the room that had been bedroom for us three boys while I was growing up. Back around 1965, Aunt Helen's boss at Kieckhefer's retired, and he offered his desk to me. It was in my Fox Hollow and Woodstown houses, so I moved that to Merchantville when we sold the Woodstown house. It was solid mahogany, and of good quality. I refinished it and it

Figure 1 Home office in Merchantville, 1988

became the center of my new office. Figure 1 shows the office.

Of course, I had to have a computer. When I left the Labs, they let me take the Macintosh computer that was still in my office, unused, but that would not support the DVI system, which was the basis for a lot of my consulting. Therefore, I bought my own Dell 310 computer, which was used by some of the people at the Labs with DVI. The Dell was my main computer, used for all my work. I also had to get a printer, which was an Apple laser printer, interfaced to the Dell PC. I got an account with

Figure 2 Business card-1989

Compuserve for my first e-mail address outside of the Labs.

Being independent, I had to have a business name. Although I could just have used my own name, I had big ideas as always, so I chose the name "Arch Luther Associates", which used my name, but left me the opportunity to have more than one consultant in my firm. I also made a business card (see Figure 2), showing myself as the President of a firm of Multimedia Consultants. I further took out a post office box in Merchantville, so I wouldn't have to reveal to my business clients that I was working from home.

Now to Find some Business

There was no lack of business opportunity for my new venture:

> Writing books
> Consulting for IBM and Intel
> Consulting for DVI customers
> Expert witness in patent litigation
> DVI software
> Non-DVI consulting

Each of these is described in more detail below.

Writing Books

I had already begun what I expected to be the world's first book about DVI Technology (it was). This began shortly after the DVI public announcement in 1987. Although I was quite experienced with writing, I was new to the book publishing world, and I needed help finding my way around that environment. I met Alan Rose at the DVI public announcement; he was a book producer (Intertext Publications/Multiscience Press, Inc.) and agent. He got me up to speed very quickly and I signed a contract with McGraw-Hill for *Digital Video in the PC Environment.* I don't remember who came up with that title, but I know I didn't! The contract provided me with a grant for writing the book and an advance against future royalties. *I found later that book contracts varied between publishers, and receiving a grant like I did for the first book was unusual.*

I wrote this book in Microsoft Word on my old Macintosh and delivered the chapters one at a time to McGraw-Hill as hard copy in the double-spaced text format that they required. That was completed in September 1988. Intertext Publications and McGraw-Hill did formatting of the material and added illustrations provided by me in sketch format. When all was done, they provided me with

Figure 3 Covers for *Digital Video in the PC Environment* books, editions 1 and 2

galley proofs for me to review. I wrote the entire book in about six months but it took nearly a year more before the book appeared in print, in 1989.

DVI Technology and its growing infrastructure changed rapidly in the year following this first book. When Intel took over the project, they moved it out of the Labs campus, which now belonged to SRI International. They went to a building down the road in Princeton; the new activity was called the "Intel Princeton Operation". The size of the staff also nearly doubled. DVI had changed so much, that McGraw-Hill asked me to write a second edition, which I completed in June, 1990 and which was published in 1991. Both editions did well in the market, and boosted my reputation as a digital video expert and writer. One area of my later work stemmed directly from the publicity I got from the book: I began getting requests to be an expert witness in patent litigations. I'll cover that later in this chapter.

My book writing did not stop with these two books. There was a lot more to tell about DVI Technology, and the "multimedia" field, as the combination of audio, video, text, and graphics on a computer had been named in the industry. The task of creating applications that utilized that collection of different media became known as "authoring". I played an important role in that field and it led to more books.

As I wrote more books, I took over more of the production process for them. I began using page formatting software, and I did my own artwork and photography. (My books always have a lot of illustrations, like this book.) Soon, I was delivering books to the publisher as "camera-ready pages", which were printed pages exactly as the book pages would look.

The publisher copied them with special cameras, the output of which was used to make the offset printing plates, from which the final book pages were printed. I had taken control of the complete book production process except the printing.

IBM and Intel Consulting

When I retired, IBM and Intel were instant clients for my DVI expertise. One thing they wanted was the result of another project on which I had been working. This was a software program called Presentation System (PS) that I had begun before I left the Labs. This program ran on a PC that contained a DVI system; it allowed easy building of demonstration sequences for DVI (for someone with programming skill). PS had already been used for demonstrations around the Labs and I was continuing to enhance the program in my spare time. Clients not only wanted the program, but wanted me to use it for them and to teach them how to use it. I wrote a 100-page manual for the program and conducted many training sessions at different locations.

It was clear that PS was a valuable asset. Technically, it belonged to Intel, because I began writing it when I was at the Labs, and all the intellectual property that pertained to the DVI project went to Intel when they bought the project. I was interested in publishing it as a software product, so I asked Intel for the rights to PS. They gave me the rights, with a royalty to them on any units that I sold.

I was also demonstrating and teaching DVI for IBM. I went to several of their locations and corporate meetings to show the technology for them. Busy with travelling and so many projects, I found the need for some help to keep everything going. Kayle had recently graduated from college, and I offered her a job with me, as an assistant in the DVI work. She had some experience with that already, and she accepted the job. She learned how to run the DVI system and how to use PS, and began going with me on some of the demo and teaching assignments. That helped considerably.

My son, Clint, who was 16 at the time, also went on one of the IBM teaching assignments. He dazzled the IBM people with his knowledge of the subject at his age. I had been tutoring him about computers every time I visited New Hampshire after the family moved there. At first, I would take a TRS-80 along and set it up in a hotel room near where he lived.

Later, I gave Clint his own PC to work with. He was very interested in the computer and spent a lot of time with it. We talked often about technical issues on the phone. Clint seemed to be on the track to becoming an engineer like me.

But That was Not To Be

In the summer before Clint's senior year of high school, he attended the St. Paul's School Advanced Studies Program at Concord, NH. This program was for outstanding high school students; it was a six-week live-in program that provided students a choice from a curriculum of advanced study subjects. Clint chose to study the Russian and Japanese languages. Also that summer, he and I visited some engineering colleges. We went to MIT, my Alma Mater, and we visited Stanford in Palo Alto, CA. He couldn't decide what he wanted to do and did not apply to any college.

In June, 1989, I went to New Hampshire for his graduation from high school. The graduation went well, and his friends were having a party at his friend Courtney Kurk's house after the graduation. Clint chose not to go to the party right away, and he and I hiked up Mt. Monadnock, which is a 3,165-ft mountain near his home. It was raining and the trails were muddy and slippery. We didn't go all the way to the top, but we were pretty muddy by the time we came down. We decided to go to the graduation party anyway.

In the fall of 1989, he decided to attend a small college near his home: Keene State College in Keene, NH. Keene was not an engineering school, but they did have a science curriculum.

In late October, 1989, Clint went to visit his friend Courtney, who was attending Brown University in Providence RI. One night he and his friends went to a party at one of the fraternities. Clint became bored with the party and announced that he was returning to Courtney's dorm. He was not at the dorm when everyone else returned. Three days later his body was found in the Providence River.

Pat called to tell me about this and said: "I have bad news. Clint is dead." I couldn't believe it, but it was true. I still wouldn't believe it; there must be a mistake. Pat went to Providence and identified the body. I could not escape the truth. My hopes for the future: a successor, someone to carry on the family name, another engineer — all dashed. It was the worst thing that ever has happened to me. Clint's death was ruled an accident. To this day, we do not know what actually happened.

Aunt Helen, Kayle, and I went from New Jersey to New Hampshire for the funeral. My brother Bill and his wife Barbara came from California. Many friends from RCA, Intel, and IBM also came. I appreciated all the support I got at that time. Even though I had been separated from my only son by divorce, I loved him and will never forget him. After nearly 20 years, there is still a sensitive spot in my heart for him.

Before the funeral, my daughters and I discussed the idea of setting up a scholarship fund in memory of Clint. We agreed to do it. At the funeral, we had a book for people to sign up if they were interested in supporting a memorial scholarship. Many signed. Later, I worked on setting up a private foundation for the scholarship, called the "Arch Clinton Luther III Science Scholarship Foundation". The scholarship would be offered to high school seniors from schools in southern New Hampshire. We would give one scholarship per year to a student who planned to study science or engineering in college.

Figure 4 Arch "Clint" Luther, III 1970-1989

The scholarship was announced to 45 high schools in southern New Hampshire for the first time in February, 1991, and was first awarded in June of that year. It has been awarded every year since then; 2008 is the eighteenth. The scholarship is administered by my daughters and myself. The 2008 announcement letter is shown below.

Award of the scholarship is based on: A lifelong interest in science or

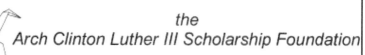

the Arch Clinton Luther III Scholarship Foundation

Trustees: Arch C. Luther, Jr. • Kay L. Luther • Nicole Luther Tatro

February 26, 2008

Guidance Department
Dear Sir or Madam:

Attached is an announcement flyer for the eighteenth annual Arch Clinton Luther III Science Scholarship, to be awarded in 2008. This letter is being sent only to high schools in southern New Hampshire.

This scholarship is created in memory of Arch "Clint" Luther, a 1989 graduate of Con-Val High School in Peterborough NH, who showed outstanding promise in science, but who died accidentally in October 1989. The objective of the scholarship is to assist a high school graduate entering college for studies in a science (*other than medicine*) or engineering curriculum at an accredited four-year college. We will make one award in 2008 with a value of one thousand dollars, with payments split between the first two semesters of the student's freshman year at college.

The application procedure requires the student to write a letter containing information as described in the attached flyer, to the attention of the Trustees of the Foundation at the address below. The letter must be received by April 21, 2008. A Selection Committee, who may require additional information or personal interviews, will choose the recipient. The final selection will be announced at the 2008 commencement exercises or awards ceremony of the recipient's school.

During preparation of an application, you may feel free to contact the Trustees at the addresses or phone numbers below for additional information.

Very truly yours,

Arch C. Luther, Jr.
Trustee

engineering demonstrated through activities, studies, or hobbies; outstanding academic performance in school; and acknowledged community service participation through school, church, or other organizations. These criteria are similar to the things I looked for in interviewing young engineers for hire at RCA except for also looking at college-level knowledge and maturity. The scholarship winners over the past 18 years have been about equally divided between male and female .

DVI Hardware

The original DVI demonstration hardware consisted of a very large plug-in for video; it extended out the top of an IBM PC/AT desktop computer by about 12". A standard desktop computer cover could not be used with this board. A second plug-in board was needed for audio, which did fit the standard PC/AT board size.

DVI was introduced to the market first in the form of a development system, for use by companies and individuals who were developing application programs for the DVI system on an IBM PC/AT. Intel provided a set of boards and software, which supported the interfacing of the DVI boards to the operating system (OS) of the PC/AT. There were three plug-in boards: the video board, containing the VDP chipset, memory, and interfacing circuits; the audio board containing the audio DSP chip, memory and interfacing; and a capture board, which had a video input that could be used to enter live video into the system.

A second-generation board was designed and provided by Intel. It consisted of a single standard-sized IBM/AT plug-in board containing the video and audio co-processors, with a piggyback audio and video capture board. This was called the ActionMedia II system (see Figure 5).

DVI Software

Initially, DVI used the original OS for the IBM PC, "disk operating system" (DOS). This was a command-line driven, text-based OS. The video screen of a DOS computer shows only text and limited graphics. *There was no mouse or windows as we know them today.*

The output of the DVI video board was displayed on a second monitor. To show the full-color capabilities, that monitor was an RGB color monitor. On the second monitor, which I'll call the DVI monitor, one could have

Figure 5 Actionmedia II DVI board

whatever display configuration they wanted to program for the system. The DVI display could have separate windows, images, areas of text, graphics, mouse support, or whatever the application required. This could all be done by programming with my PS program.

MEDIAscript

Initially, I published PS to local users at Intel and IBM and a few customers. However, I did not have the capability to market it to all the other people who were beginning to use the DVI system. I don't remember how it happened, but I partnered with a software publishing company, Network Technology Corporation (NTC), in Springfield, VA. After I obtained the rights to PS from Intel, I transferred them to NTC for further development and publishing. We decided to name the product "MEDIAscript", with the odd capitalization as shown. The first version of MEDIAscript was a fairly close copy of PS, and it ran under DOS. The manual for it was written by Kayle and myself; it was 300 pages.

Later, with some support from IBM, we re-programmed MEDIAscript for IBM's OS/2 operating system, and also added capabilities for the user to program the system simply by working with menus and windows on the programming screen. This project was done in the C programming language. MEDIAscript would automatically write the scripts necessary to run the user's application. I functioned as Chief Architect for this project. For some time, I made the 150-mile drive to Springfield, VA on Monday, stayed there all week and drove back on Friday afternoon. There was a team of about 20 people working on the project. The MEDIAscript OS/2 manual was written by a team of writers, including Kayle. Something like 1,000 copies of MEDIAscript were sold. Customer support and training was a large task. Kayle participated in the training activity, as part of Arch Luther Associates.

At one customer training session at Springfield conducted by Kayle, a customer, Jay Silber, was so impressed with Kayle's knowledge about MEDIAscript, he offered her a job at twice what I was paying. He was doing a DVI application for recertification of airline pilots. It was an interactive training application built with MEDIAscript. Kayle's title would be "programmer", which is something she had not really done on her own. We discussed that, and she was confident she could do it. My recommendation was: "Go for it!" I also offered to help her via telephone. The job was in Collegeville, PA, west of Philadelphia. She took the job. She commuted from Pennsauken where she was living, and Arch Luther Associates reverted back to a one-man show.

As MEDIAscript was now on the market, I started a third book, *Designing Interactive Multimedia*, which taught authoring techniques, and featured DVI Technology and MEDIAscript. This book was published by Bantam Professional Books in 1992.

The Market Begins to Change

Several things were beginning to happen in the marketplace that threatened the future of DVI Technology. First, other technologies for digital video and audio were being developed. But far more important was the continuing increase in processing power of CPUs. This was a direct result of Moore's Law. Some of the additional power was being devoted to enhancement of CPU instruction sets to include functions that would help video processing. This meant some degree of video compression could now be done in software running on the system CPU. It was just a matter of time before a video co-processor would not be necessary. Some of the processes that made the VDP chip set so powerful were getting built into CPUs themselves. This was the start of a progression that would eventually eliminate the need for the DVI boards.

In the long run, this was an ideal situation for personal computers. Once a task can be done in software without any custom hardware, the

Figure 6 Covers for *Designing Interactive Multimedia*, *Authoring Interactive Multimedia*, and *Using Digital Video*

process disappears into the rest of the software as far as the user is concerned. To the manufacturer, software is easier and less expensive to manage than custom hardware. Changes can be made by releasing upgraded versions of software; the customer's equipment does not have to be changed — simply load new software into the systems.

Writing about Digital Video and Audio

Because of the changes that were looming on the multimedia horizon, my next book took a somewhat different approach. Instead of focusing the presentation on a single digital video and audio technology, I began to write more generally, not wedding the book to only one technology. I wrote a lot about how the industry was beginning to create standards for multimedia in PCs, including software modules called "drivers" that could adapt any hardware to a standard software interface. With the correct driver, any hardware could be connected to any PC in a way that application software programs could use the hardware. The first book written that way was *Authoring Interactive Multimedia*, which came out in 1994 from Academic Press. This book described the multimedia authoring process, methods for each of the multimedia elements, their integration, and the selection of authoring tools, both hardware and software.

This book was also my first book that included a CD-ROM disc. The disc was produced by IBM and was called the IBM Ultimedia Tools Series. It provided a tutorial on multimedia application development, and a selection of evaluation programs (including MEDIAscript) from several

215

Figure 7 Reference CD-ROM

companies for multimedia authoring tasks.

My next book, *Using Digital Video*, published in 1995 by Academic Press, went even broader on the subject of digital video and audio, its technology, uses, production methods, and authoring. It also included a CD-ROM disc, called the *Digital Multimedia Reference CD-ROM* (see Figure 7), which contained video and audio test patterns and sample material. This disc was produced by Network technology Corporation using information provided by me.

Book Collaboration

I have mentioned my friend and RCA boss, Andy Inglis. After his retirement, he also began writing books. One of his books, *Video Engineering*, published by McGraw-Hill in 1993, was up for a second edition.

Andy decided he didn't want to do as much work as that was going to need and he asked me to collaborate with him on it. I agreed. It was a lot of work because video technology was changing rapidly, especially regarding digital video. So I took over most of the work for the revised book, producing drafts that were finalized in joint review sessions with Andy.

Figure 8 Book covers where I collaborated with Andy Inglis

Most of these sessions were held at one of Andy's locations: near Sacramento, CA, or near Bend, OR. Occasionally, we met at my location in California (see chapter 11.) *Video Engineering, Second Edition* came out in 1996. Because of all the new material, the second edition grew from 338 to 517 pages.

I collaborated with Andy on another book, a second edition of *Satellite Technology: An Introduction*, published in 1997 by Focal Press. Before he retired, Andy was President of RCA Americom, one of the pioneers in satellite communications. The second edition was another case of dealing with advances in technology and the resulting changes in business.

Still later, McGraw-Hill asked for a third edition of *Video Engineering*. By this time, Andy Inglis had passed away and I was on my own with the book. However, Andy's name still appeared on it as the founder of the book. The third edition was published in 1999. It had grown to 560 pages in a larger format. The covers of the books on which I collaborated with Andy are shown in Figure 8.

While talking about books, I have an interesting bookplate that I use on all books in my personal library. It is a bookplate design that was done for my father years ago by one of the artists at the Philadelphia Inquirer. I received it in the form of a printing plate. I scanned the plate and modified it in only one way on the computer: it showed a caricature my father with a pipe in his mouth. That does not apply to me. The plate is shown in Figure 9.

Patent Consulting

As soon as I had retired and was free of corporate entanglements, I began

Figure 9 My personal bookplate

getting work consulting as a expert witness in patent litigation cases. My role in these cases was usually based on my long experience in the video industry. I had been there and done that since the beginning of color TV.

Although I had a lot of experience with getting patents at RCA, I had no experience with the intricacies of patent litigation. Patent cases occur when someone holding a patent finds out about someone else (individual or company) using their patent without authorization. Normally, one must obtain authorization from a patent holder to use his invention.

A payment of some sort is usually required for this permission, so there is money involved. The unauthorized use of a patent is called "infringement". The patent holder notifies the infringer of the problem and offers to negotiate a settlement. If this does not work, the parties may go to court and have a judge or jury settle the matter.

Patent litigation is very complex; many books have been written on the subject, but I will explain only enough so my role in it can be understood. The two major thrusts of a patent infringement case are "invalidity": The defendant tries to prove that the patent(s) in suit are invalid, and "infringement": The plaintiff tries to prove that the patent is, in fact, infringed by the defendant's product. There are many other approaches, but these are the most common.

My role was most often in the invalidity side of the case. I might be helping the plaintiff defend his patent against an invalidity charge, or more often, helping the defendant (alledged infringer) prove invalidity. There are many grounds for a patent being invalid, for example: the invention might have been "anticipated" by an earlier patent or invention disclosure; it might not have been possible to build the invention at the time of the patent application; or there may have been legal difficulties in the processing of the application for issue of the patent.

The first step of being an expert witness is to study the case and the issues to determine whether I agreed with the position of the party in the case who wanted to hire me. Occasionally, someone wanted to hire me on a case where I just could not agree with his position in the case. Such an issue must be settled early on, before I have done any significant work and before the party in the case has spent any money on me. The only answer is for me to turn down the case.

Once I was on the case, I had to work with the attorneys for my client on what I would do. Then I must do my own research to find proof for all the assertions I want to make in the case. Basing my position simply on my own word is very weak — I need to have documented backup for what I am saying.

My positions on the case are put into writing in the form of reports. These are sent to the other side. The case has a schedule for each of the steps, going through a "discovery" phase where the parties collect information and produce reports about their findings. This is followed by a series of "depositions", where each expert is interviewed by the opposing attorneys in a formal meeting with a court reporter keeping a complete transcript of the proceeding. The attorneys for my side also sit in the depositions; they are there only to protect me from any improper behavior by the opposing attorneys who are doing the questioning. My attorneys are not allowed to prompt me on the questions.

The next step consists of hearings before the judge on certain legal steps that are taken before any trial in the case. One of these is called a "Markman hearing", which deals with a subject called "claim construction". This hearing provides information to the judge that helps him decide the meaning of the langauge used in the claims of the patents in suit. The claims are the section of a patent that provides a legal description of the invention. During the hearing, the judge may call for any of the experts to testify about their findings with regard to the claim construction. This can get very technical. The expert statements in the hearing are also subject to cross-examination by the opposing attorneys. The outcome of a Markman hearing is a report from the judge giving the official definitions of all the terms in the claims, to be used for the rest of the case.

After the hearings, the case may go to trial. On the other hand, during the preceding steps, the parties are getting a much better feeling for their positions in the case, and the possibility of settling the case before trial is constantly being tested. No one really wants to go to trial, so an out-of-court settlement is always a possibility. I participated in 15 patent cases during my career, but I never actually testified at trial. I had cases in New York, Dallas, San Diego, Omaha, San Francisco, Las Vegas, and other locations. I went to trial sometimes, but I was never called to testify. One possible explanation for that was that my written material was so good that the judge believed it without having me in court. Of course, there are other possible explanations.

The expert witness experience, which spread over nearly 20 years, was helpful for me to build self-confidence, and to learn all the legal things I have just explained above. Beyond that, it just makes good conversation, although I have to be careful about that because details about the cases are confidential.

Figure 10 Pre-school eye chart

Non-DVI Consulting

I have had one client who has gotten me into many other fields from DVI, or even video. He is Dr. Abbas M Husain MD, who was my family physician while I was in New Jersey, and has continued to be a client until today. Dr. Husain is an inventor in addition to being a physician; he has made inventions and received patents in the field of medical instruments and accessories. He is not an engineer, but he needs an engineer to work on his inventions to make models, and to create patent applications. I have done that for him. Working for him has caused me to go back many times to my fundamental education at MIT to find the answers.

One of Dr. Husain's most successful inventions is his color eye chart. He got the idea of making the common eye chart in color, in such a way that it could be used to screen patients for color blindness as well as visual acuity. I created the masters for his first charts. One further innovation that I suggested was to make a "pre-school" eye chart, where the letters were replaced by common drawings, such as a house, a car, a cat, etc. I created that chart, too (see Figure 10). He received a patent on the eye charts and they have been on the market for a number of years.

Another of Dr. Husain's inventions is a medical examination glove that has tactile markings on the index finger so a doctor can estimate distances when he or she is palpating something that cannot be seen visually. I wrote the patent application for the glove, which was issued to Dr. Husain.

A further invention by Dr. Husain was the idea to give doctors a way to augment their handwritten notes with sound recordings. Many doctors, especially older ones, are not ready to go to computer note-taking, and he felt that it would be a valuable feature to give them an easy system for adding computerized sound recordings to their handwritten notes. We jointly developed a system that used bar codes (such as those used in stores to identify products) to mark sheets of note paper; by this means an associated sound recording could be identified for each sheet of note paper. I wrote the patent application for this, and we applied jointly for a patent. We received US Patent 6,027,026, Digital Audio Recording with Coordinated Handwritten Notes, on February 22, 2000. I built a working model of the invention in hardware, which we showed to many interested parties.

I also developed a second-generation model of the system that was built entirely in software. The idea grew into a computer system for storage of medical data, including sound recorded notes. We called this "Write-n-Record" to indicate the prime feature of coordinating handwritten notes with other computer data. Unfortunately, we have been unable to generate the momentum necessary to bring the idea to market. *In the meantime, the medical community is beginning to embrace the idea of digital medical data systems. We were too early and too small to get into that game.*

More Books

By the late 1990s, DVI Technology had been superceded by other products

Figure 11 Covers of more books by Arch C Luther

in the market. To continue my writing career, I decided to write a series of books that would cover general digital technology, using my easy-to-read style that I had developed on previous books. The first of these was *Principles of Digital Audio and Video*, published by Artech House of Norwood, MA in 1997. This book was well-timed and was quite successful. It was later translated into French. *Because this book is a general treatment of the subject, it has continued to have some sales, although the rate of growth of digital technology is slowly rendering it obsolete.*

In 1998, I followed that up with *Video Camera Technology*, and in 1999, *Video Recording Technology*, both published by Artech House. These were part of the Artech House Digital Audio and Video book series, for which I was the Series Editor. Six other books by different authors were added to the series. An interesting part of being the series editor was that some of the other authors were from foreign countries. They were writing in English, but their English was not very good. That gave me an additional editing challenge. I had had some experience with doing this from editing papers by my colleague Koichi Sadashige at RCA in my Electronic Recording days. When I first started with Koichi, his English was not very good; but as we worked together and he wrote more papers, his English became very good and I became good at editing for foreign writers.

As I got older, my consulting opportunities have become fewer. I haven't done any video and audio consulting for several years. I do still volunteer as the technical consultant for my community association.

Chapter 11

Building a House in California

Once I grew up, New Jersey winters were never a happy time for me. As a child, one is protected from most of the inconveniences of winter, but as an adult, you have to deal with it yourself. I didn't like the cold; I didn't like shoveling snow; I didn't like driving in snow and ice; and I didn't like winter sports. For a long time, I felt that when I got the chance, I was going to move to a warmer climate. However, as long as I was working for RCA, I didn't see that there was any chance of getting out of New Jersey. When I retired from RCA, it would be different.

My brother Bill moved to California in 1965. After he married in 1965 in Chicago, he and his wife Johanna quit their jobs and, in true 1960s fashion, they bought an old VW van and began touring the country. After about six months, they landed in Sonoma County, California, and decided to stay. Then they had two daughters, one year later than each of my two daughters, and they built their life in Sonoma County. My brother became a designer and building contractor. Over the years, when I traveled to California on business, I always found time to visit Bill and his family in Sonoma County. I fell in love with the area. I added a stipulation to my longing for a warmer climate: It should be in Sonoma County.

Looking for Land in Sonoma County, CA

In 1990, I saw my chance to begin a transcontinental move. On a visit to California, I announced to Bill that I was in the market for land in Sonoma County. He said that a property was for sale directly across the road from his property on Joy Road outside of Occidental, CA. It was 10 acres, sloping down from the road by about 100 vertical feet. Such terrain is common in Sonoma County. I was interested and began thinking about how I could build a house on that property.

On further investigation I found that the only approved building site on that property was a 5,000 square-foot triangle directly on the road at the southeast corner of the property. The rest of the land was deemed too unstable (think mudslides) for building. The adjoining property on that side was a small farmer who raised all kinds of animals, including pigs. I didn't want to be right on the road, nor did I want to have all kinds of animals only a few tens of feet from my house. I had to abandon the idea of being right across the road from my brother. *A few years later, Bill moved away from there. I wouldn't have been next to him for very long.*

I broadened my horizons to look elsewhere in the county. Bill was very enthusiastic to help me and introduced me to a local realtor, and on my trips to California, I went out with the realtor and Bill to look at land. I had specified that I wanted some acreage, in a quiet location, away from the bustle of city or suburban life. We looked at a lot of remote places, which I liked, but nothing really seemed to be exactly what I had in mind. Some places were actually *too* remote--they were too difficult to get to, or unsecure or unsafe.

Then we went to see a lot in a community called Muniz Ranches, which was on its own private road (Muniz Ranch Road) going inland from CA Highway 1 about two miles north of Jenner. There was a security gate at the highway, with a crossbar above that is visible from Highway 1 (see Figure 1). The road went up the coastal mountains for about five miles, reaching 1,800 ft altitude, with maybe a dozen houses along the way. The property addresses were given as 1000 times the mileage from the gate at the Highway in miles. For example, 2000 Muniz Ranch Road was two miles from the gate.

We looked at a property at approximately 3000 Muniz Ranch Road. It was located at the inside of a switchback in the road, 5 acres. It was nearly a 200-foot drop from the road to the bottom of the property, which was mostly forested with oaks and redwoods. There was an almost level area near the center or the lot, which I saw as a nice

Figure 1 Muniz Ranches Gate

private building site. There was one problem, though: The realtor had been told that the property did not have a good location for a septic system. He said I would have to make a deal with a neighbor to put my septic system on adjoining land. Without really pursuing that further, I made an offer on the land. The owner turned down my offer and said he was taking the property off the market. I suspect that he had decided the price was too low and he would wait a while and then come back on the market at a higher price.

From that experience with Muniz Ranches, I did decide that it was my first choice for a location, and I continued to watch for anything coming on the market there. Some time later, my realtor advised me that three properties farther up Muniz Ranch Road had just come on the market. On my next trip West, I went to look as soon as I could. These parcels were all adjoining, they were the result of subdivision of a 46-acre parcel into three: 10 acres, 17 acres, and 19 acres. The 17-acre parcel was most interesting to me because it had the highest elevation, the best view (of the ocean and the mountains to the east), and was at the end of a

Figure 2 My lot when I bought it. The Pacific Ocean is in the background

ridge. It also had the highest price. I made an offer and it was accepted. At the beginning of 1991, I had my land, 17 acres, at 3800 Muniz Ranch Road. The lot is a 400-foot wide strip running approximately to the east down the hill. The elevation at the top is 1,400 feet, at the bottom it is 650 feet. Except at the top where there are several acres that are "level", the lot is very steep and mostly forested with a few small meadows. Very beautiful. Figure 2 shows the view from where the house was later built. The white area behind the trees is the Pacific Ocean. Now I was ready to design my dream property for my retirement.

Siting the House

Although the two tall fir trees shown in Figure 2 made a nice frame for the view of the ocean, I decided that they had to be removed before building the house. They had some fire damage on their trunks and, if they should later fall, it most likely would be to the east or north because of the prevailing winds, and that is where the house would be. The property line to the south was just behind the two fir trees. It would have been nice from the standpoint of the view to place the house as close to that line as possible. However, the house next door to the south was also close to my property line a little farther to the west, and when I walked out close to the line, that house came into view. I had to move the house back from the line to get away from that other house; that gave me a frame of other trees around my view. The area north of the proposed house site was all forest, mostly redwood. There was also a clump of redwoods back there that would be nice to have close to the entrance of the house.

Designing the House

My requirements for the house design included:

> It should be all on one level.
> There should be two bedrooms, two full baths and one half-bath.
> The master bedroom should be a separate suite.
> There should be a spacious entrance foyer.
> There should be a large area for my office and working space.
> There should be a utility room for clothes washing.
> The living, dining, and kitchen space should be contiguous.
> There should be lots of deck space
> And many other smaller requirements.

Working with floor plans for these features showed me that there was a serious problem with getting everything on one level. Because of the slope of the terrain which went down from west to east, and the space available from south to north, the eastern end of the house would be at least 20 feet in the air to achieve one level. I felt that would be too much. So I compromised on a split-level design. The bedroom area would be on the eastern (lower end), with the office area above it; the living-dining-kitchen-

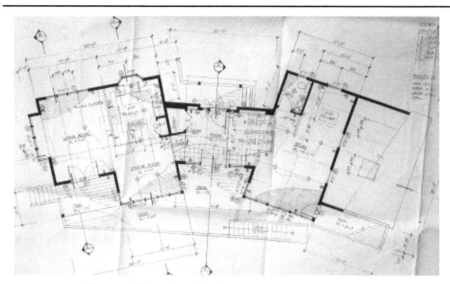

Figure 3 Floor plans for the upper levels of the house

foyer area would be half a flight up from the bedrooms and half a flight down from the office. The total square footage came out to be 2,200. The plans proceeded that way (see Figure 3).

I wanted to design the house completely by myself, but I found that California requires plans to be made by a California-licensed architect, so I had to hire an architect to work with me on the plans. Also, because of the requirement for earthquake protection, we had to have a civil engineer on the job. The civil engineer would also design the water and septic systems. My brother Bill would be the building contractor. The architect built a cardboard model of the design to help in visualizing it (see Figures 4 and 5). To the

Figure 4 Architect's cardboard model of house

227

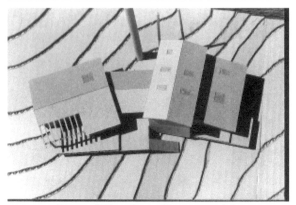

Figure 5 Top view of house model

left in Figure 4 is the ocean (south); the driveway and main entrance of the house are behind the model (north side). The master bedroom is closest to the camera, with the two-story bedroom-office unit next. The foyer is next and the living-dining-kitchem wing is farthest from the camera. The vertical poles on the model represent the redwood trees that are close to the front entrance of the house. Figure 5 is a top view, showing the angles between the wings. This was done to break up long straight lines and to better frame the view from the windows.

Because of the proximity of the clump of redwoods to the front entrance, and because redwoods have shallow roots, we felt that the foundation of the house would cut too many roots and weaken those trees. The largest tree also had what the tree people call a "sail" on its top. That is where its top had been cut off by lightning or some other event in the past and the tree had responded by branching horizontally at the top. Those branches went out 20 feet or more and created a lot of wind resistance. Since this area can get 100-mph winds sometimes in the winter, wind is of major concern. The tree man recommended to cut off the sail, which we did. The tree again responded by sprouting at the top, but this time the sprouts went straight up. *Today, the sprouts are trees in their own right, proably 40 feet high above the top of the original tree.*

Redwood trees are notorious for sprouting when they are cut. If an entire tree is cut down, the stump will send up sprouts all around. This is the explanation for the tree formations found in a redwood forest. A giant tree was cut down years ago for logging, and the stump sends up a circle of sprouts. After 100 or more years, those sprouts become trees 1 to 2 feet in diameter, producing the effect known as a "fairy ring", or "redwood cathedral". A person looking up from the center of one of these rings sees a circle of sky (see Figure 6). I have two quite nice fairy rings across the driveway from my house. There is a lot to know about redwoods.

Back to the house design, we decided to divide the foundation into two pieces: one was the living-dining-kitchen area and the other was the two-story bedroom-office area. They would be connected by a bridge, which was the entrance foyer. As it turned out on the site, one can walk standing up underneath the foyer.

Figure 6 A redwood "fairy ring" looking up

Designing a Shop Building

The plan included a second major building — a shop for my wood-working. This was a separate building from the house, 600 square feet, with a half bath, and designed to the same standards as the house. Because of the slope of the site, part of the shop is built on a concrete slab, and the rest is built over a crawl space. This building was built first and served as a base for the management of the rest of the project (see Figure 7).

Site Preparation

While all this was going on, I was still living in New Jersey. I came to California about 6 to 8 times a year and stayed for two weeks at a time. I decided to build a small cabin on the property where I could stay when I was there. This was a "non-permit" building,

Figure 7 The woodworking shop building

229

Figure 8 The cabin where I stayed when I came to CA

which is a separate building of no more than 120 square feet. No building permit is required. My cabin was a fully-finished building about 10 x 12 feet that I built mostly myself. It contained a closet and cabinets, a bunk for sleeping, and a table and a chair for eating and using the computer. Yes, a computer. I had no power from the grid at that time; they would not hook me up until my house was closed in. I bought a gasoline-driven generator to run the tools used for building, but I did not want to use that when I was there by myself because of the gas consumption, noise and pollution. I installed two solar panels on the roof of the cabin. They charged batteries, which gave me light and could run my computer and a TV at any time of the day. See Figure 8.

Heating the cabin was more of a problem. I tried a kerosene heater but in such a small place the smell of a kerosene heater was overwhelming. I could run the generator and use an electric heater — this worked well, but I had a hard time justifying burning a half-gallon of gasoline per hour just for heat. The solar system wasn't powerful enough for any heat. Mostly, I just used a lot of blankets. For cooking, I used a propane stove, outside.

Site preparation included the roads and driveways, the septic system, the water system, an underground electrical system all the way from Muniz Ranch Road, and the excavation for the buildings. My lot actually does not have any road frontage on Muniz Ranch Road. There is an easement across two other properties for my driveway, about 400 feet long. This gave me more privacy, and I considered that a desirable feature. The driveway and parking areas around the house were topped with gravel.

The water system posed some unexpected problems. An adjoining parcel was purchased shortly after I bought mine by Dr. Ken Wilkes, a physician from Marin County. He was not planning to build a house immediately as I was, but as neighbors, we agreed to share some of the site work, including the water and electrical systems. His property went down the mountain next to my property on the north and east; there was no building site on his property that would have a view of the ocean. He had only valley views. However, there was a place on my property close to the property line and about 100 feet lower and 500 feet to the east of my house, that could be an ocean view site for him. I agreed to make a lot line adjustment and give him 0.25 acres from my lot down there for his building site. This had to be drawn up and duly registered with the County. None of this can be seen from my house.

Ken's driveway shared part of my driveway across the easement, but then it cut into the side of the mountain to get down to where his building site would be. We had fun climbing along the side of the mountain in the forest with the civil engineer laying out this driveway. Then Ken spent a lot of money with an excavation contractor getting that road put in. My driveway was simple in comparison, because my terrain was nearly level and my driveway was much shorter.

Getting back to the water system, we had the civil engineer design a joint water system for us — well, pump, storage tank, and piping. When applying to the County for approval of this, they decided that we were building a "community water system", and required it to be designed to those standards. This called for upgrading to a 4" water main from the storage tank, down my driveway, and then down the hill to Ken's. Also, we had to put in water meters for each of us. This change happened shortly after we had begun work on the system, because we thought we had approval. We had to stop and revise the excavations and get new materials to complete the job to the new specifications.

Ken and I did not share septic systems. However, my system had to have a pump between the septic tank and the leach field because the leach field was about 15 feet uphill from the tank. Ken's system had a much larger problem: his leach field was 100 feet uphill from his tank. Wow.

Building the House

Building occurred during 1992. We built the shop first. It was kind of a

Figure 9 The upper level of the house under construction

trial run for the house because many of the construction features of the shop were the same as the house. My brother and his crew had to commute to the mountain every day. That was at least 20 miles each way, more for some of them. When we began framing the house itself, Bill's daughter Janna joined the crew as a carpenter.

Because I was commuting part-time from New Jersey, I was not here all the time, but I did stay in touch by telephone. Mostly, that worked. I had never before managed so important a project by remote control. Its success was surely affected by the good rapport I had with Bill, even though we are quite different people.

The house was framed with 2 x 6 lumber. There were many large wooden beams; the engineer doing the earthquake-proof design made sure of that. All vertical structure was

Figure 10 South side of house under construction

Figure 11 Finished house, south side, facing the ocean

bolted solidly to the concrete foundation, sometimes with bolts coming all the way down from the second floor. The main beams for the roof ridges were lifted by a large backhoe that just happened to be working on the site at the time the lift was needed.

The sheathing was cedar plywood. Inside finish was sheetrock with textured paint. None of the interior trim was done by the crew – that was left for me to finish later. The floor joists were 2 x 12 TrusJoists, they were decked with 1-1/8″ plywood. Floor finish was about half tile and half carpet. All-in-all, it is a sturdy house.

Figure 9 shows the upper level of the house under construction. The person standing on the deck is Bill. The other person is Kevin Lynch, one of the carpenters. The camera is facing east; it shows the view in that direction – mountains with valleys filled with fog – we are on top. Figure 10 shows the south side during construction, which faces the ocean.

Initial construction was finished in late 1992, but I still had to complete the internal trim. Figure 11 shows the outside of the house (south side) at that time.

Doing the Interior Trim

I intended to do all the interior trim myself in redwood. I developed a

Figure 12 Window trim details

Figure 13 Trim details around the entrance door

straightforward design, which proved to be quite attractive (see Figures 12 and 13 — it really takes color images to see the beauty of the trim.) This design used two types of redwood lumber: young growth redwood for the outer border of the trim, which is a light red color; and old-growth redwood, which is a darker color, tending towards brown for the inner flat surface of the trim. Old-growth, which is hard to find, is wood 300 years or more old. However, I found a source with a local wood

Figure 14 Unloading the truck at the house—1993; (inset) Drivers Janna and Kayle

collector, who had a basement full of old-growth lumber, which he had milled from old wine casks. At the start, I had only hand tools to do this work.

In 1993, my daugh-ter Kayle and Bill's daughter Janna drove a rented 10-ton truck with my woodworking shop, power tools, and other items from Merchantville to Muniz Ranches. It was quite an adventure for them, one that they vowed never to do again (see Figure 14). One important item for the shop that was on the truck was my father's workbench, which I inherited when he passed away, and which I had at the Woodstown house. When I left Woodstown, the workbench went back into the garage at Merchantville. It came from there in the truck to CA. Figure 15 shows the

Figure 15 My father's workbench in CA (with 2008 clutter)

workbench. It weighed 800 pounds and had 32 drawers filled with hand tools. All tools were still in the same locations that I learned as a child in Merchantville.

This gave me all the tools I needed for the trim work, as well as a number of items to help living in the house. However, the trim was slow work because I was still commuting from New Jersey; it took several years to complete everything.

A Cat in the House

In early 1993, my brother's wife, Barbara asked me if I would like to have a cat. Barbara had a store in Occidental at that time and one day a cat came into the store and liked it so much, he decided to stay. I am a cat person and said "Sure, but what will I do with him when I go back to NJ?" Barbara said that she could take care of him at her house during those

Figure 16 Ben

times. The cat was a very beautiful long-hair orange cat named "Ben" (see Figure 16). So I took him to the house. He decided that was good place, too and was happy to stay with me. I soon learned to be careful when petting him—if he got too much, he would bite or scratch. I could live with that.

When I went back to NJ that time, I took Ben to Bill & Barbara's house and left him. Soon after I got back home in NJ, I got a call from Barbara who said there was a problem with Ben—he was terrorizing her two other cats. I would have to find a new situation for him when I came the next time.

On my next visit, we decided that Ben could stay with Bill's daughter, Janna, who was living in a cabin on Bill's property. That worked well for about a year, but then Janna decided to move to San Francisco. There seemed to be no other option than to try leaving Ben at my house while I was back in NJ. I put a pet door on the shop and Ben would live there while I was away. I arranged with a neighbor to go in several times a week and put out food and water for Ben.

That worked until the local raccoon community found that they could enter through the pet door and eat Ben's food. I changed the pet door to one that opened only for Ben by means of a magnetic collar that activated the door. However, the raccoons learned to subvert that by using their claws. They still got the food. There were even more secure pet doors available, but they were priced about 10 times higher than the one I had, which was too much for me. I decided the answer was simply to feed the raccoons as well as Ben. Putting out more food cost less than the better pet door. I did that until I moved to CA permanently in 1998. Ben lived with me until he became ill in early 2008 and had to be put down. He was 17 years old. I soon acquired another cat.

<u>Aunt Helen Visits my New House</u>

Looking forward to moving to my California house, in late 1993, I brought

Aunt Helen to see the house (see Figure 17). I was living in the Merchantville house with her and was caring for her. She was 84. I could not move to California if she would not come there, so this visit was a test to see if she would move with me. She liked the house, but she was skeptical of its remoteness. One evening, we were going to entertain some neighbors for dinner. Dinner was all cooked, and I went out to pick up the neighbors we had invited. When I returned to the house, we found Aunt Helen lying on the floor of the foyer. She said: "I can't move." The two neighbors, who were

Figure 17 Aunt Helen in CA

retired nurses, took one look and one said: "I think she has broken her hip." A little more examination confirmed that it was probably true. I called 911.

About five minutes later, a truck pulled up outside and two men came up to the house. I was surprised, because I didn't know that anyone could get there so quickly — the nearest town that had emergency services was 20 miles away. It turned out that the two men were neighbors who had EMT training and whose houses were less than two miles down the road. They called the ambulance out from Guerneville, which got here in about 45 minutes. During this time, Aunt Helen was is serious pain, but the men were not authorized to give her anything. When the EMTs from Guerneville arrived, they took her to the hospital in Sebastopol, about 30 miles away. After putting dinner into the refrigerator, I took the nurses back to their house and apologized for the lack of a dinner. I then followed the ambulance to the hospital.

The hospital confirmed the broken hip and recommended a hip replacement. That was done. Aunt Helen came to California for a week; she got massive trauma, and stayed more than three weeks before she could travel back to NJ. I went back with her and helped her through all the physical therapy and everything else that follows a major operation. After about a year, she was back to normal. The only thing that changed was she vowed never to go back to California.

Let me explain why the accident occurred. The house plans originally showed that the floor would be level between the living-dining-kitchen area and the foyer. When we were laying out the house at the site, we found that the site slope was a little more than the plans assumed. This made the whole east end of the house too high, which would have considerably increased the cost. We solved that problem by putting in two broad steps between the kitchen and the foyer. Unfortunately for Aunt Helen, we felt that the two steps did not require a railing, and the County inspectors agreed. However, when I was away picking up our guests, Aunt Helen decided to go down to the bedroom level, but she forgot that those steps were there. You know what happens when you go over an unexpected step — you fall. That is what happened. I'm sure if I had had a railing there, she would have been holding it, and if she fell at all, it would not have been catastrophic. Hindsight. The one good thing: I put up a railing on those steps as soon as I could get the materials.

Kitchen Cabinets

I did all the trim in the house using redwood, and I also wanted the kitchen cabinets to be redwood. I had built the kitchen cabinets for the Woodstown house, but building cabinets here would have been too much for me, considering the commuting from NJ. I hired a local cabinet builder in

Figure 18 The kitchen

Figure 19 Front entrance deck and bridge

Occidental, CA (about 20 miles away) to do the cabinets for me. At first he objected to using redwood because he thought it was too soft a wood. I insisted, so he did it. The job was beautiful. *But the cabinet builder was right about the softness of the wood. After some years, the cabinets have become scratched, especially around the door handles. But I still like them.* The kitchen counters are granite, except for one work counter, which is varnished butcher-block maple. See Figure 18. This kitchen has been very satisfactory. *At one large party, there were five people working comfortably in the kitchen!*

The Front Entrance

The terrain near the front entrance was such that a bridge had to be built to get into the house. That was because the level of the foyer floor and the entrance deck was about six feet above the ground. However, the ground had a steep slope, so that about 20 feet away from the house, the driveway was level with the deck. Putting a bridge across that 20 feet made it a level walk from the driveway into the house (see Figure 19). The figure also shows the walk space under the foyer, where one can walk standing up from one side of the house to the other.

I made a collage (Figure 20) around 1995 to present an overall picture of the house. It is another example of my photography thread. I was still shooting film at that time, but all the photos were scanned and the collage was built in Photoshop. Now my dream house was complete and livable, but there was much more to do to make the rest of the property be as I wanted it. The next chapter takes that up along with other matters involved with living in Muniz Ranches.

239

Figure 20 A photographic summary of the features of my new house

Chapter 12

Living in California

Although my California house was completed in 1993, I could not move there until much later. That was because I had to take care of Aunt Helen in NJ. In fact, I had to outlive her. She passed away in March, 1998 from Alzheimer's disease at the age of 92. Her last couple of years were very difficult for me as well as her. Kayle, now a nurse, helped a lot with this, but the outcome was inevitable. I inherited the Merchantville house, which I sold as quickly as I could. It went to the son of a neighbor. My brother Bill and his wife, Barbara, came east for the funeral. When that was over, they rented a big truck and drove across the country back to California with several pieces of my father's woodwork they wanted, and all the remaining things I needed to take there.

When all my affairs in New Jersey were settled, I flew to California and planned to never look back. Suddenly, I had a new location that was totally different from Merchantville. It was like starting my life over again. Instead of the suburban environment of Merchantville, I was in a remote location on a mountaintop overlooking the Pacific Ocean. Although my closest neighbors were not too far away (150 feet), their house couldn't be seen from mine because of a redwood, oak, and fir forest. The road up to my property (Muniz Ranch Road) was 3.8 miles long, and there were only 10 other houses visible along that road before coming to my driveway. When I looked out from my decks, I could see miles of forested hills and valleys, without a single other man-made structure in view. To the south is the Pacific Ocean; on a clear day, one can see the Farallon Islands, off San Francisco, 65 miles away. And it hardly ever freezes or snows. I can garden year round, even plant tropical plants like palm trees and bird-of-paradise. Overnight, my dream house that I had built five years before became my *home*.

One thing I did as soon as I got permanently to California was to grow a full beard. This was symbolic for me, signifying the start of the transition to being a true Californian. I had never done much with facial hair except for a brief period of having a moustache in the 1970s.

There are other major differences between my California location and Merchantville, NJ. Here, it is 20 miles to the nearest supermarket (Guerneville), 40 miles to Santa Rosa for an urban shopping mall or big-box store. There is little traffic on the local roads except on summer weekends, when we get a lot of tourist traffic coming from inland towns to see the coast. That is good, because the roads are narrow, winding, mountain roads. *I have been here full-time for ten years now, and I have become so used to things here that I have trouble remembering the differences between here and NJ.*

A Lady Friend

I went to the Merchantville High School 50th class reunion in 1996. I hadn't seen most of my classmates until then. A classmate, John Smiley, and I produced and published a book about the reunion; it was like an updated class yearbook.

Among other people at the reunion, I re-connected with Louisa (Hofstetter) Lavelle. We were friendly in high school and had some similar interests. Figure 9 of Chapter one shows her next to me in a picture of the MHS class of 1946 yearbook staff. I even asked her to go to the Senior Prom, but I was too late in asking and she went with someone else. After

Figure 1 Arch and Louisa 2000

graduation, we each went our separate ways to college and had not seen each other for 50 years. At the class reunion, we met again and exchanged e-mail addresses. At that point, she was a widow and I was divorced. We began communicating by e-mail, which soon grew to every day, and we also got in the habit of talking on the phone every other day, *which continues up to the present time.* Figure 1 shows us here in 2000.

After a few years of e-mail and telephone contact, I invited Louisa to come to California and stay the entire winter at my house. She did. She was familiar with the San Francisco Bay Area because three of her sons live in the South Bay, also known as Silicon Valley. They are engineers working in the computer industry. She has three other sons and a daughter living in the East as well. Seven children! *And 16 grandchildren!!* Louisa also found time to be a school librarian. She has also become quite an artist. Louisa is definitely a major part of my life, even though we spend most of our time on opposite coasts of the US. *She comes to California several times a year and I go back east once a year, usually in July, to her place at the east coast resort town of Beach Haven, NJ. We also take a trip together once a year. Louisa travels much more than that, but you remember my comments about travel.*

Redwood and Woodworking

One of my greatest pleasures from my California location is that it is in a redwood forest. I love redwood trees and if I wanted to be a tree-hugger, I have hundreds of targets right here. Redwood trees can grow to be 2,000 years old and as much as 350 feet tall. There are none like that on my property, but I can go a few miles to a state park and see them. The largest tree on my property is one that I did not even know was there until I had owned the property for about ten years. As I mentioned in the previous chapter, my lot slopes down 750 vertical feet to a year-round stream (Russian Gulch Creek, East Branch) at the bottom that runs into the ocean. It is very steep and I never went to the bottom of the property until about 2002, when I decided to build a hiking trail to go down there. I'll describe the making of that trail a little later in this chapter. In making the trail, we discovered this large tree standing about 200 vertical feet down the hill. It is 6 feet in diameter at the base and 200 feet high. Thus, it could not be seen from the top of the hill (where the house is located). I didn't know it was there. A 6-foot-diameter redwood tree is around 500 to 600 years old, so we named it the "Columbus Tree", because it could have been a seedling about the time Columbus came to America (see Figure 2). The trail goes right next to the tree, so it is easily hugged if you are so inclined. On the property next to mine is a somewhat larger tree, about 8-feet in diameter, but it is only about 100 feet tall, having been topped by some event in the distant past (see Figure 3). It has a "sail" on top like the tree by my front

Figure 2 The Columbus Tree, oil painting by Louisa Lavelle

door had before I cut it off.

I had used redwood lumber back in New Jersey for decks and garden structures. However, the wood available there is always young-growth and relatively uniform with boring grain patterns. When I saw what old-growth redwood burl, or figured redwood was like, I fell in love with it as a furniture or trim wood. However, it is a soft and not very strong wood that requires special handling in assembly and finishing to produce durable products. I think it is worth the trouble.

Where do you get old-growth redwood? My best source turned out to be right here in my yard and elsewhere on Muniz Ranches. Redwood logs are laying everywhere. This area was last logged around 1905; for whatever reason, many logs were left here on the ground. Redwood laying above the ground easily lasts 100 years. During that time, there were a number of forest fires, which removed the bark and the sapwood (the layer just under the bark that is more yellow than red), but the red heartwood remained under the charred exterior. Logs were there for the picking. On my property near where the house was to go, there were three major logs about three feet in diameter. When the house was built, we moved those logs out of the way. Later, when I had time for woodworking, I looked for ways to cut into them to retrieve the good wood.

Figure 3 Neighbor's big tree with a "sail" on top

A chain saw is a good choice for this, but it is not very useful by itself for making boards from a log. You can make cross cuts to clean up the ends of a log and get an idea of how good the wood inside will be, but to make rip cuts along the log to produce boards, you need some kind of guide. There is a product called the Alaskan SawMill, which mounts onto the cutting bar of a large chain saw. This provides a guide that

Figure 4 Woodmizer LT15 sawmill, milling a 16 x 16 cant

can run along two boards that you fasten on top of the log. I bought a 32" chain saw and an Alaskan mill. It takes two people to run this, and it is slow going, but with the help of a neighbor, I did manage to make some rough boards from one of my logs.

In my shop, I had a small band saw that I brought from Merchantville. This could cut about an 8" wide board. However, I found that also to be slow and difficult, and the number of boards produced was very small for the effort involved. A chain saw or band saw leaves a rough surface that has to be planed smooth. I had a small planer, also from Merchantville, to do that. That worked, but all this was not adequate to deal with the logs I had and with the ones I found on nearby properties. I needed a *real* saw mill.

My Own Sawmill

At that point I discovered the Woodmizer® sawmills. These are band saw mills that have a cutting head running horizontally along a track. The log to be milled is placed on the track and suitably leveled. The saw head is raised to take a cut along the top of the log as it lies on the track. Most of the Woodmizer sawmills were out of my league financially and I could never justify their cost for my small use. However, their smallest model, the LT-15, was barely affordable to me. It was capable of a 28" cut on a log about 36" in diameter. In 1998, I bought one (see Figure 4). It turned out to be just what I needed, and I soon milled all the logs on my property.

There was the problem of moving the logs to the sawmill and getting them up onto it. Moving is done by dragging the logs with a vehicle (I had a four-wheel drive Jeep Cherokee at the time which worked for that), or you rolled them. To roll a log, you use a tool called a "cant hook", which is a long handle tool with a hook-like device at the end to grip the log as you apply rolling force. A "cant" is what you get after you mill a log down to the largest possible rectangular cross-section. Moving logs or cants takes brute strength, which was not one of my strong points. I needed help. At that time, my neighbor was Raymond Dalle, who gladly helped with that.

Raymond also brought along Jonathan Hughes, who was even more help. Jonathan is a tall, muscular man, about 45 at the time, who could pick up 300-pound planks and carry them. (More about Jonathan later.) The logs were 1,000 to 2,000 pounds, and had to be rolled, but some of the pieces we cut from the logs were around 300 pounds. Because I did not know what I was going to do with the lumber we milled, I generally did not cut the logs into boards, but into large planks or cants only small enough that we could move them by hand. I even began collecting old-growth logs from other places on the Ranch (with owner permission, of course).

The old-growth logs were not perfect. The wood was not rotten, but it often had cracks where water had gotten in over the years and caused local damage. The logs also had a lot of knots, which may have been the reason the loggers in 1905 did not take them. But between the various defects, there was some beautiful wood. Soon I had redwood lumber stacked everywhere. To prevent further damage, the milled wood needed to be stored inside. There was considerable storage space under the bedroom wing of the house, and I also built a storage room onto the shop and a large tent out in the year. All was (*and is still*) filled with old-growth redwood planks and cants.

Making Redwood Furniture

My milled old-growth redwood falls into two categories regarding its use in furniture. Some of it is either not good enough for indoor furniture, or too good for outdoor furniture. The result is that I usually buy young-growth wood commercially for outdoor projects, but select from my stock for indoor projects. Wood that I have in stock that is not good enough for indoor furniture gets used for rough outdoor projects like planter boxes.

I tried to make a business out of redwood furniture. To help that, I made a web site, www.redwoodworks.com that advertises my products. This business has not produced much work except locally, and I have not been very diligent in promoting it. *At this time in my life, I don't want too much of that kind of business anyway. I mostly only do woodworking for myself or friends.*

Figure 5 Outdoor redwood bench

Outdoor Redwood Furniture

A typical outdoor project is a bench; I have made dozens of this design (see Figure 5). I even made a fixture that I use to cut out the pieces and to assemble the legs. These benches are around my property and many other places in Muniz Ranches. They are heavy and sturdy and will endure outdoors all year with or without staining. They look prettier with stain, because it keeps the red color instead of turning gray with natural aging. However, stain has to be redone every 3 years or it will turn gray anyway.

Another outdoor project was a round table with curved benches. (see Figure 6). As shown in the figure, this was finished with an exterior varnish that was supposed to last five years. It only lasted one year, so the customer painted it green, which is a shame because it was made with expensive clear (no knots or cracks) young-growth redwood from a local sawmill. The customer paid for that, so I guess he had the right to do whatever he liked with it.

Other outdoor products include house number signs, sundial pedestals, planter boxes, trellises, etc.

Indoor Redwood Furniture

Indoor furniture was in both old-growth or young-growth redwood. Typical items were shelves, benches, tables, cabinets, dressers, or mantelpieces.

Figure 6 54-in round table and benches — redwood, varnished

These were mostly finished with a water-based interior varnish—many coats. The advantage of this finish is that it can be recoated every two hours, so you can build up 5 or 6 coats in one day, which is what it takes for durability. Varnished redwood produces a beautiful red or brown color without the use of any stain. The finish is high-gloss, but it can be hand-rubbed to any sheen the customer desires. For my major old-growth pieces, I also produced an information card giving the history of that particular piece. I built a place into each product, such as under a table top, where the customer could store the card, to be brought out whenever showing someone the piece. An old-growth coffee table I built for Louisa's living

Figure 7 Old-growth coffee table

room in Beach Haven, NJ is shown in Figure 7. The corresponding information card is shown in Figure 8.

Merchantville at Muniz Ranches

A few years after my house was finished, I got a call from Kevin Lynch (see Figure 9, Chapter 11), one of the carpenters who worked

Old Growth Redwood Table

This table is made of wood from a 350-year-old redwood log. The tree containing this log was probably felled around the turn of the twentieth century when the surrounding area was logged. For some reason, the loggers left this piece, which was originally about four feet in diameter and 24 feet long. Over the years, forest fires burned away the bark and most of the sapwood, leaving a three-foot-diameter log that is entirely heartwood.

The table top is fabricated from three pieces *quarter-sawn* from the log. That means the boards are cut approximately perpendicular to the growth rings of the log, an expensive technique that gives the closest and finest grain on the board surface. Old growth is also very beautiful when boards are cut parallel to the growth rings; this is called *flat-sawing*. This can be seen on the table legs—the wide faces are quarter-sawn, while the smaller faces show the flat-sawn patterning.

Because of this history, the wood is not perfect—it has occasional cracks, worm holes, and sometimes knots. I tried to work around all that, but some of the defects are still observable in the finished table. I think they add to its character.

Probably caused by the long aging period in the tree and on the ground, old growth redwood is more brown than red, although any artist will tell you that brown is simply a dark red. When the table is placed in bright sunlight, you can see that there is red in it. The finish is Flecto Varathane Diamond Finish, a water-based gloss varnish. The top has about eight coats of finish. No stain was used, and the finish is very clear; what you see is the natural color of the wood. Although this finish is very durable, if it should become damaged, a light sanding followed by one or two coats of the same product will restore it.

Arch Luther
Woodworker

P.O. Box 92 □ Jenner, CA 95450   September, 1998

Figure 8 Information sheet for table in Figure 7.

with Bill on my house. He said that he was working for a woman who lived about a mile up Muniz Ranch Road from me. He was in her library and saw a copy of a Merchantville High School yearbook. When he asked the woman, she said yes, she had gone to MHS. He suggested that I should contact the woman, Elena Scola. Of course, I did.

Elena graduated from MHS in 1948, two years after me. I looked in my yearbook and there she was, in a picture of the sophomore class. What are the odds of finding someone from Merchantville on a mountain 3,000 miles from New Jersey? Not only that, one of her brothers, Orlando Scola, worked for me as a machinist in Electronic Recording at RCA.

Elena and I became friends. After I moved permamantly to Muniz Ranch, we talked about going into business together. Elena is an artist (oil painting) and she had the idea that there ought to be a way on the Internet for artisans and artists to display and sell their work. This was 1998, early in the history of the Internet. We searched the Web for sites that sold the work of artists, and there were already many. However, there weren't many sites selling the work of other artisans, such as potters, woodworkers, weavers, etc. We decided to develop a web-based business that specialized in all artisanal products except paintings. A third person, Elena's secretary, Simonetta Baldwin, joined the partnership. The plan was that Elena would have the responsibility to find artisans to be on the site, I would design the site, and Simonetta would manage the finances.

In Business on the Internet

We went to work. I began the task of designing a web site for our business, which we called ArtisansWorld.com. This proved to be a massive task, which took me six months to complete. The problem was that there were not many tools in 1998 for designing web sites, especially an e-commerce web site as this had to be, and the tools that were available were too expensive for us. I ended up doing the entire site design from scratch, writing all the pages with a text editor. I learned a lot about web design on this project. I found that I enjoyed it even more than the other software projects I had done, and have designed web sites whenever I got the chance ever since then.

The ArtisansWorld site was designed to be expandable as we added more artisans. It also had to have password-protected areas for each artisan to manage their information on the site. There was a customer login feature so that customers did not have to enter their information every time they made a purchase. Purchases also could be made from several artisans and the system handled it as one order so far as the customer was concerned.

Behind the scenes, a multi-artisan order was parcelled out to each artisan separately. All this took place without anyone having to go into the site manually and make any changes. Figure 9 shows the home page of the site at an early stage in its development. Everyone felt the site was very beautiful, and they were amazed by its features, which were unusual at the time. *Today these features are commonplace and are available to site authors without any special programming or much cost.*

Figure 10 shows a typical artisan's display page that presented their products. This one happens to be products collected by Dr. Abbas Husain on his trips to India. There could be any number of such pages, depending on the number of products being sold by that artisan. I could fill many pages of this book showing

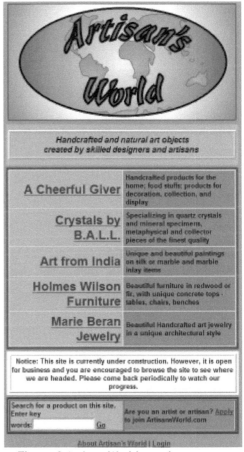

Figure 9 ArtisansWorld.com home page

all the things included in this site. For example, I wrote an instruction book for the site to be used by our people who managed the site. It was over 100 pages.

ArtisansWorld.com was online for two years. During that time, we got about 20 artisans to join the site, but the sales were very small. It was difficult to get artisans to join; many were skeptical of online selling, or they felt it would generate too much work for them. The other problem was getting customers to come to the site. I think there was the same hesitation among customers about buying over the Internet. We were ahead

Figure 10 A display page for "Art from India"

of the time about this. In mid-2000, we closed the site. We lost all of the money we invested in it. I also lost the work I put into designing the web site. At one point I discussed with my partners about trying to sell the site design to others who might want to use it on the web. With the extensibility and configurability of the design, it could have been easily adapted to other users who wanted to sell products from a multiplicity of vendors. I wanted us to make some money from the site design work. They refused to let me do it.

Muniz Ranches Property Owners Association

Muniz Ranches (MR) is in an unincorporated area of Sonoma County, so it does not have local government other than Sonoma County. We have a property-owner's association, called Muniz Ranches Property Owners Association (MRPOA). This is managed by an elected 5-member board of directors. The Association members are all the property owners on the Ranch, about 44. When I first came to MR in 1991, and the people found out my background, I began getting requests to run for the Board. My answer was: "I'll consider that once I am here full-time." When I moved from NJ in 1998, I could no longer use that excuse; I ran for the Board, and was elected.

At my first Board meeting, I was appointed Treasurer, a position I held for 9 years (I did not run in 2007). I quickly found out that being treasurer for even such a small organization was a lot of work. However, I said I would do it, and according to my style, I did it. The previous Treasurer had not used a computer at all; all the record-keeping was pen and paper. I couldn't do it that way; it had to be computerized. In addition to the finances, the MRPOA Treasurer is responsible for keeping the member data records. So I set up computer records for all that, at first using Microsoft Excel, a spreadsheet program. This still involved a lot of manual work, especially in assembling reports for the board meetings.

After a few years, I decided that the best thing to do would be to put the MRPOA records online, in a password-protected web site. There was already a web site for the Ranch, run by one member. However, he was quite anti-board and would not allow his site to become an "official" Muniz Ranches web site. After some discussion, we decided to get a new domain name and start an official MRPOA site. In the site, we put information about the Ranch, member data, and financial data. To make it possible for the site to have information of interest to members, but that the world could not see, we made everything password protected. All members were given the general password. Each member was also given a personal password that would allow them to see their personal data stored by the Association, as well as the general information. The personal data included things such as address, telephone, e-mail, their assessment status, and information about their property. They could even edit some of their personal data. This information is used by MRPOA for communicating with the members.

The people who are Board members can use their personal password to access information related to their position on the Board. The Secretary can access up-to-the-minute mailing or e-mail lists; the Treasurer can access all the financial data, including entering new transactions; and all Board members can access current financial summary reports, which are assembled at the instant they are requested. *The web site has been valuable to the Board members, who appreciate the up-to-the-minute reports, but it has not been that popular with the members. Since I left the Board, I am still webmaster of the web site.*

There are two major responsibilities of the MRPOA Board. The big-

Figure 11 The Muniz Ranches bridge across Russian Gulch Creek

gest is maintaining our six-mile private road, Muniz Ranch Road, which goes from Highway 1 up to the end of the Ranch. Since it is a gravel road, it requires periodic maintainence, typically twice a year. There is also a security gate at Highway 1 and a bridge across Russian Gulch Creek about a mile up the road. We replaced the gate mechanism and gate in 2005, and the bridge was replaced in 2006-2007 (See Figure 11). Both had previously been in place for more than 30 years.

The other major responsibility, is what is called the Architectural Control Committee (ACC). This committee is set up by the Board. The ACC reviews const-ruction projects on the Ranch to assure compliance with the requirements of our Conditions, Covenants, and Restrictions (CC&Rs), which are community rules that were set forth at the time of incorporation of the Ranch in 1971. This has proven to be a difficult and sometimes controversial job. I was a member of the ACC all the time I was on the Board.

I enjoyed being on the Board even though I was amazed at how political some issues could become even in such a small community. I resigned simply because I decided it was too much work and I had put in my time and more some.

Gardening

I have always liked gardening. I did a little in Merchantville while I was still in school, but gardening really bloomed (no pun intended) for me when I got my own house. In Fox Hollow, I tried to garden outside, but the property was so shady that few things grew well. Instead, I built a greenhouse at the only sunny spot on the property so I could garden inside all year round. When I lived in Woodstown, I was in real farm country and almost everything we planted there did well. When I moved back to

Merchantville after the divorce, I tried to do a lot of gardening there too, but again the growing conditions were not good. But then I moved to Northern California!

Here, I can grow all kinds of plants year round, and many tropicals that I only could grow before when I had the greenhouse;

Figure 12 Two deer watching my garden

here, I grow them outside. But still, there were problems to overcome. Below is my saga of gardening at Muniz Ranches.

The first consideration of gardening at MR is that there is a lot of wildlife here: deer, rabbits, wild turkeys, raccoons, coyotes, gophers, and more (see Figure 12). Many of these will devastate a garden. But the worst problem is that we have free range cattle on the Ranch. MRPOA leases grazing rights to a local rancher, who grazes some of his beef cattle on the Ranch. These animals will not only eat your garden plants, but if they find a plant they can't eat, they'll pull it out of the ground. They leave nothing. So I needed a fence strong enough to keep out cattle, small enough wire spacing to keep out rabbits, and tall enough to keep out deer. The usual answer is about 6 to 7 feet high and using a graduated fence wire that has small spacing at the bottom and larger spacing at the top.

I hired a contractor to fence a modest area on the south side of the house about 25 feet by 100 feet. The fence started at the middle of the house and went over to the edge of the shop. Figure 13 shows this right after it was done. The fence was very nice and some of it still exists. The rest was removed when I later enlarged the garden area. However, in one of those removal projects I discovered that one of the original fence posts was set right into the side of my septic tank! Because it is so rocky here, the contractor dug the holes with a jack hammer. I guess he thought the septic tank was just another rock. I repaired the septic tank with concrete and everything is now fine. Speaking of jack hammers, I found it necessary to have one of my own to deal with the rocks myself.

As Figure 13 shows, nothing was planted in that area at that time, but

Figure 13 My first fence before anything was planted, 1994.

there were some rocks in place—they were there before the house was built and we left them. Most of the rocks have beautiful lichen growth on their sunny side. The figure also shows that I was doing some minor gardening in pots on the deck.The proposed garden area was reasonably level and most of it got full sun, which was good. Unfortunately, grayscale pictures of gardens don't show much—they should be in color.

When I began to plant some things, I learned another fact of gardening at my location on the Ranch—the ground is rocky—really rocky. There is approximately 50% small rocks in every shovelfull you take up. If you want good soil, you have to dig a large hole and sift the soil and then put it back for planting. This gets to be a lot of work. Also, we had to put the sifted-out rock somewhere. I decided to start some rock berms to make level places in some of the steeper areas of the property. More work. I planted many things: agapanthus, euryops (an evergreen shrub with yellow daisy-like flowers year-round), ice plant, iris, pampas grass (a hybrid type that would not spread), roses, rock roses, salvia, primroses (in shady areas), viburnum, peach trees, and others.

These first plantings revealed yet another truth about gardening here: one must have irrigation. It was a lot to water by hand, and who would do that while I was back in NJ? I installed a drip irrigation system. For this, there is a timer unit that controls electric valves to send water to one or more "drip hoses", one at a time. These are ½" plastic tubing that runs over the ground throughout the garden. The individual plants are watered by emitters that connect to the drip hose with small-diameter "spaghetti tubing". Holes are punched in the drip hose to take a connector fitting to the spaghetti tubing. There are many kinds of emitters, and for multiple-plant watering you can use either a special hose that leaks along its length, or sprinklers can be used. These latter are less efficient because a lot of water evaporates while sprinkling and never gets to the plants. It also wets

Figure 14 The garden after one year

the foliage, which some plants don't like.

After my first plantings grew a while, I learned another caveat of gardening here: planting and irrigating close to redwood trees attracts their roots. Redwood roots are very invasive and they will quickly take all the water and nutrition from the plants. Some plants seem to survive anyway, but most don't like the tree roots. The answer to this is to build planting boxes above the ground (above the ground because redwood roots will actually grow *up* into a box placed on the ground). This is more work and considerable expense.

In spite of all these problems, my first garden was quite successful (see Figure 14); I was able to have a lot of flowers and beautiful ornamental plants. However, I had trouble when I grew edibles. My peach trees set fruit, but the critters and birds harvested the fruit before I could get it.

That was about as much garden as I could handle while commuting from NJ. However, after moving to CA full-time in early 1998, I decided that the garden was not large enough and I went into phase 2 of fencing. The existing fence was mostly taken down and moved out toward the ocean

Figure 15 The phase 2 garden (2000)

by another 20 feet. Now there was room to add olive trees, a fig tree, a windmill palm tree, a cordyline tree, lemon trees, a fremontia bush, and others. Figure 15 shows the phase 2 garden near its beginning, when not much was planted in the enlarged area.

The new garden area also required enlarging the irrigation system. I had planned the original design for this, and simply by adding more pipes, valves, and hoses I could irrigate the larger area. The new plantings grew well and in a few years I had a veritable jungle. However, I was still greedy for more fenced space and I wanted to do something to protect my edibles from the critters and birds. This led to a plan to fence in even more new area than the size of the phase 2 garden. However, that posed a problem because all the space outside the phase 2 garden had increasing downward slope. The fence would have to follow the slope. So was born the phase 3 garden (hopefully the last). On the south side, we moved the fence out to the property line, an extension of 30 to 40 feet; the fence goes up to the far side of the shop (20 feet more); and it follows the property line east down the hill about 100 feet beyond the phase 2 east side; it then goes northward about another 75 feet; turns left and goes uphill to the lower level of the house. It was 500 feet of additional fencing. The total enclosed area was more than ½ acre.

Jonathan was still working for Raymond Dalle next door, but more and more he worked for me instead. Meanwhile, his mother, whom he lived with, moved to Oregon. One thing led to another, and I allowed Jonathan to move into my house until he could find another place in California for himself. He became a resident handyman, landscaper, and gardener. He also worked for many of the neighbors on the hill.

Jonathan and I built the phase 3 fence. The new area that sloped downhill from the earlier garden area required some work to make it accessible. I had Jonathan build paths so that one could conveniently and safely reach any area of the new garden. In doing this, we learned how to do such things as make cuts into the hillside to get a level place for a path, and how to work with the local rocks to make edging and retaining walls. This led to still further path-making, including a path down the hill to Ken's property, and paths outside the fencing on the north side of the house. Jonathan did all this work with hand tools: pick, shovel, rake, and wheelbarrow. Jonathan loves hard work and exercise and really got himself into shape doing it.

The lower part inside the new fenced area was tanoak forest. We felled all of the trees and converted them into firewood. There were still a lot of fir seedlings, which we did not remove. *In the ensuing 8 years, they have grown up and some will soon have to be removed. I had thought we could use some of them as Christmas trees, but that never happened.* Because of the tanoaks, the soil in this area is quite bad. Tanoaks are evergreen, but they drop leaves all the time. The leaves don't decompose well, they just lay there and produce a very slippery surface when wet. Very little leaf mulch goes into the soil. When planting there, we had to add a lot of fertile mulch to condition the soil. Still, it is difficult to grow some plants in that area.

Cutting the tanoaks in the garden opened up the view to the east. One can now see much farther down into the valley, although not all the way to the bottom. Looking up higher, over the mountain on the other side of the valley, one can see ridges all the way down to the Russian River valley. In foggy weather, the valleys can get filled with fog, with the ridge tops floating above.

I also wanted to make a fully-enclosed area for growing edibles away from the birds and critters. We put a cage across the front of the garden about 40 feet from the house. Louisa felt that this was going to block the

Figure 16 The vegetable garden cage

view, but it really didn't because other things grew up to do that. The vegetable garden was 10 x 40 feet with chicken-wire fencing on it, even on the top, which was 8 feet high (see Figure 16). Inside, it had two rows of planter boxes, with several areas for in-ground planting. This area was far enough from the redwoods that we didn't have to worry about their roots. We moved the peach trees that had been closer to the house, to one of the in-ground areas in the vegetable garden. In the boxes, we planted peas, green beans, kale, chard, strawberries, onions, and tomatos.

However, we now had a new problem with the peach trees. They got leaf curl, which affects the new leaves in the spring. It curls up the leaves and prevents proper opening and pollinization of the flowers. We got very few peaches. *Eventually, I gave up on peaches entirely and took the trees out.*

Meanwhile, I was

Figure 17 Garden picture (April, 2008-fisheye lens, from the roof of the house)

buying plants to populate the other new areas. Jonathan did the digging, sifting, rock-moving, planting, and mulching. He often complained that I went to the nursery and bought plants without ever thinking of where they would be planted. He was right. I bought plants mostly because I liked them. I felt that there was so much area to plant, that we surely could find a good place to plant anything. I believe that a garden should look natural, and not precisely structured as so-called formal gardens are (see Figure 17). I do, however, consider the juxtaposition of colors when I decide where to plant. This haphazard strategy has mostly been successful, and the garden appears to most people to be planned, although it wasn't. Because of the slope of the terrain, it is difficult to take a picture of all of it at once without a helicopter.

The Hiking Trail

It was not long before I decided that it would be nice to use our new path-building skills to build a hiking trail down the hill on my property, and ultimately all the way to the creek. When we built the fence, we put a gate at the bottom; the hiking trail could take off from there. So Jonathan began his digging and leveling process. At the start it was a tanoak forest, with occasional redwoods. It took several switchbacks to get down to an old logging road going across my property. When we put in Ken's driveway, we connected this road to it, so I could actually take a vehicle down there. That was about 100 feet down from the level of my house.

The trail went across the logging road into more tanoak forest, although here there were some large fir trees, too. As we progressed down the trail,

Figure 18 Meadow 1

we placed redwood benches like the one in Figure 4 at strategic points, either where there was a good view, or at suitable resting places for the hiker.

More switchbacks got us down to the first meadow (see Figure 18). This is a meadow of maybe 3 or 4 acres, sloping down with at least a 45° angle. The trail went along the top of the meadow, because we didn't want to disturb the meadow itself for fear of erosion. At the top of the meadow it was very rocky and erosion was not a concern. Past the meadow, we again went into tanoak forest. Two more switchbacks brought us to the base of the Columbus Tree (see Figure 19). The trail goes right past the trunk.

Beyond the Columbus Tree, the terrain gets steeper. We put two sets of wooden steps just past the tree to take up some of the elevation and then the trail goes out to the edge of the meadow and we put in more steps made of pieces of railroad ties going down there. At this point, the trail is at the bottom of Meadow 2; it crosses the meadow here, going into yet another tanoak forest. In building the trail, we ran into a lot of poison oak, which we killed with Roundup, which pretty much removed it.

This tanoak forest had a number of gigantic trees, with low branches that spread out at 6 or 8 feet above the ground, going 50 to 80 feet in each direction. That produced a nearly complete canopy in the area. One of those trees was especially large and complex, we called it the Octopus oak tree. The trail went right around its trunk and continued down with more switchbacks. Unfortunately, about six months after the trail was built, the Octopus oak tree was blown over in a winter storm. It flipped over with its trunk in the air (see Figure 20). Examining the trunk showed that most of the roots had rotted away and it had been standing with only a few roots left. As it was, the tree left a huge hole in the forest and it fell on some of the trail; several hundred feet of trail had to be relocated to become passable again.

The trail continued down with switchbacks until it came out at the bottom of meadow 1. There, it was next to a small ravine,

Figure 19 Trunk of The Columbus Tree

263

which we crossed with a bridge (see Figure 21). All the parts of the bridge had to be hand-carried down to the site, which was about 350 feet down from the house and shop. Below the bridge, there was a small clearing and level space, which we enlarged, and equipped with a redwood picnic table. I cut the pieces of the picnic table in the shop, and Jonathan then carried down one or two at a time, where we assembled the table and benches.

Just past the picnic table was a small spring, which blocked our way. We dug out the spring and put in gravel and a pipe to carry the water away from the path. Then we covered everything up and continued on building the trail. The route passed through a slide bank that had to be cut through. This made an open-top tunnel that was 5 or 6 feet deep at some places. All the earth-moving was done manually by Jonathan. At this point, the walking distance along the trail was about 2,000 feet.

We were only halfway down to the bottom of the hill, so the trail continued. However, as best we could tell without sending a surveyor down there, we had gone off my property and onto neighboring properties. This

Figure 20 The Octopus oak tree, before and after the storm

meant that I was less interested in making a great trail, and the objective became to simply make a reasonably safe way to get down to the bottom with the least effort. But it was still a lot of work. Jonathan prevailed and he got down to where one could *see* the creek. However, the creek was still in a narrow canyon about 50 feet deep. If you walked far enough downstream, the canyon ended and you could reach the banks of the creek. We stopped there. After all the work was done, I estimated that Jonathan had moved something like 2,000,000 pounds of earth in making the trail, and it is almost a mile long.

Jonathan Hughes

I have said a lot about what Jonathan did in making the garden and the hiking trail, but I haven't said much about him. I first met Jonathan when he came to work at my neighbor Raymond's place. I saw right away that he was a different sort of person, but it took quite a while for me to understand *how* different he was. At that time, he was living with his mother in a trailer park along the Russian River. He didn't have a car and I or Raymond would have to go there and pick him up for a day of work. This was about an hour of driving to pick him up and another hour to return him. As he continued to work for me, I learned more about him. Jonathan had had a very difficult life where he was essentially abandoned by his parents at a young age to the child care system wherever they lived. His parents divorced and Jonathan was in the care of his mother, who moved around the country every year or two. Mostly he was placed with other children who were either disabled or retarded, but he was neither. He

Figure 21 Jonathan and I on the bridge

Figure 22 Jonathan carrying a 300-pound plank (left), communicating with a wild deer (right)

did have difficulties in interacting and communicating socially, and this was interpreted as disability or retardation. That was very unfortunate, and it kept him in situations where he was unable to learn normal social behavior, and to learn many of the things needed to carry on an independent life. Once he was an adult, his mother shielded him from the world (it was "too dangerous"), so his social learning opportunities continued to be limited.

Jonathan is intelligent, creative, extremely physically strong, idealistic, wonderful with animals, and an accomplished artist (see Figure 22). Some of these things don't come through to people who can't get past his communication problems. When he moved into my house, it was supposed to be a temporary situation, but his limitations have made it extremely difficult for him to find another place to live *and he is still here.*

My relationship with Jonathan is that of a surrogate father. He lives in my house and strives to take over all of it. I am constantly resisting the things he wants to do in the house and the things he wants me to do for him. The problem is that he needs to learn the skills to live independently, which takes a professional teacher. He absolutely resists any kind of professional help--from his earlier experiences he thinks all these people are incompetents who cannot see beyond Jonathan's current behavior to the underlying person who needs help. It is a catch-22 that I haven't been able to break. Having lived with him for more than seven years, I can't just throw him out on the street.

Photography

Photography is one of the threads that has been active throughout my life, beginning at about 12 years of age. Up until about 2000, I used a film camera. First it was the 4x5 Speed Graphic sheet-film camera (see Figure 8, Chapter 1), until about 1966, when I bought a 35mm during my first trip

Figure 23 My 35mm darkroom in Merchantville

to Japan. However, prior to then, I sometimes used my father's 35mm camera. In those days, it was 35mm slide film for good color. Around 1985, I switched exclusively to 35mm negative film for prints. I continued using that until the beginning of the digital era, about 1997.

I maintained the darkroom in Merch-antville for developing my 4x5 negatives. However, when I began using 35mm, the Merchantville darkroom did not have suitable equipment and I did not update it. When I changed to 35mm print film in 1985 and I was again living in Merchantville, I bought 35mm darkroom equipment and used it for developing films and making prints. By that time I had removed the old darkroom when I made part of the basement into a wood shop, so I made a small darkroom in a corner of the shop (see Figure 23). Since the shop was a dusty place and a darkroom requires cleanliness, I enclosed the darkroom with large folding doors to keep out the dust when I was using the shop tools. I had to darken the entire shop when using the darkroom. With the growing availability of 1-hour developing services, it was too convenient not to use them for developing the negatives, so my darkroom was used mostly for making enlargements.

Even before there were digital cameras, I was scanning my prints and using a computer with imaging software and a color printer. I used this approach while I was working on DVI Technology as early as 1987. I prepared many of my own photos to display on the DVI system.

My first digital camera was a Kodak DC-120, which I bought when it came out in 1997. It delivered a 1 Mpixel image (1280 x 960), which was actually interpolated up from a somewhat lower resolution sensor. I was pleased with it back then, although I still used my film camera for the best pictures. I took thousands of pictures with it and gave the camera to Kayle when I upgraded to a Nikon CoolPix 990 3-Mpixel camera in 2001. I thought this camera was pretty good, but my eyes were opened in 2005 when I bought a Canon EOS-20D digital SLR camera. I also bought an 11:1 zoom lens and a fisheye wide angle lens. This camera is 8-Mpixels, but its real advantage is the freedom from noise in the picture, even at high ISO settings. Another major advantage is the short delay between pushing the shutter button and the picture actually being taken. With the 990, that was about 2-3 seconds, which made it nearly impossible to catch anything at the right

Figure 24 Collage of Niki and her family's visit to California in 1996

time that was in fast motion. On the EOS-20D, the shutter delay is 0.5 second or less.

With the digital SLR camera, there is no advantage to film photography for my purpose, but there are many advantages to digital. Almost every picture I take gets cropped, sometimes a lot. Also, many pictures need to be enhanced for contrast, color, or grayscale rendition. With the low-noise signal from the Canon camera, these processes can be done and still retain acceptable picture quality. Even the point-and-shoot cameras now are getting better in these respects, at a much lower price. One of the things I enjoy doing with my pictures of an event is making a collage of selected pictures. I do this with Adobe Photoshop. Figure 24 is an example, a collage of pictures from Niki and her family's visit to Sonoma county in 1996. I have done many collages like that.

Cooking

When I was living with my parents, or Aunt Helen, or with my family, there wasn't much reason for me to cook other than the occasional barbeque. In fact I was often told: "Get out of my kitchen" by the reigning cook. Sometimes there was an undertone: "Engineers don't know how to cook." However, during periods when I was living by myself, such as when I lived on Scope III before getting married, I learned to cook and (as usual) amassed a great deal of literature about it. I also found out that I *liked* to cook, and developed several dishes that I have gotten a lot of acclaim for among my friends. This interest in cooking is the reason my house has a well-equipped kitchen that I use regularly.

As with everything eles in my life, I use an engineer's approach to cooking. For example: Louisa, who cooked for her family of 9 for many years, often comments about how I always follow a recipe and measure out everything exactly. She thinks that is funny. Her style for many common dishes is to measure the ingredients by feel or memory, which she calls the "creative, artistic" approach. By contrast, I follow an exact procedure, putting each ingredient in the mix as the recipe tells me to do so. I have a vast collection of cookbooks to guide me, and both I and Louisa now often look up recipes on the Internet. However, I do some things by the seat of my pants, such as measuring out oil. I usually will simply pour the oil into

---

Lemon Meringue Pie

Use a 9" pie pan and pre-heat the oven to 325°. Prepare and bake piecrust in pan according to crust directions. Let crust cool before proceeding.

Measure and prepare the following ingredients before beginning the recipe. This is especially important if you are working alone. This is because the pie filling and meringue must be prepared simultaneously, and you will be kept busy without having to measure things at the same time.

Filling	Meringue
1½ cups granulated sugar	5 egg whites
5/8 cup cornstarch	¼ teaspoon cream of tartar
1/8 teaspoon salt	½ teaspoon vanilla
1-3/4 cups water	5/8 cup superfine sugar
5/8 cup fresh lemon juice	Meringue Stabilizer
3 teaspoons grated lemon zest	(combine all in a small saucepan)
5 egg yolks (at room temperature)	1½ tablespoon cornstarch
3 tablespoons unsalted butter,	1½ tablespoon granulated sugar
cut into ½-inch cubes	½ cup water

Note: The filling and the meringue must be prepared simultaneously, so the meringue can be applied on top of the hot filling as soon as that is put into the pie shell

To begin the filling: In a medium saucepan, whisk together the **granulated sugar**, the **cornstarch**, and the **salt**. Then, whisk in the **water, lemon juice, and zest**, followed by the **egg yolks**, stirring until uniform in color.

Place the saucepan over medium heat, and add the **butter cubes**. Stir constantly with a wooden spoon during heating, until the mixture comes to a simmer. Cook for 1 minute, or until the mixture has thickened appropriately. The heating takes about 15 minutes.

To begin the meringue: Place the **stabilizer paste** over medium heat and stir regularly until it comes to a boil. Boil for 15 seconds, or until it thickens, and remove from the heat, covered. Note: The stabilizer needs to cool a little. It will not work if it is too hot.

In a clean, grease-free mixing bowl, beat the **egg whites** at medium speed until foamy. Add the **vanilla** and the **cream of tartar**; continue beating until soft but definite peaks form. Then gradually beat in the **superfine sugar** and continue beating until the peaks are very stiff and glossy but not dry.

Reduce the speed to slow and slowly incorporate the **stabilizer paste**, one tablespoon at a time. Then increase the speed to medium and beat for 10 seconds.

Assembling the pie: Pour the hot filling into the pie shell and immediately spread the meringue over it, anchoring it to the edges of the crust at all points. Bake the pie in the 325° oven for 20 minutes.

---

the pot without measuring, judging the amount by eye. My reason for that is practical — pouring oil in a measuring cup means that cup cannot be used for measuring anything else until it is washed, and washing oil out of a cup is not easy.

On the facing page is one of my recipes, written by and for an engineer. It gives exquisite detail for making my acclaimed Lemon Meringue Pie. I recommend Meyer lemons for this recipe. I have Meyer lemon trees in my garden, which produce *sweet* lemons all year round that are like none others.

Web Site Design and Hosting

After reading through this chapter you may wonder, "What happened to the video engineer?" I am still here, but the focus of my video engineering skills has changed to photography, computers, imaging software, and web site design. I am using my video skills to work with images, motion video, and the other features of Web pages. All that is software.

There are two aspects to a web site: presenting information, and asking for information. Most actual sites will have some of each. In the presentation mode, a web page is an opportunity for artistry of design, choice of media, colors, writing, etc. This is a type of challenge that I like; it is where I find web design the most fun. Translating a design to an actual page is an act of software design — produce the code that will create your page on the web. I like that challenge, too. Many people use web design tools that hide much of the software design aspect from the designer. That is ok, but I enjoy working with the code directly in a text editor. I am not hampered by limitations that someone else (the tool designer) puts in my way. If the tools have done their job, they should make the design process easier and faster than my way. Maybe so, but I find that I can do the code design nearly as fast as someone using a tool, and I can bring in a lot of features that the tool may not be able to create. Note that when a tool is made to support a lot of features, it inherently becomes more complex, and some or all of the "easy to use" aspects of the tool may be compromised.

Some web sites I have designed are listed below. All are described at www.archluther.com site under the heading of Web Site Design.

www.archluther.com, which is my personal web site. I put this online in October, 2001. It is a relatively simple design, but there is a lot of information presented. There are also private sections for showing information to special groups. One recent addition to this site is a section to promote this book.

www.redwoodworks.com, is the site for my woodworking business. That business is not very active now, but it is a comprehensive presentation of my previous work.

www.lhlavelle.us is a site to show Louisa's painting work.

www.artisansworld.com (no longer online) was described earlier in this chapter. It was for a business where we tried to sell the works of local artisans via the Internet. It was ahead of the time.

www.tvantanna.tv is a web site for the TV broadcasting antenna consulting business of Dr. Oded Bendov, who was a colleague of mine at RCA.

www.write-n-record.com is a web site I built to show the write-n-record software I designed with Dr. Abbas Husain for certain new features of medical record-keeping. This was described earlier in this chapter. This domain is no longer online. The site can be seen by going to www.archluther.com/wnr.

www.kennethwilkes.com is a web site that shows the photography of my Muniz Ranches neighbor Ken Wilkes.

I also designed a web site for Muniz Ranches Property Owners Association. It is private to the members of MRPOA and password-protected, so I am not publishing it here. I am still designing other web sites, and planning some major extensions to my personal sites.

At this point, my discussion has come up to the present time. I am happily living at my mountaintop dream property on the California coast, and I have more things to occupy me than I will be able to do in a good long time.

Observations

My chronology is now complete up to the present (2008). But before closing this memoir, I want to give my observations and comments about my life. To continue the convention I have used in the other chapters, this entire chapter should be in italics, because it is all from the present-day perspective. I will dispense with that and use normal text.

Accomplishments

The book has detailed many accomplishments during my life. They are listed below with my comments. But first, the greatest accomplishment that I did *not* achieve was to become "rich and famous". I would have liked the rich part, but I think I pre-determined the failure of that by staying with RCA Broadcast Systems for so long. However, my efforts at business after RCA did not succeed either. That may just be representative of the odds of success for a new business — I just didn't try enough times. As for being famous, I would not have liked too much of that, simply because I am a relatively private person and did not feel comfortable in the few cases when I was in the public eye. I definitely would not like being there all the time. I did learn that being constantly exposed to something (for me: public speaking and travel) teaches you how to handle it and be comfortable with it. My list of accomplishments is:

The TG-2 Sync Generator was my first major accomplishment. It gave me the confidence that my style of engineering could succeed and that I could bring a complex project to completion. I also learned some things about business from this experience.

The TR-22 Transistorized VTR was the culmination of the experience that my group and myself gained from studying the application of transistors to broadcast equipment. It was the first all-transistor major broadcast product and gave the industry its first view of the reliability and power savings of transistors. See my discussion about technology sea changes below.

The TCR-100 Automatic Cartridge VTR was an example of applying the results of market research to focus the design of a new product that solved a significant industry problem — the playing of multiple commercials during a station break. It was an industry first. As the manager of the entire project and also one of its principal innovators, I take great pride in this product. I also appreciated the industry recognition by awarding us an Emmy for the product. Although our product is now obsolete, our concept of it has been implemented by others using computers.

All my writings. This book, my 12th, has shown that writing has been a lifelong thing for me. It is a means of getting recognition and, in a group situation, it can be a way of exercising power. New engineers often are not interested in writing, but I believe it is something that everyone should learn to do and be comfortable doing it. I think writing is part of engineering. A project is not complete until it is fully documented, which means not only the engineering drawings or computer source code, but includes instruction manuals, papers, magazine articles, and maybe even advertizing copy, and sometimes, a book. Although I would not expect design engineers to do all of this, they should work closely with the people who do the writing for them. Being a good writer is one of the strong points that lead to advancement in engineering. Being able to speak well is another strong point. In my case, I was happy to get involved in any writing that was related to my design work, and do a lot of it myself if I could.

All my patents. These are another form of industry recognition. Not too many engineers acquire 34 patents. For me, it was done during only half of my career. That was because I did not have much opportunity for invention while I was in management. Applying for a patent requires some writing skill. Any engineer who has made an invention should be prepared to do the necessary writing.

DVI Technology. This was a fun project for me. An important reason for it being fun was the research laboratory environment, which I had never before experienced. During my time in Camden, I had visited RCA Laboratories many times, but I didn't realize how different it was until I worked there. In Camden, we were always under pressure: reduce our expense; reduce cost; speed up the schedule; and so on. In the view of the engineers, these things were "imposed" by upper management, who seemed to have little understanding of what effect such requirements coming from outside had our performance. In the research lab, we had the same kind of limitations, but they weren't imposed, we did it to ourselves with full understanding of the needs of the project. Everyone was respected for what they did and what they could do. I came into the project as an outsider, yet I easily found my place in it, did work I enjoyed, and had a great sense of accomplishment and fulfillment. Although I felt fulfilled in Camden, it wasn't the same. I always felt there were roadblocks to complete success and fulfillment. I spent a lot of time shielding my engineers from much of this, because I felt it would interfere with their performance on the projects.

My family. It is difficult to express what my family means to me. I look back on the early days in building a family and see pleasure only limited by how much time I could be with the family. The pressures of business life definitely impacted the family and was one of the seeds of divorce. The divorce was another one of those unexpected events that made me do things I didn't want to do at the time. But again, it freed me to make other decisions that eventually led to my situation now. Similarly, my son's death, the ultimate unexpected tragedy in my anyone's life, has changed many things about me and my subsequent life. The lesson here is that the worst thing that could happen very well may lead to better things later. You have to keep your optimisn going and not become depressed.

My various construction projects. Being an engineer made me want to engineer all the time. Apparently, doing engineering all day at work was not enough for me; I had to have engineering projects at home, too. This was not always good for the family, because it took money and time away from them. However, some of the projects such as boats and houses did lead to fun for the family. But I did not always recognize that the children were growing up during all this and their needs and interests were changing. I was stuck with the things I built, but the rest of the family walked away from them.

My California property. I have succeeded in building my dream retirement home in one of the most beautiful places in the world. Everything is great about it except I don't know how long I will be able to afford it and keep it up. Living here is strenuous with buildings spread apart and with elevation changes. I get good exercise just by walking around. I have started thinking about what I will do when the time comes that I can't continue to stay here. As I have said before, my financial planning has always been a little haphazard and I have been trapped several times by financial considerations into doing things that I didn't want to do at the time. The best example was having to sell the cottage in Maryland. However, if I hadn't sold the cottage, would I ever have built the place in California? The lesson here is: Plan your financial life better than I did, and if you do get forced into something, think about how you will recover in the future. It may turn out better than you expected.

I was able to do so many different things. I think it is an accomplishment to have done so many different things in my life. To list a few of these things in my business life: Video engineer, engineering manager, business planner, marketing manager, research scientist, software engineer, web site designer, writer, and public speaker. I did all these different jobs because I wanted to, and I learned what it took to do them successfully. In my personal life, it was house building, boating, photography, gardening, and music. Many people might look at the things I did *not* do and say I missed some of life's best activities. My children especially saw that we as a family did not do some of the things their friends did, such as travel, camping, and other away-from-home activities. However, everyone chooses what he does for himself.

Technology Sea Changes

During my career, electronic technology went through five "sea changes" — massive change that obsoleted everthing that came before.

(1) The reigning electronic technology when I started in 1950 was vacuum tubes. In the late 1950s, transistors became available. My assignment at that time in RCA was to study transistors and their application to broadcast equipment. This was a great opportunity to get in on the leading edge of the impending technology change and do ground-

breaking work in that area. Many people at that time looked at the current poor performance of transistors and could not see that they would become much better over time. They felt transistors were not worth working on until that happened. Having the vision of imminent future improvement (called technological forecasting) was essential to keep our program from being cancelled before we could achieve key results. The culmination of this work was the TR-22 tape recorder, which became a hit in the electronic recording market and the model for many other transistorized products to come. I was in the right place at the right time. Everyone should try to do this, but remember, it also takes some luck.

(2) The second sea change occurred when integrated circuits came out. Again, there was a learning curve to apply the new technology to our equipment. By that time I was in management and could not do the technical work myself. However, I encouraged my engineers to go into it. To assist that, I had to study the technology myself enough to know the places where I should push the engineers to make the change.

(3) The next sea change was personal computers. This meant not only could an engineer have a powerful computer on his or her desk, but they could also be incorporated (embedded) into equipment designs. Again, the engineers who made use of this new technology the earliest were the ones who made the most of it.

(4) Then came the change to digital video. This began even before I joined the DVI project — digital video recorders were being developed in the early 1980s. These were dedicated digital circuits, not computers. Trying to put digital video on a computer was the objective of the DVI project. We did it first, but the rest of the industry took the ball away from us. That was the price of being too early; the pioneers are not necessarily the ones who succeed financially.

(5) As computers became more powerful, more functions that were once done with hardware could be done in software. This is the most recent sea change of technology. There will be more technology changes, but I am getting away from technology and I may not have to worry about them.

Unexpected Events

Things that happen when you were not planning for them or just were totally unexpected are a fact of life. Almost everyone encounters unexpected things at some time during their life. I'm sure I had my share of them. I certainly never planned for or predicted my divorce or the death of my son. These things just *happen*. The interesting thing is that so many unexpected events that are bad at the time they occur, eventually lead to something good. The events themselves are still bad, but good things came to me later, which might not have occurred if the bad events didn't happen.

An unexpected bad event was the demise of RCA Broadcast Systems and then RCA itself. In my early years at RCA, everyone expected the Company and the business to last until our retirement and beyond. Later, we began seeing some of the seeds of demise being sowed, and the end itself became predictable. Still, there was a lot of what happened that was unexpected. The good from this, for me, was my move to RCA Laboratories, which led to me becoming an industry leader in digital video, an author, and a consultant. If Broadcast Systems hadn't ended, my later career certainly would have been different. However, no one can say whether that would have been better or worse than what I actually did.

The technology sea changes I mentioned earlier were also events that were unexpected until they were well under way in other industries. However, I was lucky about that because I managed to be at the forefront of new technology within Broadcast Systems. The message is: When a new technology that could affect your business becomes visible, find a way to embrace it, learn it, and make it work for your situation.

The Internet

The greatest information tool of our times is the Internet. You can find almost *anything* by searching the Internet. Whether you are interested in buying something, looking for information, or communicating with people of similar interests, the Internet is likely to have an answer. I use the Internet many times every day, and tell non-believers that I could not live without it. When my Internet connection does not work, I am lost. I think back to the days before the Internet and wonder how I survived in such an information-intensive business as engineering. But of course I did; the ways for finding answers were just different, and generally more difficult. There were many times that I didn't find the answers. Today it is so much easier and more effective. I'm not forecasting what will happen with the Internet in the future, I'm just expecting it to get better still.

Management

Nearly half of my career was spent in a leadership role, where I was the manager, not the doer. In my starting years in engineering, I didn't think I would ever want to be in such a position because I felt it was a non-productive job. I also believed that being the boss to other people was distasteful—I only saw the "lording over" side of management. However, when I actually got into management, I began to see that it was productive—more productive than engineering work when properly done. I felt just as fulfilled by being the manager as when I was a working engineer. Most engineering colleges today teach management as a natural part of the engineering curriculum. That is good and I think all engineering students should prepare for a management position in their future. But don't neglect the engineering subjects; being a good engineer is a necessary prerequisite for an engineering management position. Engineers work best when their leader is someone who understands engineering work.

Troubleshooting

I described my troubleshooting philosophy in Chapter 3. It is something I have used throughout life to solve all kinds of problems. The simple formula is to understand the fundamentals of whatever thing you are trying to fix, and then simply apply your mental powers to reason what can be going wrong to make the thing behave as it does. I have done this in person, standing in front of something that is not working; and on innumerable occasions, I have solved problems over the phone or via e-mail. To this day, I get calls to solve problems for my friends. It is amazing how successful that can be.

Television

My early RCA career helped facilitate the spread of color TV broadcasting in the 50s and 60s by making equipment lower cost, higher-performance, and more reliable.. During this time, I was so busy that I seldom had a chance to look at the programs my equipment was being used for. In fact, I have seldom watched TV except for the news. This is not out of disdain or anything like that—it is simply that I have better things to do with my time. I consider sitting in front of the tube to be highly unproductive use of one's time.

When I did watch TV, I could not avoid studying the picture quality, which in the early days, was often not very good. If I was visiting someone, I would often ask if I could adjust their set. They usually agreed, and when I was finished they would say that their set had never looked so good. It was just a matter of properly setting the brightness, contrast, and color controls. The industry was doing a bad job of making receivers that the average person could learn to adjust properly. As time went on, receivers became better and today most sets do not have to be adjusted at all once they are installed.

The current transition to digital TV and flat-panel displays is making this situation even better. The new HDTV standard with digital transmission is a vast improvement. I have always been an early adopter of new video electronics, so I have had HDTV for several years and have upgraded my equipment as improved devices came out. I continue to be impressed by the HD picture quality I can get from satellite broadcasting and especially from Blu-Ray Discs.

An Engineer's Viewpoint of Life

There are many jokes about how engineers are different from the rest of the world's humans. I won't try to upstage the jokers, but I believe engineers *are* different. An engineer will approach a situation or problem analytically, trying to reason his way to the answer. He or she will collect the available information before doing any analysis. If there is time, the Internet will be consulted. In the end, the answer will be based on reasoning using the collected data and the laws of physics. A lay person cannot do this; he or she doesn't know about the laws of physics and does not collect any data beyond what can be seen. His or her answer will be based on previous experience and emotional input. How well does this work? An engineer would say "not at all". How well does the engineer's approach work? A lay person would most likely say "not at all", because he or she doesn't understand what the engineer is doing. As an engineer, I would say that the engineer's approach would work more often than the lay person's approach. Of course, if the problem involves humans and their emotions, maybe the tables would be turned.

Threads

The metaphor of threads has been used throughout this book to refer to things or interests that recurred during my life. A summary of my threads is included in the Index under the subject of "threads". Everyone has threads in their life, representing their interests and activities. If my life is unusual, it is only because of the number and range of different interests I have had and how much I did with them, and also how many of them related to engineering.

Another aspect of threads is that they tie a life together, constantly recurring. The threads in one way define the person; their recurrence reminds his or her friends that certain things about that person do not change with age, regardless of what the life situation may be.

Message

In summary, the message of this book is: One can have a highly rewarding career and personal life as an engineer. Engineering interests and an engineering education put you in a position to influence the future of whatever discipline you choose. Your activities and the things you invent, even in a relatively low position, can affect people all over the world who use the results of your work. The engineering mentality also establishes you in any environment as someone who can do things and solve problems. You will always be in demand.

# # #

My Web Site

www.archluther.com

This book is publicized on my web site, www.archluther.com, which also has private pages to provide companion information for readers of the book. The latter features are password-protected and you must enter the password "erhtsda" to view them.

To see the book information, go to my site and click on the icon "See My New Book". This will take you to the home page for the book, where you can preview the Table of Contents and some sample pages. To enter the protected areas, click on the "login" button and enter the password given above.

In the protected area you will find most of the illustrations from the book in color where applicable, and in higher resolution than in the printed book. There is also contact information for communicating directly with me.

Please don't hesitate to give me your comments and suggestions about the book.

Arch C Luther

Index

Index